Wakefield Press

BROKEN SPEAR

Tasmanian Robert Cox is a former copywriter, journalist, newspaper subeditor, and magazine editor with a special interest in the history of his home state. His publications include seven other books and numerous articles, essays, short stories, and reviews, plus an unobtrusive poem or two. He has also done voice work in radio and television and written documentary film scripts.

Also by Robert Cox

History
Steps to the Scaffold: The Untold Story of Tasmania's Black Bushrangers
Baptised in Blood: The Shocking Secret History of Sorell
A Compulsion to Kill: The Surprising Story of Australia's
Earliest Serial Killers

Memoir (with Robyn Mathison)
Behind the Masks:
Gwen Harwood Remembered by her Friends

Short Stories
Alibis, Lies, Goodbyes
The Clarity of Tears
Agony and Variations

Anthologies
A Ream of Writers
Moorilla Mosaic

Monograph
'One of the Wonder Spots of the World':
Macquarie Island Nature Reserve

BROKEN SPEAR

The untold story of
Black Tom Birch, the man who sparked
Australia's bloodiest war

ROBERT COX

Wakefield
Press

Wakefield Press
16 Rose Street
Mile End
South Australia 5031
www.wakefieldpress.com.au

First published 2021
Reprinted with revisions 2022

Cover designed by Stacey Zass
Edited by Julia Beaven, Wakefield Press
Typeset by Michael Deves, Wakefield Press

ISBN 978 1 74305 867 1

A catalogue record for this
book is available from the
National Library of Australia

Wakefield Press thanks
Coriole Vineyards for
continued support

For Lou with love, admiration, and gratitude

In 1811 Governor Lachlan Macquarie, trekking through the Tasmanian Midlands from south to north during the first of his two visits to the island, remarked in his journal on the number of Aboriginal fires he saw around him. 'I saw many Native Fires in the faces of the neighbouring Mountains,' he wrote, a sentiment echoed in 1820 by Pitt Water pioneer James Gordon. 'Are there many natives in the Interior?' Commissioner Bigge asked him. 'I believe there are a good many from the fires that I have seen,' Gordon replied.

Those images of an island alive with Aboriginal families around their campfires are haunting, for it had been so for at least 35,000 years. Yet to extinguish them for ever took British rapacity just thirty-five.

Baptised in Blood, Robert Cox

The natives say when a relative dies they give themselves up to grief. They break their spears ... and mourn.

George Augustus Robinson

Contents

Foreword

Lyndall Ryan

Black Tom Birch, or Kikatapula, the subject of this biography, is a paradox in Tasmanian history. Born and raised as a traditional man among his own people, in late adolescence he becomes a member of a prominent settler family in Hobart and is baptised into the Anglican faith. Upon the outbreak of the Black War, however, he returns to his people and becomes the most feared Aboriginal man in the colony. He leads many daring raids on settlers and is known to kill with alacrity. Yet whenever he is arrested and taken into custody, he is always released and no charge of murder is ever prosecuted.

Then at a critical moment in the war, he changes sides. He joins Gilbert Robertson's roving party and facilitates capture of the guerrilla leader Umarrah. He then becomes a leading member of G.A. Robinson's friendly mission and plays an important role in the diplomatic initiative to secure the surrender of the highly respected chief Tukalunginta. When he dies five months later, Robinson is deeply saddened at the loss of a close and valued friend.

Kikatapula is clearly an important player in the Black War, yet in comparison with Musquito, who was his mentor, and Umarrah and Manalakina and the other members of Robinson's mission such as Wurati and Trukanini, we know very little about him. What we do know is mired in controversy. Was he a small boy or a young man when he joined the Birch family in Hobart? Was he the ringleader of the killings at Grindstone Bay in 1823 or was he not there at all? Was he a witness to the massacre of his people at Bank Head Farm in 1826? What were the circumstances that led him to change sides in 1828?

Robert Cox has spent several years tracking down every known skerrick of information about Kikatapula in order to understand the apparent paradox in his life. What emerges is a riveting portrait of a Tasmanian Aboriginal man who through force of circumstance becomes the leading patriot of his people and his country. In this role he is driven by a grim determination to force the colonial invaders from his homeland. Yet at a critical moment his patriotism transforms him into a champion of reconciliation.

Cox's compelling portrait of Kikatapula enables the reader to compare him with other patriotic leaders in the colonial world such as Xanana Gusmão in East Timor and Jomo Kenyatta in Kenya. Like Kikatapula, they were Christians who through force of circumstance became leaders of their Indigenous communities and conducted guerrilla wars of resistance against colonial invaders. And like Kikatapula, at a critical moment in the struggle they also became champions of reconciliation. In locating Kikatapula in such august company, we can begin to understand him not as a paradox but as a true patriot whose paramount purpose was to save his people from extermination.

Broken Spear is the first biography ever written of this most important Tasmanian patriot and is especially important for that and because he was not only the man who sparked the Black War but the most feared, effective, and enduring Aboriginal leader, one whose resistance did not cease even after he changed sides. The book is destined to become a classic of our time and I am honoured and delighted to write the Foreword.

Professor Lyndall Ryan, AM FAHA
University of Newcastle
Author of *The Aboriginal Tasmanians* and *The Tasmanian Aborigines Since 1803*

Preface

His is an untold story, although he was catalyst for and chief prosecutor of a major war in which much blood, white and black, was spilt on Australian soil. His struggle made him a seminal figure in our history and one of the most influential people in colonial Australia, yet few people have heard of him, most historians have not noticed him, and even those few scholars who have bothered to look have not seen him clearly or wholly. Serious wrong has been done to Black Tom Birch and his rightful place in history.

He was once the most feared and hated man in Van Diemen's Land. His rage at Britons' savage treatment of his people, theft of Aboriginal lands and resources, abduction and enslavement of Aboriginal women and girls, and wanton destruction of the race and its culture sparked a bloody guerrilla campaign that quickly exploded into all-out war: the Black War of 1824–1831, which has been summarised by one historian as 'per capita … one of the most destructive wars in recorded history'.[1]

Black Tom's leadership in that war was so devastating that one newspaper demanded he be lynched immediately on capture. Yet despite being three times in British custody he was neither lynched nor punished in any other way. Eventually he changed sides to aid the enemy, first as a guide for an armed party sent to round up Aborigines for incarceration (or to kill those who resisted), then as guide and interpreter for an expedition undertaking one of the longest and most gruelling but least-known treks in Australian history as it sought to conciliate, and eventually to capture and incarcerate, every Aborigine remaining in the island. He died while ostensibly assisting his former enemies with this final roundup of his people for exile on a Bass Strait island, although in reality he was surreptitiously and successfully undermining British efforts. He then became the first person, Aboriginal or European, to be buried with Christian rites in the embryonic city of Burnie. For despite his bloody record, Black Tom Birch professed Christianity. Such incongruities sundered his short life.

Incontrovertibly, he was the most significant Aborigine in Tasmanian history. His example and leadership proved far more destructive to the advance of British settlement than any other Tasmanian warrior's, or indeed than those of such mainland resistance leaders as Jandamarra and Yagan in Western Australia, Dundalli in Queensland, and Pemulwuy and Tedbury in New South Wales. Unlike them, Black Tom sparked *total war* – an eight-year conflict in which more than 800 attacks on colonists left at least 437 of them dead or wounded.[2] As a leading historian has observed, 'the recorded European death rate in the Black War equated to 15 killed per 10,000 colonists per year, averaged over the eight years of the conflict. *This was … much higher than World War II*, which on average cost the lives of six out of every 10,000 Australians in each of its six years [emphasis added]'.[3]

For the Aborigines themselves the war was cataclysmic. How many of them died during the conflict is unknowable, but it devastated their tiny population, which even before war broke out had shrunk catastrophically under the pressures of invasion, dispossession, and introduced disease. In the ultimate irony of Black Tom's conflicted life, both his leadership of resistance to the British and his eventual defection to them helped achieve the destruction of traditional Aboriginal Tasmania. Within the greater disaster of cultural genocide, his life was thus a profoundly personal tragedy.

A tragedy of Shakespearean proportions.

Today, however, a mention of Kikatapula, his real name, would elicit no more than a blank stare from the vast majority of Australians. Even his British-bestowed name, Thomas Birch, and its variations – Black Tom, Birch's Tom, Black Tom Birch – would be unlikely to spark so much as a flicker of recognition in 21st-century eyes. Yet for more than four years in the 1820s he led his people in harassing, attacking, wounding, and killing British settlers and their servants, plundering their possessions, burning their houses, and destroying their crops and livestock, and in doing so he inspired other Aborigines to emulate him. Charged with murder, he appeared in court only once but was astonishingly not convicted, unlike his comrades Musquito and Black Jack who expiated their deeds on the scaffold, for he was discharged without trial, punishment, or explanation.

A well-informed 21st-century Tasmanian asked to name a local

Aboriginal resistance leader might answer 'Umarrah' or 'Walyer', yet neither they nor any other Tasmanian had a guerrilla career anywhere near as long, as influential, or as lethal as Kikatapula's. But colonial newspapers understood his pre-eminence. They peppered their pages with news of his exploits and furious calls for his destruction, describing him as 'the chief instigator of the atrocities of the blacks', 'the man who appeared to lead and instigate [Aborigines] in these dreadful crimes', 'the man who has been the main instrument of their late attacks', 'the notoriously treacherous and infamous leader, Black Tom', 'the cause of so much mischief at the head of the savage tribes', 'the Aboriginal Native, who so long headed the sable tribes', and similar telling phrases.[4] That he was paramount in fomenting and leading Aboriginal resistance to the British invasion of his homeland cannot be doubted. The evidence is unequivocal.

Yet many historians seem unaware of his importance; a surprising number either omit him entirely from their books or relegate him to a minor role. Henry Melville's *The History of Van Diemen's Land* (1835), published only three years after Kikatapula's death, dilates on his role as a guide for the British but makes no mention of his bloody record as the spearhead of Aboriginal resistance. The 1862-published memoir of G.T. Lloyd, who lived in Oyster Bay country during the years of Kikatapula's hostilities there, mentions 'black Tommy Birch' only once, erroneously referring to him as a tracker of bushrangers, which he never was.[5] John West's *The History of Tasmania*, published the same year, confuses him with another Aboriginal man and claims he was executed in 1825 – a common mistake dating back at least to 1830, when Kikatapula was still living – while James Fenton's *A History of Tasmania from its Discovery to the Present Time* (1884) ignores him entirely. Except for two instances, in both of which the author confuses him with another man, so does M.C.L. Levy's 1953 biography of Lieutenant Governor George Arthur, a crucial player in Kikatapula's drama who, when the guerrilla leader was in custody charged with murder, chose to set him free. The six volumes of Manning Clark's mythopoeic magnum opus *A History of Australia* (1962) fail to mention him at all, whereas Lloyd Robson's compendious two-volume *A History of Tasmania* (1983) makes brief reference to his services as a British guide but appears unaware of his greater importance as fomenter and leader of Aboriginal resistance. At the time of writing, the University of Tasmania maintains a website devoted to Kikatapula's life but it is sketchy and inaccurate.[6] And almost all the books about Aboriginal Tasmania published since Robson's also miss Kikatapula's primacy in Aboriginal resistance and get the facts of his life wrong. Although Keith Windschuttle's *The Fabrication of Aboriginal History* (2002) does recognise his crucial role in resisting the British, it absurdly dismisses him as a criminal, a 'black bushranger' – an ideologically warped interpretation that would also relegate the likes of Boudicca, Pierre Georges, Hannie Schaft, Crazy Horse, and Shaka Zulu to the category of criminal rather than patriot.

The whole sanguinary story of the Tasmanian Aboriginal people's violent resistance to the invasion and usurpation of their island is little known to most Australians and virtually unknown outside Australia. Anyone now reading one of those small self-published monographs on Tasmanian regional history, often written by descendants of pioneering pastoral families, must wonder at the general absence from their pages of Aboriginal people. Such booklets always begin with the arrival in the subject region of the intrepid first British settlers; there is never acknowledgement of 35 or more millennia of Aboriginal occupation and stewardship of the land before then. When Aboriginal people – always referred to as 'the blacks' or 'the natives' – make their brief appearance in the text, it is as a pestilence like fly-strike or scotch thistle, their 'atrocities' and 'murders' – words never used about white violence to Aborigines – treated as only sporadic impediments to the progress of agriculture and the spread of Christian civilisation.

Yet for eight years those Aboriginal people fought the usurpers with an intensifying ferocity that was all the more remarkable because their population, probably no greater than a few thousands in 1803 when the first invaders arrived, began to shrink almost immediately. By 1820 it was doing so at a drastic rate, so that 'Within a single generation of British occupation of Tasmania, approximately 90 per cent of the Aboriginal people alive at the time of British arrival were dead'.[7] By 1824 and the outbreak of the Black War there were probably no more than 1000 Aborigines, including women and children, left to fight it – far fewer than the colonists they stoutly resisted, so their courageous David-against-Goliath stance was doomed to failure. But as a contemporary historian has observed, 'Although they ultimately lost the war, their resistance against a technologically and numerically superior enemy was nothing short of extraordinary'.[8]

By the end of 1823, when the initial spark for war was struck, more than 200,000 sheep were grazing Tasmania's grasslands where just a generation earlier there were none.[9] To the surviving Aborigines it was obvious that their culture was ruptured and probably irreparable, their numbers were diminishing apace, and their race's very survival was in doubt. A fight to the death was inevitable. The reasons for their subsequent violent resistance were summarised by two chiefs, Tukalunginta and Manalakina, who said they made war because they 'and their forefathers had been cruelly abused, that their country had been taken away from them, their wives and daughters had been violated and taken away, and that they had experienced a multitude of wrongs from a variety of sources'.[10] Put simply, British colonisers and their servants dispossessed Aborigines of their land, appropriated Aboriginal resources, abducted Aboriginal women and girls, and murdered Aboriginal people opportunistically, while sealers working in Tasmanian waters abducted and enslaved Aboriginal women and girls and murdered Aboriginal men who stood in the way of their abductions. This unplanned and uncoordinated two-tined assault first disrupted and then quickly destroyed the culture's ancient equilibrium.

Enter Kikatapula who, with an involuntarily transplanted mainland Aborigine named Musquito, began the fightback.

I have written before about various aspects of Kikatapula's life. In *Steps to the Scaffold* (2004) I included a short chapter on the little I then knew of him and identified him as a conduit between the first and last waves of Tasmania's so-called black bushrangers – between the first guerrilla attacks, led by him and Musquito, and the last, carried out by his acolytes Tanaminawayt and Malapuwinarana, transplanted Tasmanians who in 1841 terrorised the fledgling colony that became Victoria and paid with their lives. Researching *Baptised in Blood* (2010), I found evidence supporting a lone 1830 report that about half the members of Kikatapula's mob were slaughtered in 1826 in a surprise attack by police and soldiers and that the murders were hushed up to protect the killers. I included a chapter adducing persuasive circumstantial evidence that the killings had indeed happened, finding in it too a likely explanation for Kikatapula's extraordinary immunity from prosecution and punishment. (In this book, I enlarge on that by examining the neglected matter of his three captures and discussing why he was released untried and unpunished each time.) Then, in 2012, I presented to the Tasmanian Historical Research Association a paper titled 'Black Tom Birch: Fact and Fiction' revealing the all-important but then unrecognised part he played in the 1823 Grindstone Bay killings that were precursory to the Black War and the overlooked truth about the British atrocity that sparked them.[11] As I was finishing this book I published a newspaper article promoting Kikatapula's worthiness for toponymic commemoration in Tasmania.[12]

Over time I came to see him as a fascinating and often admirable character: an intelligent man with demonstrated leadership qualities whose riven life symbolised the life-and-death dilemma facing all Indigenous peoples in the path of invasion, violent usurpation of their country, and destruction of their culture. So I decided to write his biography, using what I already knew as a framework to be built on through assiduous research. For the last years of his life I would be able to rely on that sublimely evocative but little-known classic of Australian literature *Friendly Mission*, the published journals of George Augustus Robinson, his leader in the great expedition referred to above. As I worked, the emerging picture confirmed the need for his reappraisal, so in this book I reveal him in full and as he deserves to be seen – not absurdly dismissed as a criminal or a black bushranger but celebrated as a patriot, an inspiring leader, and one of Australia's most significant Aboriginal people. For he instigated, inspired, and fought in Australia's most sustained, intense, and bloody battle against invasion: Tasmania's Black War of 1824–1831.

Fair-minded people might call him a great Tasmanian, a true Australian patriot.

Tasmanian history during the Black War was nothing like fully recorded. Historian Hamish Maxwell-Stewart believes the paucity of records for the period evinces the extreme pressure the war put on the colony and its administrators. He cites one example: 'There are no detailed population returns for the colony of Van Diemen's Land for the period 1824–30, a product of the dislocation caused by frontier conflict'.[13] As a result of such scarcity, researching Kikatapula's story has sometimes been like attempting one of those children's puzzles in which numbered dots are joined to form a picture, only in this case many of the dots were not numbered and in some instances were absent altogether, so I occasionally had to proceed as though all the dots were present and numbered even when they were not. I can say only that, right or wrong, I have joined them as seemed most reasonable according to whatever evidence exists.

Throughout the text, Kikatapula is sometimes a shadowy figure, a phantom whose participation in particular incidents can at times only be inferred or deduced. My policy has been to name him as a participant only whenever a contemporary record identified his presence. Whenever he was not named but the geography and/or chronology of an event, or some other credible detail of it, suggested his participation, I have recorded the incident in its chronological place without naming him as definitely present – although, as I will show, he took the war to areas well outside the traditional country of his own Oyster Bay people and their allies the Big River people, indeed far outside the geographical limitations generally imposed on his resistance activities. The records make abundantly clear that Kikatapula was the propellant for serious Aboriginal resistance, that he led or participated in many attacks, that he lit the fuse for others, and that his activities were unconstrained by supposed tribal boundaries. And although his final attack on settlers was in November 1827, he passively continued resistance until his death.

One unusual element of Kikatapula's epic was his friendship with an upper-class white woman who succoured him when he was an ailing youth, cared deeply about him throughout his life, interceded to save him from the hangman, and mourned him long after he died. Although Sarah Birch Hodgson's story is even more scantily recorded than his, I have attempted where possible to redress the lack, for without her Kikatapula's life would have been shorter and his end brutal.

Broken Spear is not about the Black War per se but its sparkplug and spearhead, a man whose active participation ended four years before hostilities fizzled out. I have not reported the many attacks on settlers that occurred after Kikatapula changed sides in 1828, or those during the years of his resistance leadership where his participation is uncertain or unlikely. The history of the war itself is well told in two complementary recent books, each offering a different slant on the subject: Nicholas Clements's *The Black War* (University of Queensland Press) and Nick Brodie's *The Vandemonian War* (Hardie Grant Books). *Broken Spear* aims only to tell Kikatapula's story, to reclaim him from the shadows of neglect and calumniation, and to elevate him for the first time to his rightful prominence in history's spotlight.

When history books mention Kikatapula at all by his Aboriginal name they spell it *Kickerterpoller*, an Anglicised hearing and spelling, although Aboriginal people pronounced it something like *Keeckadapulla*, with emphasis on the penultimate syllable. In keeping with the preference of contemporary Aboriginal Tasmanians I have used Kikatapula as my spelling throughout this text except in direct quotes from printed sources. Similarly, I have used their preferred palawa kani spellings (see below for explanation), where available, for other Aboriginal names in place of the varied spellings common during the past two centuries, again excepting direct quotes.

Tasmanian Aboriginal society was devastated by Britons' avarice, diseases, and criminal acts well before any of the invaders thought it might be worthwhile to learn and record anything about it. George Augustus Robinson did attempt to do so during his peregrinations around the island between 1830 and 1834, but by then it was too late. They were the dying years of traditional culture, which had been in desperate flux for more than a decade, and the ancient norms had ceased to exist. Consequently, Aboriginal taxonomy remains anything but an exact science. Scholars generally agree that there were nine language groups of Tasmanian

Aborigines – always referred to in colonial times as *tribes* – and that each of those groups or nations occupied a particular territory whose boundaries were known and understood by other groups. Yet no Aboriginal name is known for any of the nine; the names we use were all bestowed by Britons. All are regional, meaning they were nothing more than convenient geographical tags to roughly identify the Aboriginal nation whose territory appeared to be a particular place. So those whose country was in the east in the wider Oyster Bay area were labelled *the Oyster Bay tribe* to differentiate them from those in the north of the island (*the North tribe*) or in the south-east of the island (*the South East tribe*) and so on.

Each of those nations comprised several *bands*, a term generally agreed to be the basic unit of Tasmanian Aboriginal society. A band was a group of families, consisting of 40 to 80 people 'who called themselves by a particular name, and were known by that or other names to other people'.[14] The names of those bands – at least 48 are recorded – are how Aborigines identified themselves. So I have preferred to call Aboriginal groups by their band names (where known); otherwise I have taken the line of least resistance by using the general term *people*, in the sense of Aboriginal people who lived in a particular region – viz. the Oyster Bay people. Rather than muddy already turbid waters, I have avoided the subject whenever possible and used collective names only when unavoidable.

Aboriginal names for places and individuals also present problems. Since the Tasmanians' culture was an oral one, all names had to be recorded phonetically by Europeans as they heard them pronounced by Aboriginal speakers, with obvious potential for mishearing, mispronouncing, misrecording, and misremembering, no doubt exacerbated by guesses at appropriate spellings (not to mention subsequent misinterpretation) when they wrote names down. A further difficulty is synonymy. As one authority has noted, 'It seems to have been usual for a native to have two names rather than one. In some cases an individual might have more than two names: the largest number recorded is five'.[15] Confronted with such potential impediments to clarity I have generally taken the line of least resistance and chosen names that historical usage and acceptance have made most familiar, although with palawa kani spellings when available and appropriate. And I have chosen to use every Aboriginal person's parentally given name (or the commonest of them), whenever it is known, rather than one, like Jack or Dick, repeatedly conferred by unimaginative colonists.

Many British-bestowed Tasmanian place names have changed since the 1820s, but for the sake of contemporary flavour I have left verbatim in quoted text whatever name was used and for clarity put its modern equivalent in parentheses or brackets. Other than that I have used today's place names, preferring *Tasmania* to *Van Diemen's Land* and *Hobart* to *Hobart Town* and *Hobarton*. In today's toponomy I have followed the Australian convention of omitting apostrophes from the adjectival portions of names, a practice officially adopted because they are descriptive rather than possessive, so Prossers Plains rather than Prosser's Plains, Black Charlies Sugarloaf instead of Black Charlie's Sugarloaf. (Such omissions should also render the possessive 's' redundant, but that nicety has so far escaped the notice of nomenclature authorities.)

Where necessary I have added in brackets or parentheses the metric equivalents of imperial measurements. But since one yard is roughly equivalent to one metre and one ton to one tonne, I have provided neither yards-to-metres nor tons-to-tonnes conversions. I have also resisted the temptation to tag with *sic* every oddity of 19th-century typesetting and spelling, preferring to reserve its use principally for errors of fact.

Wherever I have used the word *mob* to describe a group of Tasmanians, I have not done so in a derogatory or disrespectful sense. Australian Aboriginal people customarily use the word to mean a clan or family or group of relations or friends bonded formally or informally (as indeed many non-Aboriginal Australians do), which is the sense I have used it in.

Most important, throughout this text I have eschewed using the word *murder* in relation to Aboriginal killings of colonists because in colonial Tasmania the word and the concept represented only a European view. Murder was a concept of British law, which Tasmanians neither knew about nor would have cared about if they had. They were engaged in a war to rid their country of invaders, so the word *murder* is as meaningless in the context of Aborigines killing colonists during the Black War as it is to French or Norwegian or Belgian resistance fighters killing occupying Germans during World War II. To suggest that Tasmanian Aborigines *murdered* settlers is simply untenable and absurd. But it is correct to say settlers murdered Aborigines.

Much of the material in Chapters 15 to 20, covering the final 28 months of Kikatapula's life, is drawn from the journals of George Augustus Robinson (published as *Friendly Mission*, first edition 1966, second edition 2010). Whenever I have quoted directly from the journals, for clarity's sake I have cited the date of the journal entry rather than its page number because the second edition has different pagination from the first. Whenever the date of a journal quote is obvious from my text, I have not included a citation for its source, hoping thereby to limit the number of endnotes. But wherever a quote from *Friendly Mission* is not from the journals themselves but from such additional material as editor's notes or Robinson's notebooks, I have cited the appropriate page number in an endnote and also stated which edition it is from.

My use of the term 'broken spear' is metaphorical and not intended to suggest Tasmanian Aborigines physically broke their spears as a sign of surrender or conciliation. However, they did so when mourning their dead, in which sense it seems a particularly appropriate metaphor here.

Finally, 'One of the terms Tasmanian Aboriginal people used when referring to themselves was "Palawa"', which is the term that many contemporary Aboriginal Tasmanians prefer, so I have used *Palawa* hereafter in preference to the European-bestowed *Aborigines, Tasmanians,* or *Vandemonians*. The neo-traditional language, as presently being reconstituted by contemporary Aboriginal Tasmanians, is *palawa kani,* whose spellings I have used, where available, for Palawa personal names and band names – again except in direct quotes – and I am grateful to the Tasmanian Aboriginal Centre for providing this material. Individuals' alternative names are shown in parentheses. I acknowledge that not all my orthographical choices will be approved by every Tasmanian Aboriginal community; some indeed may be deemed culturally inappropriate. They have been used because such standardisation aids comprehension, never because of insensitivity to or disrespect for Aboriginal culture past or present.

BAND NAMES

Aboriginal palawa kani spelling	Historical European spelling
Luntaytamiriliyuyna	Loontimmairrener
Mumirimina	Moomairremenner
Muwinina	Mouheneenner
Nununi	Nuenonne
Panina	Panninher
Paytirami	Poredareme/Parradarreme
Payintaymirimina	Pyendaymairremener
Tayarinutipana	Tyerrernotetepanner

PERSONAL NAMES

Aboriginal palawa kani spelling	Historical European spelling
Kikatapula	Kickerterpoller
Kulipana	Kolebunner
Malapuwinarana	Maulboyheenner
Manalakina	Mannalargenner
Muntipiliyata	Montpeilliatter
Nikaminik	Nicermenic
Panganitalatina	Pungerneetterlattenner
Pintawtawa	Pendowtewer
Prupilathina	Probelattener (Lacklay)
Pulara (Rramanaluna)	Bullrer (Drummerrerlooner)
Pularipana	Pollerrelberner
Tanalipunya	Tanleboneyer
Tanaminawayt (Piway)	Tunnerminnerwait (Pevay)
Tikati	Tekartee
Trukanini	Truganinni (Trucaninni)
Tukalunginta	Tongerlongeter (Tupelanta)
Wapati	Wapperty
Wulaytupinya	Woolaytoopinneyer
Wurati	Woorraddy

Kikatapula (Black Tom Birch). This 1832 drawing by Thomas Bock was once thought possibly to be Umarrah. Here, for the first time, the unnamed subject is identifiable as Kikatapula, chiefly by the 'remarkable scar on his forehead' reported in the *Hobart Town Gazette* on 5 May 1827.

(Courtesy British Museum)

Prologue

Behind him, the blood of 14 of his followers glistened fresh on the ground. Ahead, he knew, a noose awaited him. So although the bayonet-point trek down the wheel-rut track from Black Charlies Sugarloaf to Sorell Town that cool and cloudy Saturday morning in 1826 was long and arduous, the tall Palawa man with the scarred forehead was not eager to get there.

Not so the constable and four soldiers responsible for the morning's slaughter and the capture of the survivors. After leaving Sorell at 11 o'clock the previous night they had tramped through chill darkness to the Palawa camp 20 kilometres away in the hills and at dawn had launched a surprise attack with guns and bayonets. Now they were tired and hungry and footsore, and perhaps sober realisation of how much blood they had spilt was starting to sour their achievement. They prodded townward the little band of shocked and sullen survivors – five men, four women, and a boy – eager for a meal, the solace of rum, the balm of sleep.

Sorell, their destination, hardly deserved then the title of town. The hub of the rich farming district of Pitt Water, an isolated frontier region north-east of Hobart, it comprised just a scattering of makeshift huts and modest houses, a school, a partly completed church and parsonage, a windmill, a cemetery, a jail, and a compact new military barracks. Toward the embryonic settlement the whites and their black captives trudged on through the day, down through hill country to the flatter stump-studded verdancy of late-spring pasture. Colonists watched with satisfaction as Chief District Constable Alexander Laing and his soldiers herded the small band of survivors into the town and along to the jail in Gordon Street facing St George's Square. Occasional approbation from bystanders punctuated Saturday-morning somnolence as the little procession trudged through, for the tall man with the scarred forehead was the notorious Black Tom Birch, the feared and hated leader of Palawa resistance to British settlement, captured at last.

After the 10 survivors of the slaughter had been crammed into the tiny jail's single cell, Laing went off to report their capture to a magistrate while the soldiers returned to the new barracks next door for food and rest, leaving Black Tom to brood on a bleak outlook. During the three bloody years of his resistance many Britons had been slain and many others wounded, stock had been slaughtered, crops destroyed, buildings burned. Only four weeks earlier, newspapers had reported Black Tom himself spearing to death a stockkeeper, for which he knew the inevitable penalty – the one suffered by his tribesmen Jack and Black Dick, hanged only three months earlier for slaying a settler, and by his comrades Musquito and Black Jack who had been executed the previous year for attacks that resulted in the deaths of three colonists.

Word of Black Tom's capture and incarceration spread quickly on the frontier, demoralising Palawa resistance. Attacks on settlers ceased completely, causing the colony's newspapers to trumpet the arrival, finally, of peace. Black Tom, desponding in captivity through all of December and into January, knew nothing of the war's suspension or anything of the eddies of social and political expediency deciding his future. Squatting on the cell floor, expecting at any moment to be taken to Hobart for trial and execution, he was mired in dread and despair at the seeming inevitability of his fate, for he had lived among the British, served them, spoke their language, and knew the prescribed and unforgiving savagery of their retribution.

Yet he was not hanged, not tried, not even taken to Hobart. Unexpectedly, inexplicably, astonishingly, he and his small mob of survivors were given food and blankets and set free. Black Tom promptly took up the spear and the waddy again, and again British blood began to flow.

Part One

The Spear and the Waddy

KEY LOCATIONS

King Island

Flinders Island

Vansittart Island

Cape Grim   Circular Head

Waterhouse Point   Swan Island

Cape Naturaliste

Emu Bay (Burnie)   George Town

Bay of Fires

Launceston

Perth

Quamby Bluff   St Patricks Head

Campbell Town

Ross

Macquarie Harbour   Lake Echo   Swansea
Tunbridge

Bothwell   Little Swanport

Melton Mowbray   Jericho   Oyster Bay
Kempton   Colebrook   Grindstone Bay

Oatlands   Maria Island

Richmond   Runnymede

Kangaroo Bay

New Norfolk   Sorell

HOBART ■

Tasman Peninsula

Colonial names now renamed:

Brushy Plains → Runnymede
Cross Marsh → Melton Mowbray
Jerusalem → Colebrook   Port Davey
Green Ponds → Kempton
Great Swanport → Swansea   Bruny Island
Gun Carriage Island → Vansittart Island   Recherche Bay

1

'A timorous, harmless race of people'

For many millennia they had been alone, isolated and unsuspecting. Although Palawa had inhabited *lutruwita*, as many of them called their homeland, for at least 40,000 years (and possibly five millennia longer) before Europeans came, rising sea levels had separated it from mainland Australia by 250 kilometres of ocean some 12,000 years before the first ships appeared.[1] So several hundred generations of Palawa had lived and died unaware that other peoples existed outside the nine discrete nations of their island. But their isolation was doomed once rapacious strangers with superior technology began to probe the great waters that moated their sanctuary. Few sovereign peoples ever suffered the shock of the new so quickly, so devastatingly, or with such finality.

Their home was an attractive find. The British writer Anthony Trollope, after visiting Tasmania in the 1870s, called it a 'beautiful island, the sweetest in climate, the loveliest in scenery, the richest in rivers and harbours' and 'a land more fitted by climate for English emigrants than ... any other on the face of the earth'.[2] Lying between 40 and 43½ degrees south, Tasmania is 64,519 square kilometres in area, about the size of Sri Lanka or West Virginia or the Republic of Ireland, and has a cool temperate climate. Roughly two-fifths of the land mass is wilderness, notably rugged, wet, cold, windy, mountainous, and densely forested, although that region, in the west and south-west, once supported at least four Palawa bands. It is now mostly within Tasmania's World Heritage Area and various national parks and reserves. Much of the rest of Tasmania is far more benign: grasslands, forests, lakes, rivers, and plateau-like mountains, with a more congenial climate and a countryside that was home to about 44 other Palawa bands. The population of *lutruwita* when the first foreigners arrived is uncertain but is thought to have been between 3000 and 5000 people.

Initially the strangers' incursions were neither numerous nor frequent, and all were transient. The first recorded was by a Dutch seaman, Abel Janszoon Tasman, whose two ships, *Heemskerck* and *Zeehaen*, made landfall on the west coast of *lutruwita* late in the afternoon of 24 November 1642. Tasman named his find Anthoonij Van Diemenslandt to honour the Governor-General of the Dutch East Indies, and cartographers and mariners and then colonists referred to his find as Van Diemen's Land until 1853, when Caucasian Tasmanians wanting to efface that name's association with what they saw as the stain of convictism (and potentially of genocide, although the word was not coined until nearly a century later) officially changed it to Tasmania. Tasman sailed around its southern tip and northward along its east coast. On 3 December he planted the Dutch flag near the present-day town of Dunalley and claimed possession of the land. During excursions ashore his men saw evidence of human occupation but no humans.

Almost 130 years passed before the next Europeans arrived, but after that they came more frequently. The second wave began with French explorers led by Marc-Joseph Marion Dufresne in the *Mascarin* and the *Marquis de Castries*. After sighting the west coast near High Rocky Point on 3 March 1772, they followed the coastline southward and rounded South East Cape, Tasmania's southernmost tip, before following the east coast northward. At North Bay, on Forestier Peninsula, they became the first Europeans to encounter and the first to kill Palawa. After an initially friendly meeting with a band of the Oyster Bay people – Black Tom's people – they fired at them during a beach skirmish when the Palawa resisted their landing. Ensign Jean Roux recorded 'several dead and many wounded', although only a single body was found, other casualties having been carried away.[3] The clash was a tragic harbinger of looming catastrophe.

The first British explorer arrived a year after Dufresne: Captain Tobias Furneaux, second in command of an expedition led by Captain James Cook. When a storm separated Furneaux, in the *Adventure*, from Cook's

A Palawa family group, drawn by French explorers around the time
of Kikatapula's birth.
(Courtesy Libraries Tasmania)

Resolution, he set course for Van Diemen's Land to replenish his water
supplies and on 9 March 1773 sighted South West Cape. Like Tasman and
Dufresne, Furneaux followed the coastline around the southern tip and
up the east coast, coming to anchor in *kabbererdy*, which he renamed
Adventure Bay, on the eastern (seaward) side of *lunawanna alonnah*, now
called Bruny Island, which Europeans at that time thought was part of the
Tasmanian mainland. Furneaux saw signs of habitation including fires and
'several huts or wigwams' but sighted none of the island's inhabitants,
the Nununi. After five days he continued northward along the coast,
discovering and naming the Furneaux Islands, before he turned east to
New Zealand and a rendezvous with the *Resolution*.

Cook himself, in HMS *Discovery* on his third and final voyage into the
Pacific, anchored in Adventure Bay on 24 January 1777 and stayed two
days. After a while Palawa approached the visitors, but an elder shooed
them back into the bush when some of Cook's crew made advances to
the women. The Nununi remained peaceable, however, and the *Discovery*
sailed away without violent incident.

Ships came more often after that. Early in 1788 Lieutenant William Bligh in HMS *Bounty* briefly revisited Bruny Island, where he had been the previous year with Cook. Some evidence exists that a few months later the two French frigates *L'Astrolabe* and *La Boussole*, commanded by Jean-François de Galaupe, comte de La Pérouse, also dropped anchor in Adventure Bay.[4] Then, on 2 July 1789, the brig *Mercury*, commanded by Captain John Henry Cox, arrived off the west coast. After naming Cox Bluff and Cox Bight on the far south coast he sailed up the east coast and anchored on 7 July in Mercury Passage, the strait separating *roleleeper* (Maria Island) from the east coast of mainland *lutruwita*. Cox stayed four days in Mercury Passage, charting Maria Island and Marion Bay, before resuming his voyage across the Pacific on 11 July 1789. One of his officers, Lieutenant George Mortimer, summed up the Oyster Bay people they encountered. 'Upon the whole,' he wrote, 'they seemed to us to be a timorous, harmless race of people, and afford a fine picture of human nature in its most rude and uncultivated state'.[5] *Timorous* and *harmless* were not adjectives that next century's British arrivals would ever apply to Black Tom's people.

On 9 February 1792 William Bligh, now in HMS *Providence*, again anchored in Adventure Bay, where he planted fruit trees, acorns, and vegetables before sailing away on 22 February.

Two months later *lutruwita* had more European visitors: a French expedition searching for the missing La Pérouse. On 23 April 1792 Rear-Admiral Bruni D'Entrecasteaux in the *Recherche* and Captain Jean-Michel Huon de Kermandec in the *Espérance* anchored in a harbour Palawa called *leillateah*, in the extreme south-east of *lutruwita*, and renamed it Recherche Bay. During five weeks of exploring south-eastern waterways the French mingled amiably with local Palawa, found the channel that separates Bruny Island from mainland Tasmania, renamed it and the island itself in honour of the admiral, explored *talloonne* (Huon River) and *rummerneegegee* (Port Esperance), the Derwent estuary and Frederick Henry Bay, and capes Pillar and Raoul before sailing away on 28 May to resume their mission. On 22 January the following year they returned to Recherche Bay, further exploring the south-east including *nibberlin*, a river they renamed Rivière du Nord, for another five weeks before leaving *lutruwita* on 28 February 1793.

Little more than a year later, beginning on 24 April 1794, Captain John Hayes in the *Duke of Clarence* and the *Duchess of Bengal* also explored D'Entrecasteaux Channel as well as Rivière du Nord, which he renamed River Derwent. Before leaving *lutruwita* on 9 June he also named the Derwent's Risdon Cove, which nine years later was to be the site of the first British settlement of Palawa country – and soon after that the site of the first British massacre of Palawa.

The next strangers arrived unwillingly. In February 1797 the *Sydney Cove*, sailing from Calcutta to Sydney and in imminent danger of sinking, was grounded on an island at the eastern end of Bass Strait, part of the uninhabited Furneaux Group. The crew survived on the island, which they named Preservation Island, until rescued six months later. Their rescuers observed with interest the abundance of fur seals around the islands, and on their return to Sydney reported the potential for rich pickings. By October the following year, five years before the first attempt to colonise mainland *lutruwita*, sealers had begun to live in the Furneaux Group. They were a motley lot, men of diverse cultural and racial backgrounds who were happy to live away from and outside the law: seamen, adventurers, deserters, emancipists from New South Wales, absconders. As the industry flourished and the number of sealers increased they built crude houses, cultivated vegetable gardens, and raised livestock. They also raided coastal camps in eastern and north-eastern *lutruwita* to abduct Palawa women and girls to be sex slaves. Within two decades sex-slaving became a remorseless malignancy that infected the heart and soul of Palawa, helping to create a serious gender imbalance among them, devastating their birthrate, and eroding their social structure.

In the meantime, exploration was continuing. In October 1798 Lieutenant Matthew Flinders and his friend George Bass sailed south from Sydney in the sloop *Norfolk*. They discovered the strait that now bears Bass's name and sailed the length of it from east to west before turning south to confirm by circumnavigation that *lutruwita* is an island. Sailing well up the Derwent, they encountered a Palawa man with two women. Although the women fled, the man appeared unafraid and accepted the explorers' gift of a swan. '[T]he quickness with which he comprehended our signs spoke in favour of his intelligence,' Flinders noted.[6]

In 1800 the French government sent Nicolas-Thomas Baudin in the corvettes *Le Géographe* and *Le Naturaliste* to map the New Holland coast. The expedition entered D'Entrecasteaux Channel from the south on 13 January 1802 and subsequently explored Port Cygnet. They had several peaceful meetings ashore with curious Palawa from the Mellukerdee or Lyluequonny bands, who behaved amicably toward them, although the French opined that the men 'have a look that is both sinister and ferocious ... corresponding only too clearly with their character'. The expedition spent more than a month exploring and surveying the area around D'Entrecasteaux Channel, Maria Island, and *tiggana marraboona* (Schouten Island) and sailed into the Derwent. They then wintered in Sydney, where British officers lavishly entertained them. Perhaps having too freely enjoyed the hospitality, the visitors confessed their enthusiasm for Tasmania, saying they intended to recommend a French colony be established there. Unenthusiastic about the possibility of a French settlement on his doorstep, Governor King of New South Wales informed Baudin that Van Diemen's Land was already a British possession, and when news arrived from London shortly afterwards that Britain was again at war with France, King decided for security's sake to nip in the bud any future French expansion. On 8 September 1803 a tiny British expedition under Lieutenant John Bowen in the *Lady Nelson* raised the Union Jack at Risdon Cove, on the eastern shore of the Derwent a few kilometres north of present-day Hobart. Five days later the *Lady Nelson* was joined by the whaler *Albion* bringing supplies for the new settlement.

Britain also established a settlement that year in Tamar Valley, at the northern end of the island about 170 kilometres away. Called Port Dalrymple, it was subsequently renamed Launceston.

In 1804, the Risdon Cove site having proved unsuitable, the southern settlement was moved about seven kilometres downriver to Sullivans Cove, on the Derwent's western shore, to a place local Palawa knew as *nipaluna*, where it flourished and grew into the city of Hobart. The Risdon Cove settlement was in the country of Oyster Bay people, some of whom were slaughtered there by Britons before the move to Sullivans Cove was complete. When a bloody resistance to the invasion began two decades later, it was incited and then led by an Oyster Bay warrior – the man the British came to know, fear, and loath as Black Tom Birch.

2

'They rushed them at their fires'

Black Tom never forgot the first ship his band saw. Their shock was great. In fear the people fled.

> [T]he blacks could not conceive how the white men came here first. Tom said he saw the first ship, that it came to Maria Island, he was a boy at this time and was with his tribe; that in the morning they saw the ship at anchor off Maria Island, that they were all frightened and run away, that it looked like a small island and that they could not tell what it was.[1]

That was how Kikatapula – Black Tom – remembered the coming of the cataclysm. In little more than a generation it would cost his race their country, then their freedom, then their lives. His own short life straddled the brief and bloody history of *lutruwita* from the time the first invaders dropped anchor in Risdon Cove almost to the final futile spear thrust and waddy blow against them.

Kikatapula, whose alternative name was Kikatamana, was born into the Paytirami (pronounced *pie-tee-RAH-mee*) band of the Oyster Bay people.[2] His parents' names are unknown, any siblings he had are unrecorded as such, and the year of his birth is uncertain. The ship that shocked his people is usually presumed to have been the Baudin–Péron expedition's, which anchored in Maria Island's Great Oyster Bay in February 1802. But Baudin's expedition comprised two ships, not one, and although they lost sight of each other in fog on 8 March and subsequently proceeded separately, that was more than a week after they left Maria Island and sailed northward. However, between 18 March and 3 April 1803 *Le Naturaliste* returned to Oyster Bay to search for *Le Géographe*.[3] If what

Kikatapula saw was indeed a single one of Baudin's ships, it was likely to have been then.

Or he might have seen the whaler *Albion* (362 tons) during its passage from Sydney to the Derwent to provision the British toehold at Risdon Cove. *Albion* lay three days in Oyster Bay in September 1803 and caught three sperm whales within sight of Maria Island.[4] If what Kikatapula saw was the *Albion*, it conjures a bitter irony: a brief distant encounter between the first wave of British invaders and a small boy who two decades later would light the touchpaper of resistance to them.[5]

Whatever ship he saw, it was undoubtedly between 1800 and 1805, from which historians calculate he was born around 1800. The date is plausible and proximate.

Because early adventurers had been impressed by the abundance of whales, dolphins, and seals in the waters around Maria Island, those resources were soon being exploited, so that first ship was soon followed by others. All too quickly, strangers and ships ceased to be a novelty for Oyster Bay people.

Kikatapula's Paytirami and their fellow Oyster Bay bands inhabited a region of abundant resources and mild climate. Their country, a sizeable portion of eastern Tasmania, encompassed much of the island's best grassland including the Midland Plain. In all, it comprised about 7800 square kilometres of land, bounded on the east by 515 kilometres of coastline southward from St Patricks Head to the Derwent estuary. The eastern bank of Derwent River as far eastward as the mouth of Jordan River at Herdsmans Cove was its southern boundary, from which it meandered north and east back to St Patricks Head.[6]

The Paytirami and the other Palawa bands were hardy people, perfectly adapted to their island's climate and resources although culturally as well as physically isolated, with simpler technology than their mainland counterparts had developed. Their spears were not barbed but simply sharpened to a point and then fire-hardened. They had no shields and neither woomeras (spear-throwers) nor boomerangs, but they supplemented the spear with the waddy, a weapon variously described as 'a club made of very hard and heavy wood' or 'a small stick, bluntly pointed at one end, and about 18 inches [46 cm] long, which ...

they are trained up from infancy to throw with surprising dexterity and precision'.[7] Later reports described waddies sharpened at both ends. Probably there were different kinds for different uses; the club type, whether thrown or wielded at close range, was devastatingly used against colonists during the Black War.[8] The other Palawa projectile weapons were stones, which colonists quickly discovered they threw with deadly force and accuracy.

The war against Palawa began early. Initially an undeclared war of attrition, it started even before the British invasion officially began in 1803, prosecuted by Bass Strait sealers' sex-slaving raids. By 1804 the islands in the strait had a population of 123 men, probably with captive Palawa women and the first progeny of their couplings.[9] A typical experience was that of a woman named Tikati, believed to have been from Kikatapula's Paytirami band, who recalled that a sealer named Hervey stole her when she was a little girl and also abducted her sister Tanalipunya; both were later associates of Kikatapula.[10] Another, Tenkotemanener from the Laremairremener band of Oyster Bay people, 'was stole away by the sealers from her people. They rushed them at their fires … Two more women was stolen with Tenkotemanener by the sealers'.[11] Some were mere infants when taken. Pulara or Rramanaluna, a Cape Portland woman who was later also an associate (and an intimate) of Kikatapula, was abducted with five others by a sealer named Munro when she was so young she could just crawl.[12] She reported that Munro had six Palawa women enslaved; others had four or five each.[13] The abductors were ruthless. Adolphe Schayer, an employee of the Van Diemen's Land Company, wrote that Bass Strait sealers 'found very useful the services of black women to keep them company; and when they refused to accompany them voluntarily … took them using force and often killed their parents or friends who tried to prevent this violence'.[14]

Kikatapula must have had first-hand experience of such raids, perhaps when Tikati and Tanalipunya were abducted from his own band. They and other Oyster Bay bands were fractured by the abductions and by the murders of any of their menfolk who objected, so it is not surprising that Oyster Bay people became noted for their hostility to Britons.

Sydney-based whalers and sealers began a separate wave of seaborne incursions a little later. Whales migrate northward along Tasmania's east coast in winter, calve, then return to antarctic waters for summer, so whalers and sealers were soon working out of Oyster Bay and Maria Island's Whalers Cove.[15] Palawa punished the intruders by attacking their makeshift shore bases. As early as March 1805, eight sealers at Oyster Bay had their hut razed, their supplies stolen, and their catch of 2200 sealskins destroyed. They were little deterred. Although only five Sydney-based ships were whaling in Tasmanian waters before 1810, within 10 years that number had tripled.[16]

The colonists' first foothold at Risdon Cove suffered no Palawa hostility. Nevertheless, in May 1804, a few months after it was established, Britons there fired a carronade – a short-barrel large-calibre naval cannon whose destructive impact caused sailors to tag it 'the smasher' – into a hunting party of Palawa men, women, and children, probably Mumirimina from the Oyster Bay people. How many were killed is uncertain. Although the number has been set as high as 40 to 50, it was probably lower, but, regardless, 'this outrage was the origin of all that happened afterwards'.[17] However many casualties were suffered, word would quickly have spread far and wide that the newcomers were murderously hostile and possessed a fearsome weapon that belched fire and smoke and killed and maimed indiscriminately. Clearly the British were to be avoided, and for a decade thereafter Palawa avoided them. Except for one or two peeps into Hobart by bold and curious individuals in 1804 and 1806, they stayed away for nearly a decade.

In the bush, however, accidental encounters were unavoidable as Britons began to explore Hobart's environs. Although there were occasional friendly contacts, skirmishes were inevitable as Oyster Bay bands in their perambulations found armed Britons hunting in their country without permission or reciprocity. They resented the hunters' theft of their resources and both sides suffered casualties in ensuing clashes. Further pressure was applied to Palawa when trusted convicts were given firearms and sent out to hunt kangaroos to feed the growing British population. Some naturally opted to abscond into the bush, and their numbers were soon swollen by escaped prisoners, for although Tasmania was a penal colony it was not a jail. Convicts were assigned to settlers as farmhands and labourers; only recalcitrants and repeat offenders spent time behind bars, on a chain gang, or at penal settlements like Port Arthur, Macquarie Harbour, or Norfolk Island. Since they were physically unconfined, assigned prisoners found it easy to abscond, so escapes were plentiful and authorities soon coined the word *bushrangers* to describe the fugitives. One early bushranger, a convict named Carrett who absconded in 1806, later bragged of decapitating a Palawa man at Oyster Bay and forcing the man's wife to wear the head around her neck. Two fugitives from the northern settlement, John Brown and Richard Lemon, ranged over Oyster Bay country for about five months in 1807–1808, committing 'many acts of barbarity against the straggling natives', bayoneting Palawa and shooting at them, using their living bodies as targets.[18] A man named Ibbens reportedly slew many eastern Palawa in sneak attacks with a double-barrel firearm.[19] In 1810 Lieutenant John Oxley reported that 20 to 30 convicts were at large and that some of them had murdered Palawa men and then forced the widows to live with them.[20]

The Big River people, whose country abutted Oyster Bay bands' around the region called Abyssinia, were also early victims. Before it received its first European settlers in 1821, Abyssinia was a favoured hideout for bushrangers. The killer Michael Howe had several battles with Palawa there before he was slain by a soldier in 1818. Another bushranger, known only as Abyssinian Tom, was said to hunt Palawa with dogs and a double-barrel gun, afterwards notching the butt of his weapon to record each victim.[21]

Reprisals were customary and certain. The first Briton to suffer Palawa vengeance was Robert Waring, a hunter slain in 1807 in an attack that had the hallmarks of payback.[22] The second was an escaped convict named William Russell who had been at large for about two years and who boasted of his skills at torturing Palawa. He paid with his life in 1810 when some of them caught up with him. His accomplice George Getley suffered the same fate.[23] But they were the last Britons to die at Palawa hands for eight years.

Nevertheless, as British atrocities continued so did Palawa reprisals, which the British fully understood as such. The *Derwent Star* noted in 1810 that 'rendered desperate by the cruelties they have experienced from our people', Palawa were attacking cattle in retaliation.[24] On 10 April 1813, during Kikatapula's adolescence, the *Sydney Gazette* reported Palawa being very hostile because their ill-treatment by escaped convicts was provoking retaliatory attacks. Two months later, after Oyster Bay people speared settlers' cattle in Coal River Valley near Hobart, the Lieutenant Governor admitted the attacks were in retaliation for Britons' abduction of Palawa children.[25] A serious gender imbalance among colonists was causing Palawa women and girls to be coerced into servitude as concubines, wives, or sex slaves, and convict stockkeepers on the frontier far from judicial eyes were willing to commit barbarities to acquire them. Such cruelties, according to a leading player in Kikatapula's drama, were at the root of all Palawa hostility. There was scarcely a single Palawa who had not had 'some monstrous cruelty' committed against his family or band, he asserted.[26] Later he was to record numerous British atrocities that his Palawa guides told him about – a sanguinary legacy that will help explain Kikatapula's rage at a mindless act of brutality to a Palawa woman at Grindstone Bay in 1823.[27]

An act that lit the fuse for a long and bloody war.

Time passed; more Britons landed. They included free settlers lured by the promise of free land and free convict labour who expropriated more and more Palawa land for agriculture, encroaching into Oyster Bay country in Derwent Valley, Pitt Water, Coal River Valley, and the southern Midlands, then radiating from the Midlands east toward the Eastern Marshes and the Blue Hills and westerly into the Big River people's country in what has been characterised as 'the most dramatic expansion of British settlement anywhere in Australia since 1788'.[28] They continued to plunder Palawa resources without permission, reciprocity, or recompense: kangaroos, wallabies, and possums for their skins and meat, seals for their skins and oil, emus for their meat and fat, swans for their meat and feathers. European livestock displaced native herbivores on grasslands that had been created and nurtured for millennia by Palawa firestick farming. Settlers' attitudes to Palawa were often racist, derogatory, and murderous. Although the colonial government frequently called for fair play and humane treatment of Aborigines, racism-justified self-interest prevailed. As a visiting Swedish clergyman was to observe,

'To kill a native of Australia is the same as killing a dog in the eyes of the British colonist'. His view was supported by a Tasmanian settler who recalled that 'it was a favourite amusement to hunt the aborigines'.[29]

Palawa distrust of Britons was well evinced in 1817 by a chance encounter between black and white in the sparsely settled frontier region between Richmond and Sorell, which was Oyster Bay country. Their anger at finding a white man near their women and children was quickly demonstrated.

> Robert Rosne, overseer to Capt. Jeffreys [of Frogmore Castle, Penna] was searching for sheep strayed from his flock, came across about 15 native women and children assembled around a fire in the Sweet Water Hills. Considering them to be an inoffensive tribe, and his mind dwelling on his pursuit, he carefully approached them to light his pipe, pleased with his reception; but on leaving this peaceful group, he met with a number of savage native men, whose ferocity had nearly been his death. One of them threw a stone at him, which struck him violently on the mouth and staggered him, but little time was given him to recover from this blow, when an ill fated volley of stones dislocated his shoulder. Fortunately, however, he was suffered to leave them alive.[30]

Yet despite all the provocations Palawa hostility during the second decade of the British invasion was generally reactive and restrained, although Oyster Bay bands' growing resentment at encroachments, abductions, and atrocities was demonstrated by the increasing magnitude of their retaliatory attacks – 930 sheep killed and burnt in one raid near Oatlands in 1815, for instance, and 500 slaughtered two years later at Rokeby on Hobart's eastern shore. The following year, while still wary of the invaders' superior numbers and weaponry, Palawa also began to attack individuals as well as livestock. In August 1816 they ambushed three stockkeepers near New Norfolk and two months later beset four colonists in a cart near Salt Pan Plains. Both assaults were repulsed by gunfire.[31]

Those years of uneasy peace were a time of great uncertainty for Palawa as the population of Britons ballooned and spread and squeezed them out of ancestral country. Unsure of how to respond beyond tit-for-tat reprisals, they continued to avoid the newcomers while watching and learning. As Wurati, a Nununi chief, recalled, 'the natives went to the mountains, went and looked at what the white people did, went and told other natives and they came and looked also'.[32]

From time to time Britons attempted to befriend Palawa by enticing them into Hobart in order to impress upon them British superiority and goodwill, and curiosity sometimes overcame caution. In mid-winter 1814 a former bushranger named Campbell and his Palawa wife persuaded four Oyster Bay people from South Arm, where the couple lived, to sample the town's wonders.[33] '[A]fter receiving several articles of clothing from His Honor the Lieut. Governor,' and other humane Gentlemen of this Settlement,' a newspaper reported, 'they were conducted through the Streets by A. Campbell ... Their curiosity ... prompted them to examine every thing with wonder and amazement ...' Campbell and his wife subsequently coaxed into Hobart 13 more South Arm Palawa 'who received every kindness and humanity from the Lieut. Governor'.[34]

In time the news spread, and the following year Hobart's chaplain Robert Knopwood recorded Palawa women and children visiting his house. They stayed overnight 'and many of the inhabitants came to see the natives', indicating Palawa were a rare sight to Hobartians.[35] Six months later the visitors returned. 'The party of natives that was at my house sometime back came again this morn', Knopwood wrote.[36]

But such visits remained so uncommon that in March the following year a visiting Sydney clergyman asked why there was such a dearth of Palawa in Hobart; he was told 'We shoot them whenever we find them'.[37] A government order issued two months later suggests the truth underlying that casual response. After noting that 'several Settlers and others are in the habit of maliciously and wantonly firing at, and destroying, the defenceless NATIVES or ABORIGINES of this Island', it forbade ill-treatment of Palawa and promised 'to Support and Encourage all Measures which may Tend to conciliate and civilize them'.[38]

That the order had any effect on settlers and stockkeepers is doubtful, yet the situation did change during 1818, a year of some rapprochement in which Hobart gained a floating population of Palawa sojourners that probably included the young Kikatapula. The British were clearly not going to go away and Hobartians were not openly hostile, so curious Palawa began to visit and linger in the town that year and engage with the inhabitants, for the little settlement was a cornucopia of wonder and novelty. Its streets teemed with strange animals: donkeys, dogs, horses, and horned cattle – so many, in fact, that a few days before Kikatapula was first recorded there the government ordered its citizens to keep the thoroughfares clear of livestock.[39] Carts and carriages were also a novel part of the streetscape's wondrous bustle and surge. As well as seeing such extraordinary sights for themselves, Palawa were curious about Britons' food, clothing, and artefacts. Possibly they saw advantages in familiarising themselves with the newcomers.

Throughout 1818 Palawa were frequently recorded in the town. On 24 and 26 February Knopwood's diary noted his taking four Palawa girls residing with him to dive for crayfish at Taroona. In April the *Hobart Town Gazette* noted that several Palawa seen about the town and its environs were being given food by charitable Britons.[40] In September Palawa watching tilling operations in Argyle Street were delighted when the plough uncovered 'a large root of a fungous nature' that they called *bringally* (native bread or breadfruit), which they eagerly ate.[41] On 14 November a Palawa woman and seven children visited Knopwood's house. When they returned the following morning four girls chose to stay with him. Twelve days later he recorded a similar visit. Again some of the visitors tarried, and next day his friend Thomas Capon sketched several of them. On 30 November and 2 December Capon visited again and both times drew pictures 'of the native girls at my house'.[42]

If Palawa women and children became common Hobart sights that year, their menfolk were also present, although not always treated so kindly. Some Britons craving entertainment delighted in bribing or provoking them to perform brutal acts. After witnessing such a performance one outraged citizen complained about 'That most shameful, cruel, and barbarous custom of encouraging the Black people to murder or mangle one another for the sport of the *learned*, the *polite*, and the *refined Europeans*; for the amusement and gratification of those who are denominated *Christians*'. He cited an example.

Last Sunday afternoon [23 December 1818], on my way from Church homewards, I was much grieved and distressed, to hear and to see that the public peace of the Town, and the holy rest of the Sabbath, were most impiously violated by the *blows* and *cries* of the Blacks, excited to uproar and outrage by the *Whites*, who take pleasure in the sufferings of their fellow men, and, who will propose and give a reward, that the unoffending may be slain, or injured, merely to gratify or indulge the diabolical passions of a base mind ...[43]

Familiarity with Hobart and some amity with its inhabitants, however, did not alter Oyster Bay people's attitudes to British transgressions in their country. On 25 October in that year of rapprochement five young Britons set out from Hobart in a boat belonging to a prominent settler named Thomas Birch, a merchant and exporter of seal skins who was about to become a pivotal influence in Kikatapula's life. They sailed up the east coast to Oyster Bay and for three weeks helped themselves liberally to local resources, collecting 136 kilograms of swan feathers, 60 swan skins, 300 kangaroo skins, 34 live swans, and 250 seal skins. On 13 November they steered their heavily laden boat homewards, putting in at Grindstone Bay, about 50 kilometres farther south. When contrary winds delayed them there for three days they decided to go back to Oyster Bay to procure more seal skins, leaving John Kemp behind to guard their booty. They returned to Grindstone Bay to find him dead at the water's edge, 'cut and mangled in a manner too shocking to relate', and their entire three-week haul removed or destroyed. As they were retrieving Kemp's corpse they were ambushed by about 20 Palawa, whom they managed to escape by hastily putting to sea. They recognised one attacker, 'A native girl, who had been some time among those at present walking about the streets of Hobart'.[44] So Hobart's 1818 Palawa visitors included recognisable Oyster Bay people. Whether Kikatapula were one of Kemp's killers is unknowable, but he was about to appear in Hobart and in history for the first time.

Almost nothing is certain about his life before then. As well as his recall of seeing the first ship, Kikatapula was occasionally recorded speaking about events that must have occurred when he was still young enough to be a member of his natal Paytirami band but old enough to have taken part in internecine fights. The example below is typical: the Paytirami and two allied Oyster Bay bands against a Big River band, the Luggermairrerner, whose country was around *yingina* (Great Lake). It helps repudiate mistaken claims, discussed in the following chapter, that Kikatapula was only a small boy when he first appeared in Hobart.

> KICK.ER.TER.POL.LER said his own nation the PARE.DARE.RER.ME [Paytirami], [with] the PY.DER.RE.ME and the LOON.TIM.MAIR.RE MER was engaged in a war with the lakes or LUG.GER.MAIR.RER.NER PAIR. RE.NER nation and that this nation killed several of their women and took some away: that [the Paytirami] fought with them and beat them and that then the LUG.GER.MAIR.RER.NER natives came upon them at night, that expecting they were coming the PARE.DARE.RER.ME people concealed themselves away from the fire, that by and by there came a shower of spears, that in the morning [the Paytirami] tracked [the Luggermairrerner] and fought with them and beat them off. This was occasioned in consequence of this nation breaking the treaty; the PARE. DARE.RER.ME had given them beads and the LUG.GER.MAIR.RER.NER would not give them the red ochre as agreed.[45]

How and why Kikatapula came to be in Hobart is uncertain, although plausible surmise is possible. During his adolescent years survivors of some invasion-shattered Oyster Bay bands were coalescing into composite new groups that Britons called 'tame mobs'. They lived a peaceful semi-traditional semi-mendicant life around their country, visiting settlers for handouts and, as we have seen, making forays into Hobart. Probably Kikatapula was a member of such a tame mob and found his way to Hobart with them toward the end of 1818, soon afterwards making his innocuous first appearance in the pages of history.

3

'Nursing Mr. Birch's children at Hobartown'

Had they known of a small rite occurring there on the afternoon of Wednesday 17 February 1819, Hobart's more superstitious citizens might have read sinister meteorological portents in the sky. 'Much thunder and lightning all the morn and aft, with showers,' Rev. Knopwood recorded in his diary that day. 'I waited upon His Honer the Lt. Govnr, respecting a native boy, who was unwell. At 2, I xtianed [christened] him'. The only Palawa baptised in Hobart that day was given the name Thomas and he was the only Palawa christened with that name in Hobart between 1805 and 1822.[1] Neither his parents' names nor any European surname was recorded, but Kikatapula – the 'native boy' can have been only he – was afterwards known to Europeans as Tom Birch, named for the man who took him into his household to convalesce.

The reasons Kikatapula had attracted vice-regal attention and was at Government House are unrecorded, and confusion is rife about how long he had been in Hobart and how old he was. Those history books that bother to notice him claim he was stolen or adopted or fostered, aged about nine, by Thomas and Sarah Birch around 1809, and an article written in 1915 by their grandson Thomas Sutcliffe appears to confirm that. (The 'small boy' concerned is identified as 'Tom' later in the article.)

> My mother, whose maiden name was Eliza Birch, was born in Macquarie House [Hobart] in the year 1816. She often told me about the wild blacks, and grandmother [Sarah Birch] was very good to them, giving them food and clothing … One of the black gins left a small boy with grandmother, to teach and make him know as much as a white fellow, in consideration that

grandmother gave her a red petticoat in return. This lad was in the Birch family for four years. He then ran away and joined the wild tribe again.[2]

Kikatapula did rejoin his own people after serving the Birch family for about four years, but that was in late 1822, so those four years began not in 1809 but in 1818–1819, which concurs with his baptismal record.[3] The only contentious issue is how old he was at the time. Sutcliffe, who was not born in Kikatapula's lifetime, wrote from hearsay that Kikatapula had been 'a small boy', whereas Knopwood, although recording him as 'a native boy' when baptising him, estimated his age that day as 17, which accords with historians' guesses that he was born around 1800–1802, so he was *not* a small boy when he joined the Birches. (Knopwood's reference to him as 'a native boy' should not mislead. As late as 1828, when Kikatapula was nearing 30, the upper echelon of British society in Tasmania – the Executive Council in this instance – still referred to him as a 'Black Boy', a mindlessly patronising term for a supposed racial inferior.)[4]

Other evidence supports his not having been a child when he joined the Birch household. The two circles on his loins that were once reported in the *Hobart Town Gazette* were cicatrices incised during pubertal initiation ceremonies – persuasive evidence that Kikatapula was still living a traditional life during adolescence.[5] Moreover, in 1821, after more than two years with the Birches, he was seconded to guide a surveying expedition into Oyster Bay country, a task he would have been unequipped for had he been living in Hobart since age nine. (In the caption to his sketch of the expedition, assistant surveyor Thomas Scott, in the customary way, referred to Kikatapula, then aged around 20, as a 'Native Black boy'.) Similarly, Kikatapula's hunting and tracking skills, which were praised during the Friendly Mission from 1830 to 1832, and which have been noted as essential to the mission's success, can have been acquired only from a traditional upbringing from infancy to young manhood.[6] Had Kikatapula been with the Birches since the age of nine he would not have had those skills or his adroitness with the spear, which was also commended.[7] Finally, George Augustus Robinson's journals note several instances of Kikatapula's recalling internecine battles he had fought in, so he was unquestionably a young warrior, not a boy, when he joined the Birches in Hobart. The erroneously claimed 1809 date probably had its origins in a simple error: a misprint, mishearing, or misremembering of 1819, the correct and documented date.

As Knopwood noted, Kikatapula was ill or injured when he was baptised, so the rite probably took place in hospital.[8] As the chaplain told Commissioner Bigge early the following year in answer to a question about Palawa children's baptisms, 'Some of them have been brought into the Hospital when *sick*, and seeing them there I have baptized them; they have also been brought in by the Settlers with whom they happen to be staying'.[9] That indicates the clergyman had not previously encountered Kikatapula, confirming that he was not already a member of the Birch household, where Knopwood was a frequent guest, until he was baptised.

What ailment took him to Lieutenant Governor Sorell's attention in 1819 is unknown, but some years later a newspaper reported that Kikatapula was identifiable by a 'remarkable scar' on his forehead, so possibly a head injury or wound was responsible.[10] Given 'Monitor's' letter of complaint, published in the *Gazette* only two months before Kikatapula's baptism, that Palawa males in Hobart were being urged to fight one another, a credible scenario suggests itself: of his being one of the curious Palawa visiting the town in late 1818 and early 1819; of his being goaded into fighting another Palawa male for the amusement of Britons; of his consequently suffering a serious head wound that left his forehead scarred; of his being treated by Birch, who was a doctor, and then taken into Birch's home to convalesce.

So Kikatapula was not, as is sometimes claimed, an early member of the Stolen Generations. He was not a terrified child acquired by force or trade by a stockkeeper or a whaler or sealer. He was a mature, intelligent, inquisitive young man bent on acquiring some familiarity with Hobart and its inhabitants. He was there of his own volition, as a Hobart newspaper acknowledged, and he was not a captive.[11]

Plausible surmise is possible about why he was there. Palawa visiting the town were collectively known to colonists as 'the tame mob'. Some were Oyster Bay people, so youthful membership of the tame mob might have been Kikatapula's route to Hobart. Since he was later known as 'a famous interpreter', time spent in such a heterogeneous coalition could also help account for his facility in more than one Palawa language or dialect.[12]

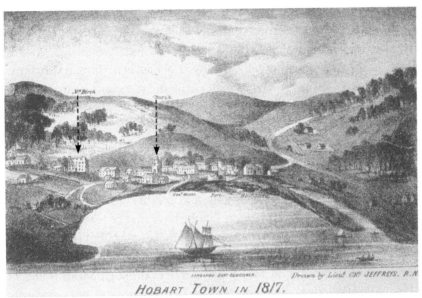

Hobart just before Kikatapula's advent. A pointer to Macquarie House
is labelled 'Mr. Birch'. (Courtesy Libraries Tasmania)

Coincidentally, the year Kikatapula was first recorded in Hobart was
also the year an exiled mainland Aborigine known as Musquito forsook
working for the British in Tasmania to join the tame mob; perhaps the
two men first met that way. Later, after he became the tame mob's leader,
Musquito would unite with Kikatapula in a brief partnership that would
earn them each a bloody place in history.

Kikatapula's benefactors, the Birches, were prominent and
prosperous.[13] Thomas William Birch, born at Kingston upon Hull,
Yorkshire, in 1774, was a surgeon who reached Hobart on 2 May 1808 as
medical officer in the whaler *Dubuc*, a year out from London via Timor
with 300 tuns of oil aboard.[14] *Dubuc* continued whaling in the Derwent
until later that year when it had to be beached at Bellerive after being
declared unseaworthy. Birch then decided to settle in the tiny colony,
founded only five years earlier. Once established, he rarely practised
his profession – Hobart already had two surgeons – instead turning
his attention to commerce. He soon interested himself in whaling, his
time in the *Dubuc* having familiarised him with the abundance of whales
and seals in Tasmanian waters. He had a 40-ton schooner called the

Henrietta Packet, and around 1816 he also acquired a bigger ship, the 120-ton *Sophia,* which 'worked locally each season and regularly took full catches of around 40 tuns of black oil'.[15] The first Tasmanian settler to enter the industry, he eventually employed 26 men in it. He 'had very large dealings, and was possessed of much acuteness', a court heard in 1838, with 'many and large transactions in money matters, which he managed entirely himself'.[16]

Birch was a decent man, if 'rather odd and eccentric; he would work sometimes as a cook, sometimes as a carpenter, sometimes as a gardener', an acquaintance recalled.[17] Another testified that 'One day he would eat and drink to excess, and be very jolly, and another, he would fast rigidly, and mope about, seeing no person. On the days that he feasted, he would rise very early, and give anything away to the people about him'.[18]

The woman Birch married a few months after settling in Hobart, Sarah Guest, is unsung in Tasmanian history, although Sarah Island in Macquarie Harbour commemorates her. Her origins were not outwardly propitious. One of six children, she was born in 1792 on Norfolk Island, a British penal settlement in the Pacific about 2400 kilometres from Hobart. Her father, George Guest, was a petty thief condemned to death for stealing 10 pigs and a horse but reprieved and transported for seven years; her mother, Mary Bateman, was a prostitute transported at 15 for stealing a silver watch. George became a successful Norfolk Island farmer with a substantial landholding and a flock of nearly 1000 sheep. When the settlement began to be abandoned, the Guest family and 300 of their ewes were shipped to Hobart, arriving in September 1805. George was granted 10 hectares of land at Macquarie Point, although the family did not live there but in Campbell Street. Despite his illiteracy he was successful in business, acquiring several Hobart properties.

Three years after the Guests settled in Tasmania 16-year-old Sarah married the recently arrived 33-year-old Thomas Birch. She was to bear him seven children, one of whom died in infancy. This remarkable daughter of illiterate emancipists transitioned with apparent ease to being the wife of one of Hobart's richest and most prominent men (and, after his death, of another high-status settler, Edmund Hodgson, with whom she had six more children) and became hostess to society's upper echelon, including lieutenant governors and Governor Lachlan Macquarie himself.

She was described by 19th-century writer James Bonwick as 'estimable', which the scanty surviving records confirm.[19] For the mother of five children, one of whom in the parlance of the day was 'imbecile', to have taken in, nurtured, and educated an ailing Palawa man also indicates a strong-minded woman of notable compassion. One, in fact, willing not only to befriend him but fight for him and even lie to protect him, as we will see she did.

In 1815 Birch built a substantial house in Macquarie Street, Hobart, on what is now the corner of Victoria Street. One of Australia's most significant colonial buildings and one of the oldest private residences in Tasmania, Birch's House, as it was first known, is thought to be Australia's oldest three-storey house and today is one of the three oldest surviving buildings in Tasmania. Originally it had a flat roof with battlements, through which poked two cannons Birch had mounted there for defence against a possible French invasion, declaring that he intended to give a good account of himself. Sometimes called Birch's Castle because of that, the house originally stood on a sizeable area of pleasant grounds that must have been salutary for the convalescent Kikatapula. They extended from Murray Street to Harrington Street and then down to Hobart Rivulet, which abounded in wild ducks and spotted trout and eels.[20] The finest house in the fledgling town, it was sometimes used as a surrogate Government House. Lieutenant Governor William Sorell chose to stay there when he first arrived in the colony in 1817, as during his 1820–1821 Tasmanian visit did Governor Macquarie, who was favourably disposed toward Birch. In 1818 he appointed the merchant one of three judges of the Lieutenant Governor's Court, the civil forerunner of the Supreme Court – a very important post indicative of his probity. In the Governor's honour Birch named his residence Macquarie House.

How long Kikatapula lived there with the Birches is uncertain. Alexander Laing, a prisoner-turned-lawman who arrived in the colony in 1815, wrote a half-century later that 'I was well acquainted with Black Tom Birch, as I had often seen him when he was nursing Mr. Birch's children at Hobartown'.[21] Kikatapula, who in 1826 was to have a lethal encounter with Laing, did serve the Birches after convalescing – Sarah spoke to Bonwick of her husband's being Kikatapula's *master*, not his foster-father as he is usually misdescribed – but 'nursing Mr. Birch's children' should probably not be taken too literally. Laing was much given to exaggeration, invention, and outright falsehood.[22]

The young Palawa undoubtedly found fascinating the many novelties of his new home, for by 1819 Hobart was one of the world's busiest whaling ports and an important Pacific base for the British navy. The ships entering and leaving the harbour, the small craft plying the river, the proliferating buildings, the red-coated military guarding convict gangs, the carts and carriages, the exotic animals, the jail (whose three-metre-high wall, built under contract by Dr Birch, extended to the corner of Macquarie Street) nearing completion on the southern side of Murray Street opposite the grounds of Government House, the new church under construction diagonally opposite (and only a few metres down Macquarie Street from Macquarie House), the gardens and orchards, the artisans' and saddlers' workshops, the grog shops and the drunkenness, the floggings and occasional executions – 10 men were publicly hanged at the upper end of Macquarie Street on a single day in 1821 – and on special occasions a musket volley or artillery salute – all must have contributed to a panorama of novelty and wonder for Kikatapula. Anything else he might have experienced of British colonial life – isolated settlers' houses and stockkeepers' huts at most – was eclipsed by the sights and sounds and smells of bustling Hobart in 1819.

Yet perhaps those very novelties, Macquarie House in particular, kindled unease in the young man. Tasmania had no more impressive example of European technology than Hobart's only three-storey building, and he must have found remarkable its size, its furnishings and kitchen, its battlements and cannons, the formality of meals and social occasions, the retinue of servants. But perhaps he also found it cause for concern. Macquarie House and all he could see from its upper windows, with their unimpeded view over the busy streets to the harbour and the steady stream of ships arriving to disgorge more beshackled Britons and armed military in full rig, might have caused an intelligent Palawa as much unease as wonder.

The Birches were caring and thorough in their treatment of Kikatapula, giving him a good basic education and a grounding in British manners and religion. Sarah, expressing a 'deep interest' in Kikatapula, described him as good and useful, obliging and gentle, honest and careful, and thoroughly devoted to his master. He spoke English correctly and could read and write, she said, and in his attendance at church and his general deportment he gave promise of true civilisation.[23] Later, after he became feared and notorious, she spoke of him as 'poor Tom'. During his stay at Macquarie House she developed a profound affection for him, which he responded to and reciprocated. Probably it was she who helped nurse him back to health, a bond consequently forming between them that was to be strengthened when she subsequently helped save him from the hangman and was further annealed when he was able to preserve her from Palawa spears only six months later.

Kikatapula learnt to read and write so well that he was able to perform clerical duties. He was, then, a man of considerable intelligence and intellectual curiosity, eager and able to learn. Religious instruction and church attendance also formed part of his Birch-bestowed education. Out of curiosity and politeness he accepted both, but Christianity played no observable part in his life before 1828, when a personal crisis caused him to open his ears to an evangelising Christian (although his baptism and consequent nominal Christianity were to help preserve him from the gallows in 1826), after which he would be recorded several times publicly espousing Christian faith. However, he was never to wholly abandon traditional beliefs and superstitions and, as in so many other ways, 'was often caught between tradition and cultural transition'.[24]

But that was only after his years as mainspring of the bloodiest war yet fought on Australian soil.

After recovering from whatever had ailed him Kikatapula stayed in Hobart working for the Birches long enough to acquire his notable literacy and fluency in English, likely for one to two years. Hobart is not known to have had many Palawa residents then, so during that period he became a familiar figure to Hobartians, a tall, prominently scarred black man proud in his European clothes, if probably barefoot. But egalitarianism and racial tolerance were not British traits, and while some Britons undoubtedly accepted him for what he was, others must have viewed him as a subject for mockery and resentment. A one-time constable named Matthew Osborne and his wife Mary, who were Argyle Street residents until 1821 and knew Kikatapula, were later to become his victims in an attack that had all the hallmarks of reprisal. They would not be the only Britons on whom he revenged himself for unrecorded wrongs, some no doubt dating from his Hobart days.

Around 1820–1821 the Birches put him to work in agriculture, intending to equip him to earn a living. T.W. Birch's success in the colony had enabled him to amass substantial landholdings including a 40-hectare farm in South Hobart, a holding near Jericho, and two grants in Coal River Valley between Cambridge and Richmond known as Duck-Hole Farm. Kikatapula was to work at both the latter two. He learnt to handle a bullock team and smoke a pipe and had his English vocabulary enriched with colourful words not heard in the refined ambiance of Macquarie House. He reportedly developed a taste for rum.

Colonists found him useful in other ways too. In 1821 a 'Native Black boy' named Tom was attached to Deputy Surveyor-General G.W. Evans's seven-strong expedition to Oyster Bay country on the east coast, charged with guiding them across rivers at traditional Palawa fording places. To have the requisite knowledge, such a guide would need to be a mature Oyster Bay man and an English-speaker; Kikatapula alone is known to have fit both criteria and be nicknamed Tom. A sketch drawn by assistant surveyor Thomas Scott shows Tom, carrying a piece of equipment, leading the party across Prosser River near Orford. He is identified by name in the sketch with a note that he 'ran away from us'. So Tom deserted them sometime after the party crossed the Prosser in September. Something, some kind of mistreatment, had seriously upset him. Even in an expedition that included at least two convicts, a 'Native Black boy' – the term itself is intrinsically belittling – would be lowest in the pecking order, liable in that caste-encumbered society to be treated with contempt or intolerance. That would have been insufferable for a prideful man who understood his own importance to the expedition, so he quit Evans and returned to Birch's farm. An early demonstration of his feisty independence, it was also the first suggestion of a burgeoning disenchantment with life as a quasi-Briton.

The journey would also have served to reinforce his awareness of settler encroachment and the scarcity of his own people in country they alone had occupied during his youth. By the end of 1821 the best grazing lands in the eastern part of the island were occupied by 7400 Britons – far more of them now than Palawa – cultivating more than 6000 hectares of what had immemorially been Palawa country, with 170,000 sheep, 35,000 cattle, 5000 pigs, and 550 horses occupying it and fences and buildings erected on it.[25] The world he had known since boyhood was visibly vanishing, as were his people. Kikatapula must have pondered their future and his own with growing unease while he walked the many kilometres back to his workplace, mulling his grievances all the way.

But more galling treatment was to follow. Shortly after his return, a new farm labourer was assigned to Birch: John Guinea, a 21-year-old career criminal who had arrived in the *Malabar* on 21 October 1821 with a seven-year sentence. He and Kikatapula were to be co-workers for a year that proved increasingly toxic for the Palawa farmhand.[26] Twice charged with violent assaults on fellow prisoners, Guinea was a belligerent man, one who through harassment or physical violence might readily intimidate and humiliate a young black man.[27] Although no specific details have survived, their cohabitation was so uncongenial that Kikatapula did not hesitate to kill Guinea when their paths crossed years later.

Samuel May was another co-worker who seems to have earnt Kikatapula's enmity. After arriving in the *Countess of Harcourt* in 1820 with a 14-year sentence May was 'many years in the service of Mr. [Edmund] Hodgson', who in 1822 became manager of all Birch's properties.[28] Seven months after Guinea died in agony, May too became a victim of Palawa spears. From their time as co-workers he was able to identify Kikatapula as his assailants' leader.[29]

And other storm clouds were gathering. On 1 December 1821, soon after Guinea's advent, Thomas Birch died, aged 46, leaving a fortune of about £40,000.[30] Although his death made no immediate difference to Kikatapula's day-to-day difficulties, their exacerbation began three months later on 1 March 1822, when the *Castle Forbes* sailed into the Derwent at the end of a tedious six-month voyage from England.[31] Among the disembarking immigrant gentlemen were two who would directly affect Kikatapula's life. One, a descendant of the chief of the Clan Robertson of Kindeace, was Gilbert Robertson, a Trinidad-born Scot whose mother was a black slave. He was 'a man of powerful frame [who] possessed qualities admirably fitting him for a leader' and was 'of independent character'.[32] His dark skin probably helped endear him to Kikatapula (though not to racist Britons, who tended to despise and disparage him). Granted 160 hectares of land in Coal River Valley adjoining Duck-Hole Farm, Robertson would become Kikatapula's friend and ally.

Not so the other new arrival, Edmund Hodgson. Born at Hawkshead, Lancashire, in 1792, he had come to Tasmania to work in an executive capacity for Thomas Birch, who died while the *Castle Forbes* was at sea. Once he learnt of Birch's death Hodgson quickly ingratiated himself with the wealthy young widow. Soon his name was attached to a mixed-goods retail business Birch had been operating from Macquarie House, and late in 1823 he and Sarah were married. It proved an unfortunate match for the bride. Although Hodgson was a teetotaller who professed religiosity, in reality he was a sanctimonious man notorious for incurring and then ignoring huge debts. He was also a bully. An 1848 court case heard that Sarah was compelled 'by coercion and misrepresentation' to bail him out of debt with £6000 – an enormous sum then.[33] A correspondent to the *Colonial Times* confirmed the coercion, saying Sarah had been subjected to a course of severe treatment by her husband to compel her to give him the money.[34] And Hodgson had a violent temper. When one of his creditors felt compelled 'through his evasive and shuffling tricks, to tell him my mind by using strong language', Hodgson attacked the man and tried to throttle him with his own neckerchief.[35] A witness in another court case testified 'that a misunderstanding had occurred between himself and Mr. Hodgson, in consequence of Mr. Hodgson turning Birch's children out of doors'.[36] The reason for such immoderate treatment of his stepchildren is unknown, but it demonstrates his quick-tempered tendency to violence, as does this report of yet another court hearing.

> Mr. Hodgson appeared to answer the complaint of Mr. Luckman charging him with assaulting one of his little boys; Mr. Hodgson was bound over to keep the peace.[37]

Well before their marriage, Sarah appointed Hodgson to manage all Birch's landholdings. He leased Duck-Hole Farm to a neighbouring landowner, his fellow *Castle Forbes* passenger Gilbert Robertson, who thereby gained Kikatapula as a farmhand.[38] But when Robertson was evicted for falling behind in his rent – he had no capital and soon lost his own grant – Kikatapula found himself subject to Hodgson's abrasive and mercurial governance.[39] Coupled with Guinea's hectoring, it brought his place in white society into sharp and uncomfortable focus. What sort of life could he ever have with people who treated him badly because he was black? Was he Briton or Palawa? Black Tom or Kikatapula? A catalysing force appeared in 1822 when the wandering tame mob camped on Robertson's land.[40] Musquito, now their leader, fed the young man's disaffection. He encouraged him to drink, poisoned his mind against Europeans, and painted a bleak picture of his present and future as a farmhand.[41] Better to join his own people, be Palawa again. The attraction proved irresistible, not least because the tame mob's women would provide sexual gratification not available to a black man living among whites, and Kikatapula was a lusty man. In later years his rampant libido was repeatedly troublesome for George Augustus Robinson, who believed a black woman enticed him to quit Hodgson.[42] But far stronger impetus was noted by another of Kikatapula's British acquaintances. 'Black Tom was forced to take the bush and join his own people,' John Batman wrote, 'because of the manner he was treated by his White Master and his servants'.[43] Embittered by their treatment, Kikatapula needed little prompting. When Musquito's mob departed Coal River Valley in late 1822 he doffed his European clothing and departed with them.[44] And although there had been no attacks on settlers in south-eastern Tasmania since mid-1819, an unexpected burst of hostility startled the colony.[45]

> Within these past few days the black Natives of the Colony have been rather troublesome among the settlers in the interior. With their spears, they have wounded two men, and killed one, named Simmonds, a lime-burner.[46]

Simmonds was slain at Bruny Island's Barnes Bay, but there is no mention of others being assaulted in the same attack, so it seems the two woundings, jointly or severally, took place elsewhere.[47] Colonists knew that Palawa attacked them only in retaliation, as Lieutenant Governor Sorell had observed in 1819, and reprisals were always to follow Kikatapula's suffering British insult or ill-treatment.[48] Whether he and the tame mob were responsible for either of those two woundings is unknowable, but because they occurred so unexpectedly after three years' comparative peace and around the time Kikatapula fled Britons' maltreatment, they have relevance.

Regardless, he and Musquito would be blooded the following year, tame no more.

4

'They are very dangerous and troublesome'

Musquito's followers were heterogeneous. They included Paytirami and other Oyster Bay people, several women from bands of the Big River people, and at least one Nununi woman from Bruny Island. They comprised one of several such groups that peacefully coexisted with colonists during the second decade of British occupation. One landowner recalled tame mobs passing through settled areas, occasionally camping nearby for a few days and accepting settlers' handouts of bread, potatoes, and clothes. But only one of those mobs left bloodstains on history.[1] A year after recruiting Kikatapula they became the first to conduct the repeated retaliatory attacks on colonists that mushroomed into the Black War. Because of that singular importance they are usually known to history simply as 'the tame mob', distinguishable from all others by the definite article.

They habitually traversed Oyster Bay country, criss-crossing Pitt Water, Coal River Valley, Risdon, the east coast, Clarence Plains, and the Midlands, also making forays into Big River country farther west, all without causing concern to settlers. Britons came to know them as 'the Oyster Bay tribe', and some set down their recollections. 'Constant friendly intercourse took place between the two races,' east coast settler George Meredith junior reported, adding that Musquito generally divided his time between the Palawa and the British, roaming the bush in summer and spending winters in Hobart.[2] John West, a 19th-century historian, claimed their visits to Hobart were to get bread, tobacco, and rum from the inhabitants.[3] Thomas McMinn, a servant of Captain Blythe near Oatlands, testified that between 1820 and 1823 Musquito and the tame mob often visited his hut.[4] Robert Evans, who farmed at Muddy Plains between Melton Mowbray and Jericho, stated that for six years a mob of 18 to 20 Aborigines frequently visited his house 'until Musquito behaved ill to his wife, and he was the cause of their going away'.[5] The *Hobart Town Courier* in 1830 provided a retrospective view of them that was devoid of any suggestion of menace or malice, if not of hyperbole.

> Musquito ... acquired such a command over the Oyster Bay tribe, that he led them wherever he pleased, and in two or three instances made them actually perform some simple agricultural labour ... He certainly had the qualifications of sable nobility in his veins, for he both considered himself to be so and acted as a great man. He has been known frequently to enter the cottages of the settlers, ordering his followers to the amount of perhaps 150 or 200 to await his motions on a neighbouring bank, and having seated himself with all the familiarity, or rather with all the claims to the rights of unbounded hospitality at the board of the landlord, would help himself bountifully to the best fare of the house, and cast with an air of condescension the bones and offals to his people, who submissively and thankfully gathered them up from his hand.[6]

Not all settlers felt obliged to help or even tolerate those whose land and resources they were arrogating. Some were unfailingly hostile. One, a Scot named Adam Amos, selected land at Waterloo Point, on Great Oyster Bay about 30 kilometres north of Little Swanport (and now the site of the town of Swansea) in 1821. He was initially granted 405 hectares – more than four square kilometres – of Palawa land, a holding that eventually grew to 2590 hectares, about 26 square kilometres. From the outset he was notably antagonistic to Palawa, readier to be aggressive than to offer friendship or tolerance. As early as May 1823, despite the passage of four years without report of hostilities in the region, he displayed animosity to a small group of peaceful Palawa after repulsing them from his land with pre-emptive gunfire.

> My house was surrounded by natives, one a woman came to the door. I made signs for her to go away – she did and in a short time about six made their appearance amongst the brush in the river close to my house. I fired small shot at about 50 yards distance[;] they run off. I fired another piece

[firearm] loaded with ball over their head to let them know I had more pieces than one ...[7]

A former army officer, Amos later became an occasional Palawa target, but even before that he was never inclined to recognise the rights or the humanity of the people whose land he had usurped. His view of them was caustic. He called them the last of the human species, derogated them because they were hunter-gatherers rather than producers, and opined that 'They are very dangerous and troublesome'. He also noted that the warriors were strong and agile and could throw a spear 50 metres with enough force to give a man a mortal wound.[8] Settlers were soon to discover the painful truth of his observation.

After departing Gilbert Robertson's Coal River Valley farm, the tame mob resumed their meanderings. They remained peaceable, continuing to interact with colonists without giving any cause for alarm. In March 1823 Dr John Ross saw them at Lake Echo, 60 or 70 Palawa whom he was familiar with because they sometimes visited Hobart for handouts.[9] Three months later, on 3 June, while they were camped at Pitt Water, a Wesleyan missionary named William Horton encountered them. It was a mere five months before they lit the fuse for war, but in Horton's scathingly Eurocentric view they were nothing but passive and indolent.

This ... was what the settlers denominate as the tame gang, in allusion to their inoffensive conduct ... This gang is ... governed by a Native of Port Jackson named Muskitoo ... The party, like the rest of their race, never work, nor have any settled place of abode, but wander about from one part to another, subsisting on what is given to them by the benevolent, and on kangaroo, opossums, oysters &c – which they procure for themselves, and lodging in all seasons around their fires in the open air. Though they have now been accustomed for several years to behold the superior comforts and pursuits of civilized men, they have not advanced one step from their original barbarism. All that they have imbibed from us is a smattering of our language, and a fondness for tobacco and spirituous liquors ... I found them perfectly naked, sitting around their fires, where they had slept the preceding night, and eating roasted potatoes. Some of them had their hair, which is cut very short and curly, as well as other parts of their body[,] besmeared with red gum and animal fat. A few were tattooed upon their shoulders but I could not ascertain the reason of this distinction …

While I stood conversing with them, several young men returned from hunting, bringing with them a few opossums and kangaroo-rats. These they kill with a small stick, bluntly pointed at one end, and about 18 inches [46 cm] long, which they call a Waddy, and which they are trained up from infancy to throw with surprising dexterity and precision … I asked them many questions of a religious nature, but the only reply I received was 'I do not know,' accompanied sometimes by a vacant laugh. Indeed, I am not at all certain that they have any idea of a supreme Being, or that they have any religious rites whatever. I asked Muskitoo if he was tired of his present mode of living, and if he was willing to till the ground and live as the English do. He replied that he should like it very well, but he thought none of the rest would.[10]

One of those 'demoralised savages' was Kikatapula, still festering about his treatment at British hands. He had been with Musquito for less than a year, although a writer not noted for accuracy in his monographs claimed a much earlier connection, asserting that Musquito lured Kikatapula away from Birch's employment in 1819, after which Lieutenant Governor Sorell let it be known that if Kikatapula led him to Musquito's hideout, he would be rewarded and his own malfeasances overlooked.

Black Tom took the Governor at his word and came down to interview him, with the result that he was sent off with a band of soldiers whom he was to lead to the hiding place. After two days marching they drew near to their quarry up in the highlands but, happening to pass a disreputable little grog shop, called in and ended by drinking so much and shouting and laughing so loudly that Mosquito got wind of the matter and made his escape with Black Tom.[11]

Objections to that story abound. Although Musquito did forsake white society at that time, he was an exile, not a prisoner, and because he committed no verifiable offence in Tasmania before November 1823 he had no need to be in hiding. Nor did Kikatapula have reason to escape from white justice in 1819, having only just joined the Birch household to convalesce. Further, he did not join the tame mob until late 1822, and no evidence exists of either his or Musquito's attacking Tasmanian settlers before late 1823. The writer compounded the fatuity of his story by claiming Black Tom – Kikatapula – was executed with Musquito when in fact that was another Paytirami, a man remembered only as Black Jack.[12]

Oddly, Musquito's leadership of the tame mob is sometimes disputed, but there is evidence from Lieutenant Governor Arthur himself.

> It is not a matter of surprise that the injuries, real and supposed, inflicted upon the blacks, have been revenged upon the Whites, whenever an occasion presented itself: and I regret to say that the Natives, led on by a Sydney black, and by two Aborigines of this Island – men partly civilized … have committed many murders upon the shepherds and herdsmen in remote situations.[13]

When Arthur wrote that in 1828, Musquito, 'the Sydney black', and Black Jack, one of the 'two Aborigines from this Island', had been dead for three years. The other man, their associate and the tame mob's subsequent leader, was Kikatapula, who at the time Arthur was writing was in jail awaiting trial for his leading part in those 'many murders'.

Musquito was a Gai-Mariagal man, a native of the Sydney–Broken Bay region of New South Wales, who had become notorious by the early 1800s for guerrilla attacks on settlers in Hawkesbury Valley. In 1805 he was exiled without trial to the Norfolk Island penal colony where he spent about eight years working as a charcoal burner before being shipped to Tasmania in 1813. A very tall slim figure with a wiry frame, he was initially peaceful and hardworking, sometimes aiding the authorities by tracking runaway prisoners.[14] In 1814 Governor Macquarie approved his repatriation to New South Wales, but it did not eventuate. Musquito subsequently worked for settlers in the Clyde River district near Bothwell and continued to track absconders, making him so unpopular with convicts that in 1817 Lieutenant Governor Sorell, noting that Musquito had been extremely useful and well conducted, again requested his repatriation. Again the administration did nothing. In September 1818 Sorell sent him to track the bushranger Michael Howe, promising repatriation to Sydney as reward. Musquito duly located Howe but the bushranger escaped from the Briton sent to capture him. Back in Hobart, Musquito awaited the promised repatriation but again the government reneged. Seething with resentment, he brawled with a convict who called him a 'hangman's nose'. He was collared by a constable and spent a night or two in a cell, but he had had enough and in 1819 joined the tame mob. Kikatapula later confirmed what other Palawa told Gilbert Robertson: that convicts' resentment of Musquito's bloodhounding had driven him into the bush.[15] Robertson himself opined that 'The breach of faith on the part of the government to Musquito when sent in pursuit of the bushrangers, was the cause of all the subsequent murders'.[16]

However, Musquito was no angel even then. Mytermoon, one of his women, said he 'killed plenty of [Tasmanian] blackfellows and black women'.[17] His belligerence and strength soon elevated him to the tame mob's leadership, for Palawa had no hereditary chiefs but allowed 'the bully of the tribe' to become leader.[18] Under his chieftaincy they continued to live the same peacefully semi-mendicant existence they had for a decade. Despite claims to the contrary, Musquito does not appear to have been actively hostile at first to the British in Tasmania.[19] Not a single attack before one at Grindstone Bay in November 1823 can verifiably be attributed to him, although he has been blamed (without proof) for killing John Kemp at that place in 1818.[20] And although he did not start the Black War, he was blamed and continues to be blamed for doing so. 'The darkies were as quiet as dogs before Mosquito [sic] came,' one colonist remembered, a belief shared by settler Robert Jones, a target of several Palawa attacks.[21] 'I believe the Blacks were put up to many wicked acts by Mosquito [sic] and Black Tom, both of whom were half civilized,' he wrote.[22] But compelling evidence revealed below shows the spur for the killings that led to the Black War was not Musquito but Kikatapula, and that they were in retaliation for an Englishman's act of wanton brutality to a Palawa woman.

That those killings happened late in 1823 is unsurprising. That year Britons were given more than 1000 grants totalling 1757 square kilometres (175,704 hectares) of Palawa land – the greatest alienation of land in any single year in Tasmanian history. Moreover, during the seven years to 1823 the sheep population had nearly quadrupled, from 54,600 head to 200,000.[23] The nomadic tame mob saw the changes and noted with concern and resentment the vanished Palawa presence. By 1823 they frequently had to ask permission to camp on their own country. And some of them, Musquito and Kikatapula in particular, were nursing gnawing personal grievances. Late that year, at a place called *pryhappenner* or *walelelabackkenner*, which whites had renamed Grindstone Bay, resentment became rage when a brutal act of staggering stupidity struck the spark for war.[24]

5

'Oh my God,
the black-fellows have got me'

A fine cool spring morning in 1823. A remote and isolated sheep run on the east coast many kilometres from other settlers. Two stockkeepers, one English, the other Tahitian, are going about their work while a third man, a convalescent young English convict who had joined them the previous day, is resting nearby. Suddenly, a mob of about 65 Aboriginal people appear. The men are armed with spears and waddies but they have their women and children with them, so their intentions are not warlike. Nevertheless, the Englishmen and the Tahitian are nervous, although it has been a year since any Aboriginal attacks were reported and nearly four years since Palawa hostility caused general concern. The older Briton, a tall man with prominent eyebrows, is the overseer. He recognises some of the newcomers and greets them cautiously. Their leader, who speaks some English, tells him they are on their way to Oyster Bay, farther north. He asks for and is given food. Still wary, the overseer asks him if he intends killing any of his master's sheep and is further reassured when the answer is *no*. Somewhat more relaxed, the two stockkeepers resume their chores while the Aborigines make camp across the creek that runs through the property. A short time later the Aboriginal leader reaffirms his goodwill by taking the overseer an old tin pot he has found in a disused hut there *lest any of the blackfellows should steal it*, he says. Later in the day he has the convalescent convict shave him. By nightfall an air of relaxed amiability prevails.

Yet within two days the convalescent and the Tahitian are dead, the overseer is severely wounded, two Aboriginal men are on a road to the end of a rope, and a spark has been struck that will soon flare into a years-long conflagration costing hundreds of British lives.

And the spark that lights the fire is sex.

For the 4½ years from April 1819 to November 1823 no Palawa attacks are identifiable in the Oyster Bay and Big River country that the tame mob constantly traversed. After such a long peace even the spring weather encouraged complacency. A typically tempestuous October – heat alternating with cold, rain, and late snow on *kunanyi*, the mountain with Hobart at its foot – had blossomed into the sort of season that fostered relaxed optimism. 'Vegetation appears to be uncommonly forward for the season of the year,' the *Hobart Town Gazette* observed on 8 November, 'and not the least blight either in the field or garden has this year been experienced. The apple and peach, as well as all other kinds of fruit trees, promise a greater abundance of fruit than has been for years'.

For colonists, however, fruit of a more bitter kind was to ripen only a week later. Adam Amos recorded its appearance.

> November 20th, 1823. I have heard that a large Mob of Natives has killed one of Mr. Gatehouse's men at Grindestone [*sic*] Bay and also Mr. Wm Hollyoak, who was on his way here from the Hospital, and wounded another who got away from them and fled to pitwater [Pitt Water]. His master and some of his men came after them to Mr. Talbot's, where they found them last night and fired on them, when they all scattered. A native of Sidney, Meskity as he is called, was with them and got off too, who is a dangerous fellow as he is akwainted with fire arms and has the Natives at his command.[1]

The killings were on Saturday 15 November, two days after Musquito and his mob appeared at Silas Gatehouse's Grindstone Bay sheep run. A grassy plain abounding in game, it was a favourite hunting ground for Oyster Bay people.[2] Gatehouse's farm, established in 1819, was a bare-bones enterprise consisting of little more than a stockkeepers' hut and adjacent stockyards beside the freshwater creek that flowed eastward into Grindstone Bay. It was the first British expropriation of Palawa country on the east coast, and although other colonists followed two years later, they chose land about 50 kilometres farther north around what is now the town of Swansea.

In charge at Grindstone Bay was John Radford, a farm labourer transported for theft. Born in Exeter, Devonshire, in 1798, he had arrived in Hobart in the *Lady Castlereagh* in 1818. Granted a ticket of leave, he became Gatehouse's overseer the following year. By 1823 he was acquainted with Musquito and one of his lieutenants, the Paytirami he called Black Jack, and he had also come to know Kikatapula, possibly as early as 1821 when Evans's surveying expedition reached Grindstone Bay.

The other Gatehouse employee was a Tahitian named Mammoa, about whom nothing is known except that his 'features were peculiar', perhaps an allusion to facial tattoos.[3] The convalescent visitor was William Holyoake (or Hollyoak), a 19-year-old convict with a clean conduct sheet and a character officially described as *orderly*.[4] Sentenced to death at the 1820 Warwickshire Summer Assizes for horse theft, he was reprieved and transported for life, leaving a wife and child in Birmingham. After arriving in the *Medway* in 1821 he was assigned to Oyster Bay settler George Meredith, from whom he had taken leave in mid-September 1823 to seek medical treatment in Hobart. Now, two months later, he was walking back to Meredith's – total distance about 140 kilometres – but had stopped at Gatehouse's on Wednesday 12 November because he was too weak to walk the last 50 kilometres.[5] His frailty and two fatally stupid mistakes he was about to make were to cost him his life.

The only known records of this pivotal event are two accounts given by Radford, the lone survivor: his 1824 court testimony, as reported in a newspaper, and an oral version he gave 18 years later to George Meredith junior, who wrote it down.[6] Each broadly resembles the other. The first, given only a year after the killings, is possibly the more accurate (despite some anomalies), although the later one includes extra details that help clarify the order of events. The following narrative is compiled from both.

On Thursday 13 November, the morning after Holyoake's arrival, Musquito and the tame mob appeared at Gatehouse's. They had come from Hobart where W.T. Parramore, a newly arrived English lawyer, had seen them earlier in the month and derogated them as poor-looking creatures.[7]

The stockkeepers and the Aborigines spent a congenial day together before Musquito retired for the night. Next day, Friday, he returned to the stockkeepers' hut, taking two or three women with him, which Radford admitted in court but failed to mention to Meredith. He did not tell the court why Musquito took the women to the hut, but it was undoubtedly to barter their sexual favours for food, as he often did. (The jury at Musquito's trial, all military officers, would have understood that; no need to spell it out.) Musquito asked for victuals and then ate breakfast with Radford. After that, however, Radford's testimony is conspicuously silent about the women, making no further mention of them. Radford told the court only that after breakfast Musquito lingered 'about the plains' with his followers until mid-afternoon, then went away to hunt. That evening, Friday, he returned to the hut and shared another meal with the stockkeepers. He also handled a musket that stood by Radford's bed, one of two firearms in the hut. Radford told the court nothing else about that evening, yet in the light of the following morning's events his silence has the force of a shout. For by then Holyoake had made the first of his fatal mistakes.

Next day, Saturday, 'the blacks were in the sheep-yard, sitting around a fire at their breakfast' about 5.30 am, Radford testified. To Meredith he said they were 'having a corrobery, dancing and singing' about 150 metres from the hut. The corroboree, however, was more likely a summon-up-the-blood ritual or ceremony preparatory to fighting, and perhaps also a diversionary tactic, because overnight the Aborigines' mood had changed ominously, and it is significant that all three stockkeepers were well aware of it.

Mammoa went out to watch them and was followed by Radford, who first warned Holyoake to take the firearms with him if he left the hut. But Holyoake failed to do so – his second and final fatal mistake.

Corroboree over, around 6 am Musquito, armed with two waddies, summoned Mammoa to join him across the creek, but the Tahitian was notably apprehensive. He hesitated, asking if the Aborigines would spear him if he did. Musquito replied *no*, so Mammoa went over to him. He and Musquito and the Palawa then spent a few minutes in a verbal exchange before several spear-carrying warriors plunged into the creek, heading for the hut. Suddenly concerned, Radford and Holyoake raced them to it but found their firearms had disappeared. *Did you put the guns away?* Radford demanded. *No*, said Holyoake. Now thoroughly alarmed, Radford called to Mammoa with the same question and got the same answer. The fear in

Radford's voice sent the already edgy Tahitian wading through the creek toward the safety of the hut, pursued by Musquito and the remaining warriors, who positioned themselves to hinder the stockkeepers' escape.

Their plight was now desperate. On one side of the hut, Radford told Meredith, 'was a deep creek; on another side was a brush fence; and on the third stood the natives, with a space of about ten yards left clear, through which was our only chance of escape, as it was now plain to us that they meant mischief, and were trying to close in the open spaces'. When Musquito's seized the stockkeepers' dogs and Mammoa objected, the Palawa instantly raised their spears to attack. *Run!* yelled Radford, and he and Holyoake took to their heels, with spears raining after them. Black Jack hurled one that penetrated Radford's side as he dashed by the corner of the fence, but he kept running. Another shaft plunged deep into Holyoake's back, causing the convalescent to falter. He cried out to Radford to come back and pull it out. Radford had sprinted ahead, pausing only to rip his boots off, but he raced back to help Holyoake before both resumed their terrified dash, with the Palawa only 30 metres behind and closing. More spears flew, one piercing Radford's thigh. He was forced to stop and pull it out before he could continue his flight. '[W]e ran together; I often waiting for Holyoake,' he told Meredith. 'We ran thus for some six hundred yards, when the blacks overtook Holyoake, and some passed him, running after me'. Now lagging 200 metres behind Radford, the sorely wounded Holyoake cried out in anguish, 'Jack, don't leave me!' but the overseer continued his frenetic rush. When he heard Holyoake scream, 'Oh my God, the black-fellows have got me,' he looked back to see Palawa surrounding the convalescent, whose bloodied body bristled with spears. He was trying to keep his attackers at bay by flinging sticks and stones at them. 'Seeing I could be of no service to him,' Radford said, 'I used my speed to save my own life, and succeeded in escaping'. Holyoake did not. Of Mammoa, Radford simply said, 'After the start I never saw [him] again; he must have been killed at once'.

Even this dovetailing of Radford's two tellings is clearly problematic. Both lack something crucial: an explanation for the overnight souring of the Aborigines' mood – a motive for their homicidal anger next morning. Two days of amiable coexistence had ended in bloodshed, although Radford swore there was no apparent reason for the hostility. 'I believe their sole motive was the plunder of the hut,' he told Meredith – his only recorded explanation for the violence. But Radford lied. His testimony clearly shows that when Musquito summoned Mammoa across the creek the Tahitian was leery. He sought assurances he would not be speared if he complied, meaning he knew the Aborigines were angry. But Musquito's words were sufficient reassurance for him to cross the creek, which seems to have been part of a ploy to divide and then disarm the stockkeepers. Radford implied that it was Black Jack who stole the firearms, testifying that Black Jack 'had gone into the hut several times, and I saw him in it on the Saturday morning, three quarters of an hour before the body of blacks came to it'. So the Aborigines' strategy is plain: Musquito would split the three stockkeepers by persuading Mammoa to cross over to where he was waiting (probably intending to strike the first blow), Black Jack would steal the firearms while the stockkeepers were diverted by the corroboree, and the attack would follow.

Like Mammoa, Radford was inexplicably edgy that morning, and you sense that for some reason all three stockkeepers were expecting trouble despite the Aborigines' previous cordiality and Friday's affability. His unease is obvious from his warning to Holyoake: 'I had desired the deceased to bring the guns, should he leave the hut before my return.' But Holyoake did not, sealing his fate and Mammoa's.

Neither of Radford's narratives explained why he and Mammoa were so plainly disquieted that morning. Yet something had obviously so enraged the Aborigines that all three stockkeepers' apprehension is evident from Radford's testimony. At Musquito's trial a year later Radford swore, in response to a query from a jury member, Samuel Hood, that 'neither the deceased or myself had offered any offence, or wanted to take any liberties' with the Palawa women and 'no provocation was given to the natives, or any violence shown by me, or to my knowledge by the deceased'. Yet *something* had triggered Aboriginal anger, and Radford's testimony shows that on the Saturday morning all three stockkeepers were aware of it and alarmed by it. Hood probably knew the truth and asked his question to get into the record Radford's denial of stockkeeper culpability, thus ensuring all blame fell on the two accused in the dock, Musquito and Black Jack. Because of that, the Grindstone Bay killings are commonly ascribed to Aboriginal treachery. Musquito is usually blamed for the deaths – he was hanged for abetting Holyoake's – and because the killings are often considered to have started the Black War he is usually blamed for that too. But the truth is very different. Two hostile acts by the stockkeepers, which Radford deliberately omitted from his testimony, were what caused the overnight deterioration in relations, and Kikatapula was the man responsible for urging violent retaliation. None of those acts started the Black War, but they set the stage for its beginnings soon afterwards.

The truth about what happened began to emerge only in 1831 when Kikatapula and George Augustus Robinson were passing through Gatehouse's farm. Kikatapula told Robinson what had triggered the killings there and Robinson recorded the details in his journal.

> [We] saw the graves that contained the bodies of two white men killed by the natives. One [Mammoa] was killed by Mosquito and Black Jack … The other was Meredith's man [Holyoake] that shot the Brune [Bruny Island] native. Tom said he was stopping at the hut with the mob and that as one of the women was walking away, they [that is, Holyoake] fired a quantity of small shot into her back which made a wound as broad as his hand. Tom said it was as cruel a thing as he ever saw done.[8]

Kikatapula's statement, which was not readily accessible until Robinson's journals were published in 1966, confirms that Radford perjured himself by swearing that 'neither the deceased or myself had offered any offence' and 'no provocation was given to the natives, or any violence shown by me, or … by the deceased'. Kikatapula's words, however, explain what really ignited the violence. Holyoake, on the Friday, had taken the shotgun from the hut and shot a Nununi woman in the back. The mindless brutality of the act was too much for Kikatapula, still smouldering at his own ill-treatment by Britons. In his first known act of leadership he exhorted Musquito's warriors to avenge the shooting, and two stockkeepers died.

Evidence of his incitement exists. In a letter, Land Commissioner Roderic O'Connor informed W.T. Parramore, who by then was Lieutenant Governor Arthur's private secretary, that Kikatapula was guilty of 'inciting his Companions to murder at Oyster Bay'.[9] O'Connor arrived in Tasmania in May 1824, six months after the killings, which means he was repeating something that was common knowledge, at least in government circles. So Radford's silence about Kikatapula's role is further evidence of his perjury because, as the sole survivor of the attack, only he could have informed the authorities about who was responsible for inciting it. That report led to Kikatapula's apprehension by the British months before Musquito and Black Jack were captured.

Why did Holyoake shoot the Nununi woman? It was almost certainly connected with the sexual assault of one of Musquito's wives by one or more of the stockkeepers. Musquito himself reported that in an autobiographical narrative.

> I stop wit white fellow, learn to like blanket, clothes, bakky, rum, bread, all same white fellow: white fellow giv'd' me. By and by Gubernor send me catch bushranger – promise me plenty clothes, and send me back Sydney, my own country: I catch him, Gubernor tell too much a lie, never send me. I knockit about camp [Hobart], prisoner no like me then, givet me nothing, call me b——y hangman nose. I knock one fellow down, give waddie, constable take me. I then walk away in bush. I get along wid mob, go all about beg some give it bread, blanket: *some tak't away my 'gin:' that make a fight*, mob rob the hut: some one tell Gubernor: [now] all white fellow want to catch me, shoot me … [emphasis added].[10]

Because that account summarises verifiable events in Musquito's life in Tasmania until the Grindstone Bay killings made him a fugitive, it rings startlingly true, the italicised phrases affirming what began the conflict: the seduction or rape of one of his own women. He was unmistakably referring to the fracas at Gatehouse's because that was what caused 'all white fellow want to catch me'.

There must have been a causal link between the sexual encounter and the shooting, but what it was is unknown. Nevertheless, a realistic chain of events can be constructed. On the Friday morning Musquito went to the stockkeepers' hut, taking two or three women with him to trade their sexual favours for food or tobacco. As a settler recalled, 'Musquito had three wives or gins. He would not allow any man to have intercourse with them. The other gins were allowed to prostitute themselves to white men for bread and other things.'[11] So any offence against one of Musquito's own women was serious. But at some stage during that day, maybe during late afternoon while the Palawa men were away hunting, one or more stockkeepers had a sexual encounter, probably forced, with one of Musquito's wives, presumably the Nununi. After that, for reasons unknown, Holyoake shot her in the back. The victim might have been Nelson (real name unrecorded), a Nununi known to have been associated with Musquito, and Holyoake might have shot her as she was fleeing the assault, although no evidence exists of that (or of any other reason for the shooting) or any permitting positive identification of the Nununi as Musquito's stolen wife, although it is a logical conflation.[12] It does not matter. The damage was done. Next morning, fired up by Kikatapula's exhortations, Musquito's warriors exacted bloody revenge.

Clearly, then, the history books are wrong. Clearly neither Musquito nor any Palawa fired the first shot in the Black War. The metaphorical weapon was primed by the three stockkeepers and the trigger pulled by William Holyoake. He paid with his life.

So did Mammoa. He may have been primarily responsible for what happened because on the Saturday morning it was he who was summoned across the creek to where Musquito and his warriors waited, he who was apprehensive about complying ('He ... first asked if the blacks would spear him'), he who appears to have been questioned by the Aborigines immediately before the violence ('They talked to Mammoa for a few minutes, then took up their spears'), he who was first to die.

John Radford too must share blame; his guilt was manifold. Regardless of whether he took part in any sexual encounter, he was in charge at Gatehouse's, knew Musquito, but failed to prevent both the assault and the subsequent shooting. Further, by deliberately omitting crucial facts from his testimony and lying about what provoked the bloodshed he exonerated himself and the two slain men while encumbering the Aborigines with all blame (possibly pressured by colonial authorities, since he was still a prisoner, to ensure a conviction). It cost Musquito his life, but the perjurer went on to enjoy longevity and considerable prosperity. He was granted his certificate of freedom – that is, fully pardoned – in August 1825, just months after his perjury sealed Musquito's fate.[13] In 1833 he eloped with landowner Thomas Buxton's daughter Mary Ann and from 1841 to 1858 was a hotelier at Little Swanport. At the time of his death in 1883, aged 84, he was seised of a substantial 3600 hectares of

Palawa land. The lies that looped a noose around Musquito's neck harmed Radford not at all.

But for Kikatapula they quickly led to a confrontation with British justice.

Reading Kikatapula's oral account of what caused the killings necessarily raises the question of his part in them. Having incited them, he could not have stood back and let others carry them out; he would have had to back his exhortations with action. And while his account blames Musquito and Black Jack (both of whom had been executed by the time he gave it) for killing Mammoa, the dead man's injuries – 37 spear wounds and a fractured skull – were too numerous to have been inflicted by only one or two assailants. It is notable too that Kikatapula deliberately did not name Holyoake's killers, an omission pregnant with implication. By the time he recounted events to Robinson he had witnessed enough executions to know not to admit personal culpability for a capital crime, but it can hardly be doubted that his were among the spears that avenged the shooting of the Nununi woman.

Radford told Meredith the Aborigines chased him for about five kilometres before abandoning pursuit, after which he made his way to a stock station (apparently another of Gatehouse's) at Prossers Plains, about 30 kilometres distant. From there word of the attack was sent to Nonesuch, Gatehouse's Wattle Hill home, about 14 kilometres from Sorell, and Gatehouse immediately assembled an armed party, which included George Wise, Chief Constable of the eastern part of Pitt Water, to pursue the killers. Apparently mounted – Gatehouse had several horses – they reached Grindstone Bay late on 17 November, only two days after the killings, and made camp. Early next morning, weapons cocked and ready, they warily advanced on the stockkeepers' hut. But it was empty, its door open, its contents strewn around the bush. (Musquito: 'mob rob the hut'.) Of Aborigines, Holyoake, and Mammoa there was no sign. Wasting no time, the posse hurried in pursuit.

Musquito's mob, after concealing the stockkeepers' bodies, had resumed their casual journey toward Oyster Bay, neither fleeing nor attempting to hide. The killings were not a declaration of war, simply payback for offences against them, so their actions in the immediate aftermath were not hostile. They continued northward to George Meredith's Swansea farm Red Banks, where nothing was yet known of the killings, and were given permission to camp there after Musquito promised 'that neither he nor any of his tribe would frighten the cattle or commit any damage'.[14] They camped peaceably 200 metres from Meredith's house for some time before moving to William Talbot's Malahide, about four kilometres away. News of the killings had not reached Malahide either, so when Musquito asked permission to make camp on the banks of the lagoon there, Talbot's overseer granted it. But that evening, four days after the killings, Gatehouse's avengers caught up with them and attacked. The over-eager Gatehouse gave the order to fire well before they were in range, and at the sound of the first shots all the Aborigines plunged into the lagoon and escaped unharmed.[15]

Gatehouse's men failed to capture any of them despite searching the immediate neighbourhood. However, when they left, one of Musquito's women went with them to Grindstone Bay to show where the bodies were hidden.[16] On 23 November Chief Constable Wise found Mammoa's near-naked corpse buoyant in the creek and pulled it out, finding it 'not very offensive'. The ferocity of the Aborigines' retaliation was obvious. Mammoa's head 'was very much bruised, and the body wounded in many places', Wise testified. 'Seven small holes were in the left side within about the compass of [my] hand, and there were eight or nine holes in the neck. Altogether [I] counted 37 wounds about the body, which [I] supposed to have been given by spears … The cranium was fractured …'[17] Near the hut were several broken spears smeared with blood, and many more spears stained with blood were found 350 metres away, presumably where Holyoake had died.

Radford returned to Grindstone Bay two days after Wise found Mammoa's body. Although Gatehouse's men had supposedly been shown where to find both corpses, Radford claimed it was he who found Holyoake's covered with sticks and partly consumed by carrion. Several spears were broken off in it.[18] The cadaver took him a strangely long time to locate: six days after Wise found Mammoa's.

After escaping from the attack at Malahide, Musquito's mob split into two parties, one of which severely assaulted him, perhaps blaming him for Gatehouse's attack on them. Alone and injured, he made his way to Bellbrook, John de Courcy Harte's farm on Wye River. Harte had heard of the killings but did not try to detain his visitor, although he did not offer him any help. Then Musquito disappeared from view for nearly two months, while the tame mob began the series of reprisals against east coast settlers that eventually mushroomed into the Black War. Honour had been satisfied at Grindstone Bay, so they had not expected violent retribution. Consequently, Gatehouse's surprise attack was instrumental in fomenting a state of hostilities.

It began in early December when the mob regrouped to make their first reprisal raid. The attack was on Mayfield, the home of Thomas Buxton, a Great Swan Port settler. He was absent, but his wife and six children were at home with a servant and a visitor. They were alerted early in the morning by their dogs' commotion and found hostile Palawa surrounding the house. Unaware that the whites had no firearms, the Palawa maintained their siege from early morning until late afternoon when, tiring of the impasse, they set fire to a brush fence adjoining the house, hoping to force the Britons out. As the flames neared the thatched roof some of the beleaguered inhabitants rushed out to extinguish them. The visitor was immediately speared in the back and the servant was fatally wounded by a spear in the stomach. Emboldened by this success, the Palawa set fire to the thatch by throwing firesticks onto it from the cover of trees close to the house, but Buxton's elder son managed to extinguish the flames and sprint back into the safety of the house unharmed. The Palawa now started a fire on the ground and used it to set fire to their spears, which they handed to those hidden in trees close to the house. With the region's only other settlers many kilometres away, the inhabitants seemed doomed to a fiery death. But a party of soldiers searching for bushrangers chanced onto the scene, and the attackers broke off and vanished.[19]

Tit-for-tat reprisals were quickly ballooning into a hit-and-run guerrilla war. After moving a little farther north to Cranbrook, near Adam Amos's

Glen Gala farm, the Palawa launched more attacks. Amos's diary provides an account.

> December 14th, 1823. The Natives who has of late been in the woods near my Hutt have this day set the Grass on fire near my farm. I thought it prudent to frighten them, having heard that they had thrattened at Mr Talbot's to burn my corn when circumstances gave them opportunity. I sent my eldest son who was joined by two of Mr. Meredith's men, who fired on them and wounded one. The Mob, who appeared numerous, fled over the hill. They purshoud them for some time & returned after dark with a quantity of spears, etc.[20]

The threat to burn Amos's corn is important because it shows Palawa, tutored by those like Kikatapula with agricultural experience, understood how loss of a crop could set back a farm, even causing its abandonment. Crop destruction was to be a recurring strategy in the forthcoming war, as were killing livestock and setting fire to buildings, haystacks, sawn timber, and fences.

The following night the Palawa returned and again tried to burn Amos's corn, but the settlers extinguished the blaze before major damage was done. A fortnight later, around 29 December 1823, Palawa tried again, with the same result. Then they vanished from the coast.

How many of those attacks Kikatapula took part in is uncertain because at some time subsequent to Grindstone Bay Musquito persuaded him to return to Hobart. There he was seized, accused of inciting the killings, and given a sentence that even hardened criminals feared: imprisonment at Macquarie Harbour penal station.

6

'Poor Tom Birch was soon captured'

Tasmania's cold, wet, ruggedly inhospitable west coast was the site of the Macquarie Harbour penal station. Extremely remote, it could be reached only by sea and passage through a narrow harbour entrance known colloquially (and appropriately) as Hell's Gates. As a place of secondary punishment it was notorious, dreaded by prisoners because of its isolation, harsh climate, and brutally coercive regime.

Several 19th-century books and newspapers state that Kikatapula once served a sentence there, although none recorded when and how he was captured or why he was punished. The killings of Holyoake and Mammoa were not reported in the *Hobart Town Gazette*, then the colony's only newspaper, until Musquito and Black Jack stood trial for them in December 1824, more than a year after the bloodshed; even then Kikatapula was not named.[1] Yet well before that, in the wake of Grindstone Bay, he and Musquito had become infamous throughout the colony. Seven months after Holyoake and Mammoa died, and a month before Kikatapula's name first appeared in the *Gazette*, Matthew Osborne, a settler in the Lower Midlands about 80 kilometres north of Hobart, could speak of him as 'a murderer' and 'the notorious companion of Musquito'. His notoriety had obviously been broadcast by word of mouth and was now well known, yet the circumstances of his sentencing to Macquarie Harbour are vague, although enough clues exist to enable a credible scenario to be sketched.

This first collision between Kikatapula and British justice happened, as we will see, while Musquito was still at large, so Kikatapula's apprehension must have been after the Grindstone Bay killings, his first known hostile act, and before 12 August 1824, when Musquito was captured. Radford's reporting the attack to the authorities would have been the trigger for his apprehension, although the overseer's only comment about his actions after he had outrun his attackers was what he told Meredith: that he 'made his way to another stock station at Prosser's Plains'. Once safely there and sufficiently recovered from his wounds, he would have walked to the nearest magistrate, James Gordon, 30 kilometres away at Forcett, to swear a deposition about the attack for forwarding to the Colonial Secretary for action. The deposition would have made its gradual way to Hobart, where preparations were under way for a major society wedding, while Radford limped the 70 or so kilometres back to Grindstone Bay, which he reached on 25 November. Four days later, the day Radford said he found Holyoake's body, Rev. Robert Knopwood married Sarah Birch to Edmund Hodgson at St David's church – a society event notable enough to be reported in the *Hobart Town Gazette*.[2] Given the upper-class mores of the day, her elite social status, and her well-known relationship with Kikatapula, it is doubtful Sarah would have proceeded with the marriage that day if Kikatapula's role in the killings had been publicly known or had he already been in custody; her concern for him in such a situation would alone have ensured the wedding's postponement. So it is improbable that Kikatapula was apprehended before the end of November.

Very soon after Mrs Birch became Mrs Hodgson, however, he found himself in custody, face to implacable face with British justice, for which James Bonwick blamed Musquito's skulduggery. He wrote that when Musquito was wanted for the killings he 'was impressed with the notion that he might seek his own pardon by betrayal of his black acquaintance', presumably meaning that he sent Kikatapula back to Hobart on some pretext.[3] 'Although the rascally chief long kept his own neck out of the halter by his duplicity and unscrupulous sacrifice of his confederates, poor Tom Birch was soon captured.'[4] The word *soon* indicates that it was not long after the Grindstone Bay killings, the first (and at that time the only) hostile act known to have involved Kikatapula, so December was most likely when he was seized.

Because of Musquito's perfidy (which Kikatapula seems never to have learnt about) the young Palawa found himself in British custody, although he was not tried for murder. Tasmania did not have an operative Supreme

Court until mid-1824, so, except for the rare occasions a New South Wales Supreme Court judge visited to preside over a Tasmanian Criminal Court, capital cases could be heard only in Sydney.[5] And although local magistrates could punish minor offences with floggings and terms at Macquarie Harbour, newspaper reports of magisterial hearings in Hobart between November 1823 and February 1824 fail to mention Kikatapula. Probably he faced some sort of drumhead court hearing, most likely military (as Musquito and Black Jack did a year later), at which he was 'sentenced to the dreaded convict settlement at Macquarie Harbour', according to Bonwick. But Sarah intervened and 'was able to preserve his life from the law's demands'.[6] Jorgen Jorgenson, who knew Kikatapula, agreed. He asserted that 'Tom Birch was captured and transported to Macquarie Harbour for his natural life for sheep stealing' – if true, probably a surrogate minor charge so he could be dealt with quickly and without too many legal niceties. Roderic O'Connor also confirmed the sentence to Macquarie Harbour, although he said it was 'for inciting his Companions to murder'.[7] So throughout the 1820s and beyond, people believed a Palawa guerrilla who had lived with the British (and was therefore 'half civilised') had once been incarcerated at Macquarie Harbour.[8] That could be no one but Kikatapula. No other Palawa was ever given that sentence.

But Bonwick also wrote that Kikatapula managed to escape from there, subsequently joining the 'Abyssinia Mob'.[9] Again Jorgenson concurred. 'He soon effected his escape,' he wrote, 'and joined the Big River tribe; then in his restless disposition he went to his own mob at Abyssinia. He again joined Mosquito [sic], but succeeded in keeping himself out of the way of the whites.'[10]

Kikatapula, however, did *not* escape from Macquarie Harbour – because he was never sent there. Tasmanian Convict Indexes do not record a prisoner called Kikatapula or any spelling variant of that name, and all the prisoners there named Thomas Birch are identifiable as transportees from Britain. The surviving archives of the penal station, which include four convict musters between 1823 and 1825, do not record any Palawa prisoners.[11] Moreover, a list of all escapees from Macquarie Harbour between 3 January 1822 and 16 May 1827 does not include a Thomas Birch, any variation on that name, or any prisoner identifiable as Palawa.[12]

So what did happen? Roderic O'Connor provided the necessary clarification. Kikatapula, he wrote to Parramore, 'was raised by Mrs Birch ... and when on the point of being sent to Macquarie Harbour for inciting his Companions to murder at Oyster Bay, was restored to liberty by her interference'.[13] His 'escape', then, was not from Macquarie Harbour but from being sent there. And Sarah's pleading was what gained him his liberty.

Early in 1824 Adam Amos transcribed into his diary a police notice recording the government's initial response to the killings.

Police Office Hobart Town 6th January 1824

Whereas Musquito a Native of Port Jackson, and Jack a Native of Van Diemans Land, Blacks, stand charged on the Oath of John Radford with the wilful Murder of William Hollyoake assigned servt of George Meredith Esqre and Mammoa a Native of Otaheite, at Oyster Bay on the 17th [sic] of November last – all constables & others are hereby required to use their utmost Exertions to apprehend the said Musquito & Jack, and lodge them in safe custody.

Despite the government's knowledge of Kikatapula's complicity, the notice included no mention of him – because, unlike Musquito and Black Jack, he was no longer a fugitive. It is clear that by 6 January he had already been apprehended, 'punished', and freed – further evidence that his capture and release were in December 1823. And circumstantial evidence revealed in the following chapter points to his involvement in killing a stockkeeper at Abyssinia soon after that, in the first weeks of the new year.

The general belief that he had been imprisoned at Macquarie Harbour is explicable: the government simply kept quiet about his release, not wanting it known that a killer had been freed unpunished after influential strings were pulled on his behalf. His subsequent return to hostilities was easy to account for: he had somehow escaped from Macquarie Harbour, as Bonwick and Jorgensen believed. But O'Connor, a government insider, knew the truth.

At large again by early January, Kikatapula quickly put Hobart and the British behind him and headed for Abyssinia, the sparsely settled region around Bothwell, to rejoin Musquito. Angry and revenge-bent, he took up the spear again, and, in what proved to be a typical post-release reprisal, a colonist promptly died at Palawa hands.

Significantly, the killing was at Abyssinia in mid-January 1824, the culprits were Musquito's mob, and the victim had a likely Kikatapula connection.

7

'The notorious companion of Musquito'

Within days of the publication of the Police Office notice Musquito's mob were identified in the attack on the farm of G.W. Evans, whose surveying party Kikatapula had deserted two years earlier.[1] Evans's farm, also called Abyssinia – it took its name from the region's – was about seven kilometres south of Bothwell. The attackers slew Evans's unnamed stockkeeper and burnt his hut.[2] Possibly he had been a member of the 1821 survey party and was killed in revenge for whatever made Kikatapula desert it. The synchrony of his slaying at Abyssinia with Kikatapula's rejoining Musquito there, as reported by Bonwick and Jorgensen, adds to the likelihood of his involvement.

Another killing soon followed, and not far away: about nine kilometres south-west of Evans's farm. Although Kikatapula was not identified as complicit – he was supposedly still imprisoned at Macquarie Harbour – he was a likely participant when Musquito's mob slew Patrick McCarthy, who had 20 hectares at Hollow Tree, on Macquarie Plains. The circumstances and precise date of his killing are not known, but Adam Amos transcribed into his diary a Police Office notice that points to McCarthy's death having been in early February.[3]

Murder. Two hundred dollars reward.

Police Office Hobart Town February 27th 1824

Whereas Musquito, a black, a native of New South Wales stands charged with heading a party of the natives of this Island, and with attacking and plundering many of the remote stock-keepers – and whereas the said party, among whom is Jack, a native of Van Diemans Land, are charged on the Oath of John Radford, with the wilful murder of William Holyoak ...

and Mammoah in November last and whereas the said Musquito and party stand further charged with the murder of Patrick Macharty [*sic*] at the River Ouse, a reward of one hundred dollars each is hereby offered ...[4]

Musquito was never charged with McCarthy's murder, but Black Jack was convicted of it on 21 January 1825, although the date and circumstances of his capture, like details of his trial, are unrecorded.[5]

Despite the slowly rising tide of blood on the frontier, pinpointing a precise date for the beginning of what Britons came to call the Black War is difficult, although Musquito's execution in February 1825 was its catalyst. Intermittent Palawa attacks during 1824 were to intensify early the following year into a widespread state of hostility to all Britons, which continued to intensify and was to last for another five or six increasingly bloody years. A settler named Richard Dry made pertinent (if Anglocentric) observations about the metamorphosis from sporadic reprisals to all-out war. In earlier years, he wrote, Palawa attacks were restricted to the 'Tribe or family' that they originated in having been 'excited by some Temporary Aggression of the Whites' – revenge or reprisal attacks. Later, 'a determined spirit of hostility [had] been manifested by the whole of the Black population, and acts of outrage committed by them, on the lives and property of the settlers in almost every settled District on the island'.[6] Significantly, all the attacks involving Musquito after the beginning of 1824 appear to have been unprovoked acts of war rather than reprisals.

Contemplating the relative numbers of the antagonists in that cataclysmal year is sobering. The British population was just over 12,000, but reckoning the number of surviving Palawa can never be more than guesswork.[7] It has been put as low as 340 for all Tasmania, although that is probably too few, and a recent estimate suggests 1000 is more likely.[8] If that is correct, the Palawa were outnumbered at least 12 to one as their random flickers of retaliation flamed into war, and their population continued to collapse even as the number of Britons, bond and free, ballooned with each new ship arrival – to 14,192 in 1825, 14,992 in 1826, 16,833 in 1827, 18,128 in 1828, 20,015 in 1829, and 24,279 in 1830.[9] In 1831, as the last futile spears were flung, George Augustus Robinson, who had spent most of 1829–1831 scouring Tasmania for Palawa and was well placed to make an informed guess, believed there were only 500–700 of them – men, women, and children – left in all Tasmania.[10] That included the remote west and south-west where there were very few Britons.[11]

But that was seven years away. In 1824, as Palawa began to fight for their very existence, it was already too late. They were hopelessly and irrevocably outnumbered.

While it is impossible to be precise about Kikatapula's whereabouts during the early part of 1824, it was a likely time for an internecine incident involving him to have occurred. He related the story to George Augustus Robinson, who recorded it in his journal while they were camped between Bothwell and Oatlands years later.

> While sojourning here the chief MANNALARGENNA [Manalakina] mentioned the circumstances of a native, a big man, who had been killed not far from here … and who had been placed in a tree. MANNALARGENNA said Tom's mob or the Oyster Bay tribe had killed this man. Tom then related the circumstances. Said he was present, that [the victim] was [of] MAN.NE.LE.LAR.GEN.NER's or the TY.ER.RER.NOTE.TE.PAN.NER [Tayarinutipana] nation [a band of the North Midlands people], that they had met and that the Oyster Bay people had preconcerted a plot, that some of them were to talk with the beforementioned people and that whilst they were so doing other of the Oyster Bay people was to go behind a tree and spear this big man. This was fully carried into effect, and Tom took up a spear and went behind a tree and shewed me the way they did it … that when the man was speared he run and cried, and that he was then followed by others who soon despatched him. Tom said PARWAREATAR alias Lawyer [a Tayarinutipana] was there and that they would have killed him also but that he got away down a creek.[12]

Kikatapula's manner as he re-enacted the killing led Robinson to comment that 'probably Tom was the man that did it'.[13] Although impossible to date with certainty, it sounds like something an ambitious young man would do to assert his right to leadership, in which case it credibly belongs in the months after Kikatapula's release. Manalakina's contention that the perpetrators were 'Tom's mob or the Oyster Bay tribe' points to

Musquito's mob when Kikatapula was flexing his leadership muscles. Or perhaps he was already leader and had used a chance meeting with the Tayarinutipana, his traditional enemies, to reinforce his ascendancy by killing two of them. In 1828 Kikatapula was to have another potentially lethal encounter with Parewareatar, but The Lawyer would escape unharmed from that too and would outlive Kikatapula by a few years.

Because Musquito's mob were known to be responsible for the November attacks on the east coast and the January and February killings south of Bothwell, armed parties set out to hunt them. One party, comprising three constables and two volunteers, decided to search in Oyster Bay country on the east coast. They reached Swansea on 9 March and, after being provisioned by Adam Amos, continued searching. A few days later they went back to Amos for more provisions before setting out on 15 March for St Pauls Plains, farther north-west. After returning to Amos 10 days later without having encountered their quarry, they left Swansea on 29 March to return to Hobart.[14] Probably it was they who were the subject of a newspaper report on 9 April that 'the strongest, if not the only party who were in pursuit of Musquito and his companion, have returned unsuccessful, after a search of five weeks'.[15]

Even as posses were combing the countryside there were fresh attacks against settlers in Oyster Bay country. In March, at Mount Seymour (east of Jericho), Palawa slew James Doyle, and at Salt Pan Plains their victims were two stockkeepers, whose bodies were buried at Tunbridge, one at each end of the old bridge over Blackman River.[16] They also seriously wounded James Taylor at Old Beach (in Derwent Valley some 20 kilometres north of Hobart). A newspaper reported: 'It does not appear that Musquito or Black Jack were seen with this party, though there is reason to believe they must have been near the spot'.[17] That suggests Kikatapula was the attackers' leader, because only two months later he was to be recorded in that role for the first time.

At Oyster Bay on 6 June 1824 Palawa slew one of George Meredith's employees, the fifth killing that year.[18] The sixth quickly followed, and although Musquito was initially blamed for it, Kikatapula was incontrovertibly identified as its leader.[19] The attack was at Pooles Marsh (now Lower Marshes) in the Lower Midlands and the victims were

63

Matthew and Mary Osborne, who lived a short distance from the Hobart–Launceston road about six kilometres north-west of Jericho. Late on 9 June 1824, just after Matthew had returned from several days in Hobart, an unidentified convict servant of a nearby settler called at the house and offered to sell Mary a kangaroo, which she agreed to pay for with tobacco.[20] Unaware that her husband was back, the convict was startled when Matthew spoke to him. 'Oh, Mr Osborne,' he said, 'is it you? I thought you were in camp [Hobart].' He told Osborne he had come to ask for food for two poor blacks nearby who were in need. Mary was immediately fearful. 'What could you mean by bringing them about the place?' she gasped. 'Did you mean them to murder me?' The convict assured her that they were tame. He had been sitting peaceably at their fire for the last two hours, he said. At that moment a Palawa man appeared whom Osborne recognised as 'Black Tom, the notorious companion of Musquito'. He was immediately apprehensive. 'You must be a very bad fellow to consort with such a murderer,' he said fearfully, 'especially knowing how many acts of barbarity he has lately committed'. The convict said he didn't care. 'I would not betray him for three free pardons, and £50 besides.' Thoroughly alarmed, Osborne gave a dish of potatoes to the convict, who took it to Kikatapula. Both then went away.

Next morning, as Mrs Osborne was at work in the dairy, her husband rushed in crying, 'Oh Mary, Mary, the hill outside is covered with savages!' The terrified woman prepared to flee but Osborne managed to calm her, telling her not to be frightened but to go into the house while he stood guard outside. As Kikatapula led the Palawa toward him, Osborne, armed with a musket, asked what they wanted. Are you hungry? 'Yes, white man, yes,' Kikatapula replied. The jittery Osborne said that if the Palawa laid down their spears and lit a fire he would bring them potatoes and butter. He also called to his wife to cut up a large loaf of bread and give it to them, but she was so rattled that she could do no more than break it in two. Again Osborne asked the Palawa to lay down their spears. 'We will,' Kikatapula said, 'if you, white man, put down your musket'. After a brief parley both parties laid down their weapons. The Palawa then came up to be given potatoes, which they ate after roasting them with their firesticks. Some Palawa then went into the house and asked for more, which Osborne went outside to fetch. But as he stepped back inside he saw that his musket had disappeared. 'I'm a dead man!' he groaned. Kikatapula, following him back into the house, began pointing at various household items, saying, 'I must have this, I must have that'. Very much in command, he snatched Osborne's hat and put it on his own head. The settler was momentarily relieved when two Palawa grasped his hands in apparent amiability, but as they did a warrior behind him plunged a spear so forcibly into his back that he screamed and bounded forward before falling dead. Shrieking 'Murder! Murder!' Mary fled, pursued by Palawa who speared her in the head and side before beating her senseless with waddies and leaving her for dead. But she did not die. Despite her wounds and loss of blood she managed to crawl about five kilometres to the hut of a neighbour, John Jones. He took the badly wounded woman to Jericho, where Dr John Maule Hudspeth nursed her back to health. When Hudspeth and others went to the Osbornes' farm they found only Matthew Osborne's corpse and a hut stripped of possessions.[21]

Until mid-1818 Matthew Osborne had been a constable in Hobart and in 1821 he was still living there, in Argyle Street, and it is obvious that he knew Kikatapula. His immediate dismay when Kikatapula first appeared on his farm confirms that he also knew of his now-nefarious reputation – 'how many acts of barbarity he has lately committed' – although neither the Grindstone Bay killings seven months earlier nor Kikatapula's part in them had been publicised in the colony's newspaper, and police notices about the killings of Holyoake, Mammoa, and McCarthy had not mentioned him. Kikatapula's belligerence to Osborne, coupled with Osborne's immediate disquiet on seeing him, suggests their previous acquaintance had not been amicable, and nothing about the attack appears opportunistic or impulsive. The attackers' clear intention was to kill both Osbornes, so revenge for some past insult was a likely motive, and Kikatapula's next raid, immediately afterward and not far away, had the hallmarks of such a revenge attack. The Osbornes were probably targeted for a similar score-settling. The attempt to slay Mary Osborne supports the likelihood because it was unique: the first recorded Palawa attack on a European female and, significantly, the last for more than four years – indeed, until well after Kikatapula had ceased hostilities – so there must have been a serious reason for the attempt to kill her, although her dying would of course also prevent her identifying her assailants' leader, who had escaped a possible death sentence only six months before. It might also have been intended to demonstrate or ratify his ruthlessness, his fitness to be a leader.

Those he led were identifiably Musquito's mob. The Osbornes' neighbour Robert Jones deposed to Oatlands magistrate Thomas Anstey that they 'consisted of the Blacks who were in the habit of visiting Hobarton, and getting provisions and other things there'.[22] The *Hobart Town Gazette* concurred. After identifying Kikatapula as their leader, it observed that the only troublesome Palawa were those corrupted by Musquito. It was confident that a posse of police and soldiers now in pursuit would soon hunt them down.[23]

Yet the attackers could not be found despite a continuing trail of British blood. To add to the confusion, a fortnight after reporting Osborne's slaying the *Gazette* published an anonymous follow-up item that was to perplex historians – and this writer – for decades.

> We learn that the native, named 'Black Tom,' alluded to in our report of Mr. Osborne's death, was not [the man] brought up by the late Mr. Birch, whose servant so called, still remains in the family, not at all inclined to ramble, but very steady.[24]

The item proved to be a deliberate ploy to falsely exculpate Kikatapula. There can no doubt he led the Osbornes' attackers. His height, his 'remarkable scar', and his command of English made him easily identifiable to people who had lived in Hobart when he did, and both Osbornes plainly recognised him. Yet the puzzling *Gazette* item proclaimed his innocence and supported the claim with an alibi that on the day of the Osborne attack he was still living with and serving the Birch/Hodgson family. Only a member of that family could have made such a claim and been believed, and only one of them would lie to protect him: Sarah Hodgson. Her claim of mistaken identity was so effective that by falsifying the truth it has misled people for nearly two centuries. Kikatapula had not *remained* with the family, as she stated, but had *rejoined* them for his own security just after Osborne's killing. Shielded by her false alibi, he was now havened with Sarah at Lovely Banks, a Hodgson property, safe from pursuit and prosecution. The circumstances were recounted by her grandson Thomas Sutcliffe.

Two years later [that is, two years after Kikatapula had abandoned European society, so 1824] ... he was the means of saving grandmother's life. It appears that grandfather [Sutcliffe's step-grandfather Edmund Hodgson] had left Macquarie House, and had taken up abode at the Lovely Banks, which I understand belonged to him. The blacks being on the warpath, surrounded the house at Lovely Banks, and grandmother [Sarah] noticed her blackboy Tom among the warriors, all over yellow mud in true war fashion. She called loudly to him to save her life, and he was greatly surprised to see her there, not knowing she was living there. Tom's influence soon checked the evil doings of the others, and instead of killing the inmates of the place as they intended, they partook of a great feast ... and by her influence with Tom she got him to cease the war trail.[25]

Although Edmund Hodgson was undoubtedly the raiders' target that day, he was not there. Early in 1824 the Hodgsons had let Macquarie House to Robert Stodart (who turned it into a hotel) and, with Sarah's six surviving children, moved to Lovely Banks, about five kilometres north of Melton Mowbray and 10 kilometres from the Osbornes' farm. It was to be their temporary home while 'Mrs. Hodgson's new house' in Macquarie Street, South Hobart, was being built.[26] Consequently, when Musquito and Kikatapula attacked Lovely Banks, expecting to find Edmund there, he was back in Hobart, probably overseeing construction of the new house. Newspapers record his presence in town from at least May to November that year, and advertisements in the *Gazette* on 4 June and 25 June show he was resident in Harrington Street when Musquito and Kikatapula beset Lovely Banks. His absence saved his life.

Because Kikatapula was unaware that Sarah was now Mrs Hodgson, he was shocked to encounter her instead of Edmund at Lovely Banks shortly after Matthew Osborne died – a killing she would not then have known about. Six months earlier she had boldly fronted colonial authorities and persuaded them not to imprison Kikatapula at Macquarie Harbour; now, with her own life at stake, she boldly confronted his war-painted warriors to persuade them to cease hostilities and him to settle peacefully at Lovely Banks. He did, and Musquito and the others moved on without him, after which life at Lovely Banks returned to normal.[27] But less than a month later the *Gazette* published its graphic account of Kikatapula's attacking the Osbornes. Sarah could not have doubted the identification; his assault on Lovely Banks was ample evidence of his militancy that month. Although the news about the Osbornes must have horrified her, her affection for him hardly wavered. She knew what she had to do. He had saved her life by prevailing on his warriors not to harm her, and she could return the favour by providing him with a false alibi to exonerate and protect him. She picked up her pen ...

Kikatapula's about-face and brief peaceable interlude as a farmhand are substantiated by an entry dated 10 October 1824 in a surviving Lovely Banks record.[28] Verbatim it reads:

Tom Clear Taking a cart & 6 Bullocks over to Hobart

No record exists of any man, convict or free, named Tom Clear or Thomas Clear in Tasmania in 1824. However, in the 18th and 19th centuries *clear* could mean *fully* or *completely* or *unentangled*, so a full stop was obviously intended after the payee's name.[29] The entry's meaning, then, was:

Tom. Successfully Taking a cart & 6 Bullocks over to Hobart

Other entries on the same page similarly lack full stops after payees' names. They also include unnecessarily capitalised words (like *Taking*) where they do not indicate the start of a new sentence. (See illustration.) Further, every other entry records the payee either by his forename and surname or by surname alone. Only the 'Tom' entry differs. So on 10 October 1824 a man significantly known only as 'Tom' was paid 12 shillings for driving a team of bullocks to Hobart earlier that month. In the light of the otherwise puzzling *Gazette* paragraph of 30 July and the revelations in Sutcliffe's article, it is evident that 'Tom' was Kikatapula.

'Tom' is not otherwise mentioned in the Lovely Banks journal. That single entry provides the last sight of him there because when he drove the bullocks to Hobart in early October he made a discovery that rekindled his anger and sent him back to Lovely Banks to collect his pay before

But hostilities continued without him. On 21 October 1824, little more than a week after Kikatapula abandoned Lovely Banks, about 20 Palawa, part of a mob nearly 200 strong, attacked James Hobbs's much-harried stockkeepers in the Eastern Marshes, although both managed to escape.[35] Possibly the newly at-large Kikatapula was among the attackers, already filling his former leader's place, for he was about to lead Musquito's mob into Hobart on a mission of mercy.

Their entry on 3 November startled Hobartians. George Augustus Robinson, a London builder new to the colony, recorded the visitors' appearance.

> At ½ 3 pm 64 black natives came into town. They were naked ... At 8 pm they were placed in the market house [now the site of City Hall]. They were formed into 3 circles with a fire in the middle of each. On one side of each circle elevated about 3 feet [1 m] above the rest sat a person whom I supposed were their chief. One out of the 3 of these chiefs could speak broken English.[36]

He commented on their upright bearing, noting that some were 185 centimetres tall, although scabby.[37]

The visitors were made welcome with blankets, clothing, and bread. Four constables were ordered 'to guard their repose from interruption' as the Lieutenant Governor contemplated how best to befriend and civilise them.[38] But the Palawa, 'their enmity ... evidently unabated', were not there to be civilised. They were there with a single objective: to solicit a pardon for Musquito.[39] 'The Tasmanian natives had become deeply attached to him', according to a 19th-century writer. 'They interceded for him, but in vain, and his death deepened their hatred of his slayers.'[40]

Informed by onlookers who recognised some of the visitors, Robinson reported that they were the Oyster Bay tribe, which is indisputable because nobody except Musquito's own followers would have reason to solicit his freedom. Kikatapula, when he rejoined them the previous month after quitting Lovely Banks, would have told them about Musquito's murder charge and its likely outcome, explained the possibility of intercession, and persuaded them to support him in pleading for Musquito's life. He knew from his own experience that intercession could get a sentence commuted and a prisoner freed, but it is hardly credible that any other Palawa would have known that. So, as a prominent historian has posited, it was almost certainly Kikatapula who led them into Hobart.[41] He was well known to many Hobartians, and by November 1824 his high status within Musquito's mob was unequivocal. Moreover, he – and uniquely he – combined substantial knowledge of the British with the confidence and the command of English necessary to advocate for Musquito's life, plus the authority with Musquito's followers to lead them in the attempt.

The day after they arrived the Palawa were moved to huts at New Town, about four kilometres from Hobart, where they stayed for two days. Parramore encountered three of the men, presumably the chiefs, wearing long greatcoats but nothing else, and thought they were 'mightily vain of their dress'. He observed that on the third day the Palawa, perhaps aware now that their intercession had been unsuccessful, were rather sullen and were refusing Britons' requests to sing the kangaroo song. They moved off early the next morning.[42]

It might be wondered why Kikatapula was not immediately arrested and charged over his well-publicised complicity in Osborne's killing. But neither Lieutenant Governor Arthur, who had been in the colony only since May, nor Robinson, who had arrived just four months before that, was likely to have known him. Even had any onlooker recognised him from his years in Hobart, Sarah's false alibi, published three months previously, countered any notion of his guilt. And Kikatapula knew he was safe – after all, he had been to Hobart only the previous month delivering a team of bullocks and had come to no harm.

Arthur, who had several discussions with the visitors, quickly set up an establishment for them on the opposite side of the Derwent at Kangaroo Point (Bellerive).[43] He ordered huts built there where they could be housed, fed, and clothed in hope the establishment might become permanent like the one at Parramatta, New South Wales. But as Arthur informed London, 'After stopping a few days ... the tribe went back to their haunts'.[44] He did not report – perhaps did not understand – what moved them to leave: on 1 December Musquito was sentenced to death. As soon as the Palawa at Kangaroo Point heard the news they angrily decamped.

Reprisals were inevitable and swift. In the first, on 6 December, a stockkeeper was slain at Jordan River.[45] A few days later the Palawa who had been at Kangaroo Point were identified as responsible for a second raid. They – 'the tribe of Aborigines, who recently visited Hobart' – were about to spear a servant of Edward Lord of Lawrenny (between Hamilton and Ouse) when an overseer named Burrell rushed forward with a firearm and rescued him. The attackers 'had the blankets and military caps which they took from town'.[46]

Then followed a puzzling 10-week hiatus in hostilities. But during the first week of January 1825, about four weeks into that long and inexplicable lull, an unusually large Palawa mob startled Launceston with a visit. The appearance of so many heading for the little northern settlement, population under 2000, caused great alarm. The visitors included women (and therefore children) and they were unarmed, so their intentions were peaceful. Nevertheless, colonists fired on them as they crossed Patersons Plains, but the visitors were undeterred. They neither fled the shooting nor retaliated but proceeded into the town, their purpose firm and unshakeable. Yet what it was is unknown, for the only record of this signal event was a few lines in a Launceston newspaper that did not mention their motive.

> In the course of last week about 200 of the aborigines made their appearance in the Town of Launceston, and immediate neighbourhood, encouraged no doubt by the kindly reception, and civil treatment, which their sable brethren recently experienced on the other side of the Island.[47]

As the newspaper noted, they seem to have known about the visit to Hobart, knew of the welcome Lieutenant Governor Arthur had extended, and perhaps expected similar largesse in Launceston. That suggests Kikatapula's involvement. During his years as resistance leader he travelled well outside Oyster Bay country – as far as Lake Echo, beyond Campbell Town and Ross, and, significantly in this instance, to Western Tiers (Longford/Cressy), less than 30 kilometres from Launceston.[48] Given his experience in Hobart three weeks earlier, he would have expected no less a welcome in Launceston, whatever his motive might have been. So many Palawa in one place at one time indicates a coalition of several bands or remnants, possibly including sometime enemies, which in turn suggests an authoritative organiser, a leader redoubtable enough to rally those remnants – one, moreover, who could speak English well enough to communicate with the townspeople. The fact that both the Hobart and the Launceston visits were so close and took place during that remarkable hostilities-free hiatus, which prevailed everywhere, supports the hypothesis. But if it *were* Kikatapula, his purpose in amalgamating such a cohort and taking them into Launceston must forever remain a mystery. For what transpired while the Palawa were there and how long they stayed – not long, apparently – are not recorded.

But as they were leaving the town 'one of their women, in its immediate vicinity, was used [by whites] in a manner, which, for brutality, beggars description'.[49] Payback was inevitable and swift. On 11 January the visitors attacked two men cutting blackwood at nearby Lake River. The sawyers were working in an area so thickly wooded that their hut 20 metres away was hidden from view. About 10 minutes after leaving it, one man went back and discovered their musket and ammunition had disappeared. He was not initially alarmed; he and his companion thought it was just a prank – until they spied Palawa waiting in ambush among the trees. One sawyer immediately sprinted for the safety of the hut but found his way blocked by Palawa, who attacked him with spears. Despite being wounded in the back he managed to escape to a stock hut three kilometres away. His companion, meanwhile, had run for the shelter of the trees in a barrage of spears and waddies. Although wounded, he escaped to the same hut.[50]

Peace prevailed everywhere for several weeks after that. But on 25 February 1825 Musquito and Black Jack were hanged with six Britons on the high scaffold within the walls of the Hobart jail. One of the Britons was John Logan, convicted of attempted murder. He had worked for George Augustus Robinson, who witnessed the hangings and recorded that they were bungled and that the condemned men's sufferings were prolonged and torturous.[51] The news enraged Kikatapula. A fortnight later vengeful spears flew again, and two more Britons died.

8

'Fire, you white cowards'

The year 1825 marked the full flowering of the Black War, and what expanded it from the sporadic raids of 1824 into outright conflict was the execution of Musquito and Black Jack. Kikatapula was emphatic about that, and Gilbert Robertson relayed the information to the Aborigines Committee.[1] Knowing who truly bore responsibility for the violence at Grindstone Bay, Kikatapula made no secret of his anger at Musquito's hanging, and more colonists paid with their lives.

The first reprisal was on the afternoon of 13 March 1825, a fortnight after the executions. About 80 Palawa slew stockkeepers John Johnson and James Taylor at Jonathan Kinsey's farm on upper Macquarie River near Ross while they were moving their belongings from an old hut to a new one. Their bodies were not found until three days later, when 'it was deemed expeditious, from the decay which had taken place, to inter them on the spot'.[2]

The attackers, reportedly Kikatapula's mob, then moved on before camping for the night.[3] Next morning they stripped an unoccupied hut and that afternoon they surrounded William Stocker's hut where an unnamed stockkeeper was alone inside. Alerted by his dogs' barking, he went outside to investigate and found the hut encircled by about 80 Palawa. Two who were highly painted appeared to be chiefs. He ordered them to go away, which they ignored. When they attempted to enter the hut he produced three loaded firearms and again ordered them to depart. As a Palawa man stepped forward and menaced the stockkeeper with his spear, saying 'me will, me will', another spear was flung at the Briton from behind, but he managed to evade it. In desperation he fired but his shots were ineffectual, and he was saved only by the arrival of another stockkeeper who, coming up some distance behind the Palawa, fired his weapon, causing the attackers to disperse. Reporting both attacks, a correspondent to the *Hobart Town Gazette* noted 'It was clearly ascertained that many of these men, were of the party recently participating in the Christian benevolence of the Government' – that is, the Kangaroo Point Palawa: the Oyster Bay mob: Kikatapula.[4]

About mid-March they returned to attack Stocker's cattle, and 'after slaying and roasting a calf, were found eating it, as if the use of European food was quite familiarized to them'.[5]

In mid-April a colonist named Temple Pearson, who farmed on Elizabeth River near Campbell Town, was driving a cart through the bush when Palawa suddenly showered him with spears. He abandoned the cart and fled on foot. The attackers ignored the cart and its contents and pursued Pearson, flinging their spears at his back. One man, running close behind him, yelled, for unknown reasons, 'I'll give you pepper!'[6] The pursuer's irascibility and command of English, especially his abstract threat, strongly suggest Kikatapula.

Although the attackers failed to catch Pearson they lingered nearby and on 23 April raided him again. They stripped a shepherd's hut of its contents and drove a flock of his sheep into the river, then started spearing them. Many were killed, others wounded, and the rest driven off. 'It is somewhat curious', a newspaper reported, 'that of those wounded the greatest proportion is in the eye! A fine young bull came home the same day, with a spear of very considerable length in his side.'[7]

In June Palawa attacked John Jones's hut at Sideling Hill near Bothwell, 'put the people to flight', and took from it blankets, clothing, and knives.[8] Palawa hostility was otherwise hibernally abeyant, and it was not until early spring, probably in September, that there was another attack in Oyster Bay country, although it was not reported in a newspaper until a year later. Two Britons had been slain at Kempton. The paper also mentioned two more killings around the same time that, like the Kempton slayings, were recorded nowhere else, although it did not report the victims' names or where and when they died.

[A]bout twelve months ago [that is, around September 1825], an old Norfolk Islander, named Kingston, with another man, who were either sawing or splitting palings in the woods, were unexpectedly attacked and speared to death, by a tribe, in the neighbourhood of the Green-water Ponds [Kempton]; and that about the same time, two more men shared a similar fate in the interior ...[9]

Geography suggests that an otherwise undated 1825 killing might also have been around September. That it involved Kikatapula was evinced by settler Robert Jones, who testified that Daniel Bamber, a stockkeeper, was slain at Michael Howes Marsh, north-west of Oatlands, by the Palawa responsible for Matthew Osborne's death.[10]

Uneasy peace prevailed throughout an especially wet October. Nevertheless, the few Hobartians who braved a wild wind-driven downpour to venture outdoors on Saturday morning the 22nd of that month were alarmed and astonished to see a mob of about 50 Palawa entering the town.[11] No one recorded why they were there or how long they stayed, but they departed after being given food. Although their visit was not reported in the *Hobart Town Gazette*, it prompted a correspondent to that newspaper to complain about their nakedness. 'Would it not be practicable,' he asked rhetorically, 'to give them to understand, that unless they are covered to a certain extent, they will not be admitted into the Town, or receive any food?'[12] The visitors' numbers and audacity suggest Kikatapula's leadership. As a later edition of the newspaper observed, 'the [mob] most confirmed in barbarism is probably that which occasionally visits the habitations of the settlers, and comes into Town'.[13]

Musquito's former acolyte was perhaps disdainful of his British enemies and cocky about his own invincibility. But his luck was not to last.

The following month brought an especially well-documented attack by Palawa who were clearly identified in a magistrate's report as 'One of the hostile Aborigines tribes, headed by Thomas Birch, alias Black Tom'.[14] The intended victims, Robert Jones and his family, who farmed at Pleasant Place near Jericho, were Kikatapula's target more than once.

In 1830 Jones testified that 'Tom Birch's mob made attempts to burn my hut and I had much difficulty to prevent it'.[15] In the November 1825 attack the Joneses were saved from annihilation only by a small child's extraordinary courage.

Jones had gone out at night to look for some sheep and had just returned home next morning when his young son ran in to warn him of Palawa nearby. Jones seized his musket and went outside, where he saw two Palawa warriors. He pursued them toward a nearby tier but spotted other Palawa waiting in ambush among wattle trees. His wife, standing in the doorway with a loaded pistol, called to him to turn back. As he was hurrying back the waiting Palawa pursued him, swearing at him in good English while using the cover of trees near the Joneses' house to work closer. A Palawa warrior was on each side of the house with lighted bark in his hand, there were Palawa women and children up on the tier, and more warriors were working their way toward the house.

The settlers were in a desperate position. A high flood the day before had filled the marshes with water, hemming the family in at the back, while the Palawa had them trapped at the front. Jones's wife kept the attackers from entering the house by pointing her pistol at them, which so exasperated them that Kikatapula, 'he who was taller than the rest, and seemed to be their chief', angrily exclaimed: 'As for you, ma'am, as for you, ma'am, I will put you in the river, ma'am'.

Deadlocked hours passed. Trapped in the house with the desperate and fearful Joneses was a seven-year-old servant named Sarah Bellinger who offered to run to a hill more than a kilometre away to fetch sawyers working there. Jones forbade her to do so, but she slipped out, crawled along the fence-line until she was clear, then ran to alert the sawyers to the family's plight. When the Joneses realised she had gone they waited 30 minutes, then coo-eed. Still some distance away, the sawyers responded by firing their weapons, causing the attackers to retreat. 'We pursued them,' Jones recalled, 'and I got very close to one as he stooped under the boughs of a fallen tree, and I could see no more of him ... We then observed the Blacks ascending a second tier, and then we quitted a further pursuit, as it would not have been safe to have left the house and the family unprotected for such a long time.' The siege had lasted four nerve-racking hours.[16]

'Fire, you white cowards'

Magistrate Thomas Anstey's report to the Colonial Secretary showed the attack had an unexpected humorous side and also provided invaluable glimpses of Kikatapula's appearance and temperament.

> Before the arrival of the sawyers the tribe was on the opposite banks, only the Chief was on this side. He kept threatening Mr. Jones and Mrs. Jones, exclaiming 'fire you white cowards – fire you white ———-'. Had the guns been so discharged, a rush would immediately have been made. Meanwhile the Chief cut a number of capers, and not perceiving that he stood on the edge of the bank, he fell backwards with his head foremost into the river. This caused the tribe to set up a loud laugh, which so enraged the Chief that he flew into a mighty passion, stamped his feet on the ground, he cried to Mrs. Jones 'as for you, ma-am, I'll put you into the river – I'll burn your hut ma-am'. He is described as a fine looking tall man, and by his speaking English, it was supposed that he belonged to one of those tribes who had frequently had intercourse with the colonists.[17]

The final recorded attack of 1825 was on the last day of the year at Western Creek, about nine kilometres west of present-day Meander. Palawa thrice speared James Cupit, an Irish convict from County Antrim who worked for William Stocker, but he managed to drive them off with gunfire. About 160 Palawa were said to be involved in what was undoubtedly a reprisal attack, for Cupit 'had killed a number of the Natives, and they ... made many attempts upon his life, and speared him in many places.[18] On one occasion as he was escaping from them they cried out to him in English "We will have you yet"'.[19] Cupit was so seriously wounded in the New Year's Eve spearing that the *Colonial Times* reported a fortnight later that 'the recovery of the poor man is very doubtful, one of his wounds, between the neck and shoulder, being four inches [10 cm] deep'.[20] But he did recover, only to be wounded again in 1831, his ninth spearing. Both tough and lucky, he survived that too, and died of natural causes in 1857, aged about 70.[21]

In all, nine Britons were killed during 1825 in attacks either identifiably involving Kikatapula's mob or attributable to them by geography and circumstance. And that tally was about to increase dramatically, for 1826 was to be the bloodiest year yet – and not only for Britons.

9

'Parrawa, parrawa! Go away!'

That Palawa violence, much of it with Kikatapula in the van, surged in 1826 is not surprising. By then, Tasmania's vast Midlands Plain, ideal country for fine-wool production, had experienced a major British expansion. More than half-a-million sheep were pasturing on prime grasslands that two decades earlier had been Palawa hunting grounds. Arable and browsable Palawa country everywhere was being usurped, always without permission or recompense and sometimes with Palawa blood secretly shed. Palawa hunting grounds, immemorially firestick-farmed and needing little or no clearing, were ideal for grazing. So many Europeans settling with great numbers of sheep on prime hunting grounds gave Palawa an unprecedented shock. With settlers came their families and convict labourers. Soon buildings, fences, stone walls, stockyards, hedges, orchards, crops, and gardens were impeding Palawa movement. That their anger would finally boil over was inevitable, and in 1826 it did. At least 23 colonists were slain that year, beginning on the Clyde in January when George Scott and Patrick McCarthy were killed.[1] It portended a bad year and moved the *Hobart Town Gazette* to suggest some land be reserved exclusively for Palawa as a means of alleviating their anger.[2] The newspaper had no doubt about who was responsible for the intensifying violence: the mob 'which occasionally visits the habitations of the settlers, and comes into Town': Kikatapula's mob.[3]

On 14 March 80 to 100 Palawa camped across the creek from Mayfield, just north of Little Swanport. Mayfield was farmed by Thomas Buxton, a Derbyshire-born former naval officer who had arrived in the colony with his family in 1821. At first the Palawa appeared peaceable. Some who could speak English visited Buxton's hut and assured him they were tame. But later that day two of Buxton's daughters noticed the leader had painted his face with red ochre, an ominous sign. They ran with the news to their father, who was assisting his men to thatch a haystack. All rushed to the hut to fetch their weapons but Palawa were already removing its contents, firearms included. One Palawa man was still in the hut holding a loaf of bread. Buxton grabbed him by the throat and shook him until he dropped it. At that moment one of Buxton's men, badly wounded, staggered into the hut and gasped that the Palawa had killed his mate.[4] The seriously outnumbered settlers now had only a single weapon, a pistol one of the Buxton girls had hidden, and dared not leave the hut. But at nightfall one of the beleaguered Britons crept out and made for Swansea to get help. In response, George Meredith junior assembled a party of his father's men and set out to relieve the siege at Mayfield, 30 kilometres away.

Buxton and his people had spent a sleepless night in the hut. At first light, Palawa carrying firesticks ran toward the haystack. Buxton charged at them, shouting and waving the pistol; the others also charged out shouting. The Palawa withdrew some distance, setting fire to the haystack as they did. But Meredith's men arrived in time to help extinguish the blaze. That night the settlers attacked the Palawa camp, killing several people, scattering the rest, and recovering most of Buxton's belongings.[5]

The following month two more colonists died at Palawa hands. Although one death did not involve Kikatapula, its far-reaching consequences did. A convict bullock-driver named Thomas Colley, who worked at John de Courcy Harte's farm near Oyster Bay, had whipped a young Palawa known as Jack.[6] A very old Oyster Bay man called Richard or Black Dick quickly exacted revenge by spearing Colley to death.[7] Both were to pay with their lives, and their executions were to further stoke the fires of Kikatapula's anger.

The second killing that month was on the 29th at The Bluff, Dromedary (in Derwent Valley north of Hobart). About 30 Palawa, including five who could speak English, slew a stonemason named James Browning, almost severing his head with a tomahawk. They also attacked his servant Richard Smith, cutting him severely about the head. Believing him to be dead, they threw the unconscious man into the fireplace and covered him with ashes before removing all the weapons, ammunition, food, and blankets from the hut. Some of the attackers wore pieces of blanket, leading the *Colonial Times* to opine that they included 'some of the Natives frequenting the townships'. The *Times* also reported that Browning lost his head because he refused to relinquish a Palawa woman he cohabited with. Smith, who survived the attack, said he could recognise several of his assailants.[8] Another newspaper noted that 'Mr. Browning ... had uniformly shown this tribe of natives, which has long been known for its barbarity, the greatest hospitality, frequently affording them provisions'.[9] A tribe long known for its barbarity meant Kikatapula's mob. A military party in pursuit of the attackers supposedly wounded several of them but failed to recover the firearms they had taken.

In May Palawa wounded a stockkeeper named James Rowe and attacked the hut of David Mackie at Carlton, in the Pitt Water district.[10] They also harassed an unnamed colonist at Bagdad, plundering his hut.[11] That month Lieutenant Governor Arthur decided the two Oyster Bay men Jack and Black Dick were responsible for killing Thomas Colley. On 27 May, after a two-day trial, they were sentenced to death.

In June Kikatapula led an attack at Colebrook, in Coal River Valley, that was provoked by a stockkeeper named Johnson's 'gross misconduct' – a widely understood euphemism for sexual assault of a Palawa woman. The attackers wounded Johnson and threatened three other stockkeepers.[12] Also in Coal River Valley in the middle of that month 150 Palawa dug up a large potato crop at Tea Tree. They carried away what they could and destroyed the rest.[13]

In early September Palawa entered a farmhouse at Pitt Water while two farmhands were in sight ploughing a field. When a servant in the house tried to stop their pilfering they beat him on the head with their waddies.[14] The attackers' leader spoke good English.

Farther north, Palawa killed Samuel Perry and Patrick Hallan near Pipers Lagoon on 12 September. Both men were found with 'their heads beat in a most inhuman manner, and speared in several parts of their bodies – one in the loins, five inches [127 mm] deep, and the spear broken off in the wound'.[15]

Next day Jack and Black Dick were executed in Hobart. Black Dick was so old and feeble that he had to be carried to the scaffold and sat on a stool to be hanged. Both executions were bungled. The cord tying Jack's hands to his sides slipped up to the elbow as he was dangling. He 'reached up his hand to his neck, and bled profusely from the nose' as he, like Black Dick, slowly, agonisingly strangled.[16] Although the Lieutenant Governor believed the hangings would deter further Palawa killings, his confidence was wholly misplaced.[17] Outraged by the executions, Palawa who had been sojourning at Kangaroo Point promptly decamped. 'The Oyster Bay tribe never came [back] to Kangaroo Point after Dick and Jack were executed,' Rev. William Bedford told the Aborigines Committee.[18] Kikatapula made no secret of his fury at the hangings. He considered both men, like Musquito and Black Jack, to be 'martyrs in the conquest of their country'.[19] The *Colonial Times* confirmed that 'the recent execution ... has kindled their animosity against the whites', and throughout October and November settlers on the Clyde paid dearly.[20] In Kikatapula's most sustained retributive campaign, lasting nearly seven weeks, so did others nearly as far north as Perth.

His reprisals on the Clyde were launched on 6 October 1826 when 150 Palawa fiercely besieged George Thomson's stock hut. Aided by the timely arrival of a well-armed bushranger named Patrick Dunne, Thomson's stockkeepers managed to repulse the attackers. Dunne, a particularly noisome individual whose pockmarked face was wreathed in red whiskers, captured a Palawa woman and forced her into a hut, where she was gang-raped before escaping.[21] Further enraged by her ordeal, Kikatapula's warriors went after Dunne and found him trying to get away by swimming across Ouse River. As he heaved himself out of the water he was shocked to be met by vengeful Palawa, but he managed to keep them at bay for five hours before escaping (only to be hanged the following January for bushranging).[22]

Honour unsatisfied, Kikatapula's furious fighters sought vengeance nearby. On 7 October they attacked Francis Burrell and William Tidwell who were driving a cartload of split timber.[23] Burrell jumped into the swollen River Clyde and escaped unhurt, but Tidwell was not so lucky. Although he too plunged into the river, he had a spear thrust through his thigh and 'must have perished from the effects of his wounds in the stream, down which he was seen, from a distance, to float, with a crowd of natives around to hasten his cruel death'.[24]

But Kikatapula's anger was unassuaged. He was far from finished with the Clyde. On 10 October a convict servant of Edward Nicholas of Nant, near Bothwell, rushed into the military barracks in the town and gasped that Nant was under attack and needed immediate help. The military, however, declined to assist. No magistrate was available to grant them a warrant, they said, and they could not respond without one. When the apprehensive servant returned to Nant he found the Palawa had gone after stripping the hut and destroying whatever they could not carry away. One of his co-workers was dying from a spear wound; another, who had tried to flee, had disappeared and was never seen again.[25] The attackers were 'headed by one Black Tom, who was reared by Mrs. Birch', a newspaper reported, also stating that Palawa had robbed many huts in the neighbourhood at this time.[26]

A nervous lull followed, during which there were no attacks on Britons anywhere in Tasmania. But after three weeks the bated-breath peace was violently shattered. On 2 November, with unprecedented ferocity, Kikatapula's warriors again assailed Thomson's run. Terrified stockkeepers fled into the safety of the house, locked the door and the windows, and tried to keep the attackers at bay by poking their muskets through cracks. The Palawa were undaunted. 'Fire, you white buggers!' they shouted. One attacker broke open the front door as others clambered down the chimney. Despite having only two charges of powder and shot, a farmhand fired, bringing down one warrior, but it had no effect on the others. They pressed their attack even more fiercely, forcing the stockkeepers to flee for their lives.[27] Yet even that was dangerous. Kikatapula's mob had a great many dogs, perhaps 60 of them, which they had trained to surround the hut and attack the stockkeepers as they fled.[28] Somehow the Britons got away.

Shortly after sunrise next day, as fearful shepherds crept out to their flocks, more than 200 Palawa shouting *Parrawa, parrawa!* Go away, go away!' stormed Thomson's farm and Robert Pitcairn's neighbouring run.[29] James Scott, a free employee of Pitcairn's recently arrived from Scotland, was 'speared, butchered and mangled, in a manner too horrible to relate'. One of Thomson's servants later confirmed that the Palawa wanted blood. 'Some weeks ago,' he told an inquest, 'Dunne, the bushranger, brought a native woman to our hut. He brought her by force. The same woman was with the tribe of natives when they attacked and plundered our hut last Thursday, and she was with the party who threatened us with death on the following day, about the same time that Scott was killed.'[30] Scott, who had taken no part in assaulting the woman, was a big man, 188 centimetres tall, but he was unable to withstand the furious onslaught. His arms were badly bruised as he tried to protect his head from waddy blows and he was speared in the thigh, the side, the cheek, and the right eye. His skull was holed in several places and some of his front teeth were knocked out.[31]

The rest of Pitcairn's men, with Thomson's, Ross's, and many others in the vicinity, abandoned their livestock and fled to the safety of The Hermitage, Ross's stone house.[32] A military party was urgently summoned from Bothwell, about 18 kilometres south, 'and the different settlers dare not stir out to collect the sheep until they arrive', it was reported. 'Nearly all the huts in the vicinity have been robbed, and it is much feared that two men left in Mr. Pitcairn's hut, have shared the fate of the unfortunate Scott.'[33]

If such a wholesale flight of settlers was a signal victory for Kikatapula, it was nevertheless fleeting. As the military neared the bloody scene the Palawa melted away, leaving their pursuers no trail to follow. '[T]hey immediately remove to a considerable distance from the scene of their barbarity', a Bothwell-based military officer wrote in frustration, 'as I have never been able to fall in with them in the neighbourhood when they commit any outrage, and in such a country as this it is quite impossible to ascertain which direction they may have taken'.[34]

His vexation was with good reason. Relying as usual on speed and mobility, Kikatapula's guerrillas put an astonishing distance between themselves and the Clyde in a very short time, striking remarkably soon afterwards about 100 kilometres away in the Central North. 'That dangerous tribe of natives headed by black Tom which has of late annoyed the neighbourhood of the Clyde and Shannon so much, has commenced its ravages on the stock-keepers at Pennyroyal Creek [Liffey River]', a newspaper reported.[35]

Three days after that was published Kikatapula had his long-sought revenge on an old enemy. The circumstances were vividly recalled by a witness, James Rush, in a deposition made to Police Magistrate James Simpson nearly two years later, when Kikatapula was about to be tried for murder.

[I]n November 1826 I resided upon the River Isis [Liffey] … on a farm [between Campbell Town and Perth] belonging to George Simpson Esq. as overseer. Upon the 7th of that month my party was attacked by a party of the black natives headed by Black Tom Birch, commonly called Black Tom. The natives came up to me in three different ways, the first party about 20 had no spears, they ask'd for Breadly and Tatery. I gave them all some bread and potatoes. I had with me in the hut two men Fr. S. Shone a shepherd and a man by the name of John Guinea a fencer both crown prisoners; being without firearms I immediately dispatched Shone for the military … by this time a part of the tribe whom I had given bread to came up to us again accompanied by about 80 more who had torches in their hands drawing close to a stack of wheat, myself being anxious about the wheat I went up to them and prevail'd upon them to lay down their torches, John Guinea [who] was close to me at this time … observ'd at short distance an immense number of natives coming up arm'd with spears and waddies [and] immediately said Black Tom is there and that we must take care of ourselves as he headed the savage tribe of natives. Guinea and myself went to the hut and locked up the house door and, in this about 10 minutes elaps'd. We were watching the natives who were nearly all round us, Black Tom and two others appeared at the end of the hut and immediately threw their spears. Myself and Guinea was not more than 10 yards [away?]. Guinea received a spear wound from Black Tom in the left side; he was an extreme sufferer for about 30 hours until he expired in the greatest agonies. Guinea had a personal knowledge of Black Tom having lived a twelve-month with him, he also said on oath on his death bed that Black Tom murdered him.[36]

Guinea was the only Briton recorded slain by Kikatapula himself. Rush escaped with slight spear wounds.

After emptying Simpson's hut the Palawa sped south-east, later that week striking Lewis Gillies's farm on Elizabeth River a little west of Campbell Town. With their waddies they clubbed Gillies's shepherd, an old man named Reynolds, and left him to die.[37] Then, working their way along Macquarie River, they wreaked more havoc, leaving behind them a total of three dead and five wounded Britons.[38]

Four days after killing Guinea, Kikatapula's mob appeared at Valleyfield, on the Macquarie about 20 kilometres north-west of Campbell Town, and ambushed George Taylor junior. The third son of his family, Taylor had distinguished himself two years earlier by helping repulse a gang of bushrangers. On 11 November he left his father's stock hut on Lake River but failed to return that night. A search party set out next morning and found his body that evening a few kilometres from the hut. He had suffered many spear wounds and his head was shattered.[39]

The continuing trail of blood moved the *Hobart Town Gazette* to fulminate about Kikatapula.

> [T]hey are a lawless, debased, brutal mob, under the guidance of this black Tom, who had, at a former period, voluntarily become a member of this community, who lived many years as a free servant to one of our settlers, and who now with the basest treachery turns the very weapons which he then acquired, in the destruction of that society whom he had deceived into confidence. He is therefore, not a deserter, but a rebel, a civil or internal enemy, and those who have joined him are alike guilty with himself.[40]

By the time the report appeared the ever-evasive Kikatapula had changed direction again and was on his way back south. Early on 21 November he appeared in Cockatoo Valley, about six kilometres from Allenvale, near Gretna, where with 20 other Palawa he peaceably approached John Riseley's sawpits. He struck up a conversation with two employees, William Priest and James Rochford, who were relieved to find the visitor friendly and agreeable to their offer of food and tobacco. Smoking a pipe with them, Kikatapula casually inquired if they were armed. No, they said. Shingle-splitters working some distance away had taken all their firearms. The Palawa then departed. Soon afterwards John Monks and Thomas House joined Priest and Rochford at breakfast, but as the four were enjoying their meal 50 Palawa burst in without warning and attacked them. Monks was quickly slain, his head beaten in, as the terrified Britons attempted flight. Priest, although speared in the neck, managed to escape, but House was later found dead.[41] Rochford was never seen again.[42]

The killings provoked more editorial outrage about Kikatapula.

The man who appeared to lead and instigate [the Palawa] to these dreadful crimes was called Jack, although it is believed that he is the same who has called himself Tom on other occasions, these two names appearing to be indiscriminately given to such natives as have acquired some knowledge of civilized life and a smattering of English. This man was seen to be distinguished by two circles marked or tattooed upon his loins, and which would seem among these ignorant people, to be a mark of distinction for him who takes the lead.[43]

Kikatapula's cockiness was undiminished. He did not bother to withdraw from the Hamilton area after slaying Monks, Rochford, and House and, on 22 November, beset a stockkeeper about five kilometres from Allenvale. Luckier than Monks and his workmates, this man escaped with his life. Colonists pursued the Palawa and reported killing two.[44]

Kikatapula now led two attacks in the nearby Bothwell region. In the first, two shepherds at Dennistoun survived by leaping a fence and sprinting to safety. Then, in the last week of November, Kikatapula's mob, much enlarged by a temporary coalition with Big River people, attacked a stockkeeper at Abyssinia. The man quickly locked himself in a hut, shutting the doors and barring the windows, and kept his attackers at bay for some time by poking a firearm through a crack. When they tried to set the roof ablaze he fired, hitting one attacker. After carrying the victim away the Palawa renewed their firestick assault and set the roof alight. Facing certain death either by fire or by spear-thrust and waddy-blow, the desperate Briton fired again, felling another attacker, which caused the Palawa to abandon their attack and allowed the besieged man to douse the flames.[45] Between 100 and 160 Palawa were reportedly involved, one of whom spoke very good English.[46]

The coalition then split up. The larger part, the Big River people, headed westward into their own country while Kikatapula's mob, believed to be 20 to 30 strong, set out north-easterly. On 26 November they denuded a sawyers' hut near Melton Mowbray after its two inhabitants fled to safety.[47] The *Colonial Times* reported that 'the natives are much worse than the ... bush-rangers; and that *Black Tom*, and those with him, declare that they will murder every *white* man that they fall in with'.[48]

One who did fall in at this time with Kikatapula was a Coal River Valley emancipist named Zachariah Sponsford. In late November he left his farm under Gunnings Sugarloaf, about six kilometres north of Campania, to buy cattle from William Stocker in the Western Tiers, intending to drive them to the Hobart market for Christmas. He went alone and did not return in time for Christmas but disappeared. 'From the circumstances of between 50 and 60 head of Mr. Stocker's cattle having been found with spears sticking in them', the *Colonial Times* reported on 5 January 1827 after Sponsford had been missing for four weeks, 'it appears but too probable that Mr. Sponsford has fallen a sacrifice to these barbarous savage people'.

Mr Sponsford, however, was unusually fortunate. He had indeed encountered hostile Palawa and only with difficulty escaped from them.[49] It sounds like a tale worth telling, but no other details of his brush with death have survived. Since he had collected the cattle from Stocker he must have been driving them through the southern Midlands when he ran into hostile Palawa. The location is unrecorded, but it appears his route and Kikatapula's converged at the beginning of December. Heading south-east, Kikatapula's mob had left Melton Mowbray on 26 November and next appeared at Bank Head Farm, between Orielton and Runnymede, on 8 December, so their route must have taken them through the region Sponsford and his cattle were traversing when he disappeared. Moreover, when they reached Bank Head Farm a few days later Kikatapula's warriors had no spears left, and 50 to 60 of Sponsford's cattle had spears in them.

However, the route to Bank Head Farm led Kikatapula's mob to another encounter the same week, one that was to prove very costly for them.

For Kikatapula himself it should have been fatal.

10

'You white bugger, give me some bread'

As 1826 drew toward its close, public outrage at Kikatapula's exploits reached a peak. Colonists were clamouring for his capture and execution, and not necessarily after the formality of a trial. On 17 November the *Colonial Times* demanded that 'a reward be offered for the apprehension of Black Tom [and] that he be immediately gibbeted on the very spot, which has been the scene of his atrocities'. The newspaper was giving voice to a widespread belief, not only about Kikatapula. All Palawa were seen as a threat.

> These violent outrages, in addition to the murders of Mr. George Taylor, Mr. Osborne, James Scott, the shepherd, and many (we may safely venture to say twenty) others, call loudly for redress. Something, it is very evident, must be immediately done, to stop these alarming proceedings ...[1]

In its following issue the *Colonial Times* thundered on. Noting 'There are two parties who have committed outrages – the Oyster Bay and the Shannon parties', it continued: 'THE GOVERNMENT MUST REMOVE THE NATIVES – IF NOT, THEY WILL BE HUNTED DOWN LIKE WILD BEASTS, AND DESTROYED!'

Yet when a constable with a small party of soldiers captured Kikatapula at Pitt Water on 9 December 1826, he was not lynched, not even tried for murder and subsequently executed, as Jack and Black Dick had been only three months earlier. Instead, after brooding in jail for a month he was quietly released with a supply of food and blankets, free to resume hostilities.

It is a curious tale.

The story began after Kikatapula parted from the Big River people – 'the Shannon party'. His mob – 'the Oyster Bay party' – continued south-easterly after their raid on the sawyers' hut and their brush with Sponsford. When they reached Bank Head Farm, near Black Charlies Sugarloaf (just south of Runnymede), they had no weapons, having exhausted their spears on Sponsford's cattle, so they were possibly on their way to Blue Hill Bluff, north of Prossers Plains, a favoured source of spear-making wood.[2] The *Hobart Town Gazette* followed their progress.

> Since our last, little has transpired respecting the natives. It is believed that the chief part of them [the Big River component] has crossed the Derwent, and proceeded to the unexplored mountains in the west. A small party [Kikatapula's] is however thought to have pursued their way toward the Coal River and the Hollow Tree [Cambridge] and some vague reports of outrages committed by them there, have reached town, but nothing which can be relied on.[3]

On Friday 8 December 1826 Kikatapula's mob descended on a lonely stock-hut on remote Bank Head Farm, the property of Alexander Laing, a convict who had acquired ersatz respectability as Chief District Constable of Sorell, a rudimentary town about 20 kilometres away – the same Laing who later wrote that he had seen Kikatapula caring for Thomas Birch's children in Hobart years before. The Palawa leader menaced Laing's stockkeeper Robert Grimes, who gave them all the bread he had. Momentarily satisfied, they made no more demands for about two hours. Then Kikatapula confronted Grimes again. 'You white bugger,' he said, 'give me some bread, and fry some mutton for us.' The terrified Grimes baked more bread and cooked three-quarters of a sheep, all of which the Palawa ate. In the afternoon they went away to hunt possums, giving Grimes a chance to send for help. When the Palawa returned, Kikatapula went alone to the hut and ordered the fearful Briton to prepare more bread and mutton for them by next morning. 'Grimes had another damper ready,' the *Colonial Times* reported, 'but Mr. Black Tom was deprived of partaking of it, as Mr. Laing and the military happened to call upon him before breakfast, and his next meal was eaten in the cell in Sorell Gaol'. Nothing in that or any other report suggested the circumstances of Kikatapula's apprehension were anything but innocuous.

On Friday evening last, the 8th instant, Mr. Laing, the Chief District Constable at Sorell, received information that Black Tom, the native Aborigine, commonly called Birch's Tom, was encamped within about one hundred yards of a hut on Mr. Laing's farm, occupied by a man named Robert Grimes, near the Brown Mountain. Mr. Laing left Sorell at 11 o'clock, p.m. with a party of four soldiers of His Majesty's 40th Regiment, and arrived at Grimes's hut, a little before day-break, on Saturday morning; and at day-light they proceeded to the spot where Tom and his party lay, and got upon them unperceived. They secured Tom and his companions, consisting of four other black men, four women, and one male child; who made no resistance; neither had they any weapons or dogs with them. On being asked where his dogs were, [Kikatapula] replied he had lost them. The natives were then conducted to Sorell Gaol, where they now remain, until orders are sent from His Excellency respecting them.[4]

The following day's *Hobart Town Gazette* reported the capture in an oddly offhand way, given Kikatapula's notoriety and the clamorous demands for his demise. 'The native named "Black Tom" has been apprehended with four other blacks at Pittwater, and safely lodged in the Gaol at Sorell Town' was all it said.[5]

Sorell jail gave Kikatapula his first taste of incarceration.
(Courtesy Libraries Tasmania)

Neither report mentioned that the capture involved killing 14 of Kikatapula's followers.

The omission is not surprising. Newspaper stories about regional events at that time were written not by professional journalists but by a witness to or a participant in some newsworthy event, or by someone who had spoken to a witness or a participant.[6] Such reports were usually published verbatim and either anonymously or pseudonymously and because of that could be usefully self-serving, imparting only what information – factual, false, or redacted – the writer wanted publicised. So neither newspaper report mentioned any slaughter of Palawa, and three years were to pass before the first evidence surfaced that there had been killings at Bank Head Farm. That was in 1830 when Kikatapula's friend Gilbert Robertson, now Chief Constable of the Richmond police district (which by then included Sorell), testified to the Aborigines Committee that:

> The Richmond police, three years ago, killed 14 of the Natives, who had got upon a hill, and threw stones down upon them; the police expended all their ammunition, and being afraid to run away, at length charged with the bayonet, and the Natives fled.[7]

Lyndall Ryan, in her seminal book *The Aboriginal Tasmanians*, was the first to link those killings with Kikatapula's 1826 capture. Others have disputed the connection or denied there were killings, but Robertson was too credible an official for his report to be offhandedly disavowed. He was sympathetic to Palawa and their plight and 'had a compulsion for telling the truth ... no matter how detrimental to his personal interest'.[8] Another writer noted that Robertson 'had the boldness to expose evils, and the temerity to confront authority'.[9] He was also very familiar with the Richmond police district. By 1830 he had been living there for about eight years and he was its Chief Constable (and the by-then-demoted Laing's boss) from November 1828 to February 1832. His testimony of 'three years ago' indicates a likely date between September 1826 and September 1827, during which period there was only a single recorded clash between Palawa and police in the Richmond police district: the capture of Kikatapula and his mob at Bank Head Farm on 9 December 1826. So that must have been what Robertson was referring to. He would have had no reason, in a report intended for the British parliament, to invent the slaughter of 14 people.

But the Aborigines Committee showed no interest. Lieutenant Governor Arthur had established it to examine Palawa depredations, not British atrocities. Moreover, in 1830 the drawn-out Black War was still raging. Twenty-five colonists were slain that year and many more wounded, so sympathy for Palawa was non-existent. Robertson himself was unpopular, a litigious pest to the government and some influential settlers. The committee ignored his testimony.

The killings were not something he himself had witnessed, only what he had been told about. He was not part of the Richmond police in 1826 and so was not involved in the capture. Details of the incident, as he related them, are clearly told from a white participant's viewpoint, so Laing himself might have been Robertson's informant. Once Sorell became part of the Richmond police district in 1828, Robertson became Laing's superior and was in a position to question him about the capture after having learnt of it elsewhere.

The most likely source of Robertson's information, however, was Sorell magistrate James Gordon, 'Robertson's friend and political ally', to whom Laing reported Kikatapula's capture.[10] The *Colonial Times* report was obviously written by someone who knew such precise details as the hour Laing left Sorell and the composition of his party. The writer was also evidently someone used to compiling reports, someone experienced and literate enough to gloss over anything unsavoury without leaving an obvious gap. Gordon fits that picture. A few years later he and Laing were reportedly colluding to purloin building materials from government stores that Laing, Sorell's commissariat storekeeper, had charge of.[11] Such a partnership might well have begun with Gordon's covering up Laing's responsibility for Palawa deaths at Bank Head Farm.

Gordon was to be police magistrate at Richmond from September 1829 to March 1832 – that is, during the greater part of Robertson's term as Chief District Constable. As friends, their official and social intercourse must have been frequent. And because Gordon (as will be shown) was instrumental in covering up what happened at Bank Head Farm, Robertson, once he learnt of it, was constrained from trying to take the matter further because it would have incriminated his friend. Besides (as will additionally be shown), the government knew of the killings and was complicit in suppressing news of them. And it was Gordon who was crucial to having Kikatapula released without trial or publicity. So Robertson's hands were tied. All he could do was find some way to put the matter on public record, which he did in his testimony to the Aborigines Committee.

Despite the committee's lack of interest, the matter did not entirely disappear. Robertson and George Augustus Robinson were reportedly arch-rivals, yet Robinson believed Robertson's testimony, perhaps having Kikatapula himself confirm the facts during the 28 months of their close daily colleagueship 1830–1832, and thought it important to try to keep the matter alive. In 1838 he took to Sydney *The Report of the Van Diemen's Land Aborigines Committee* and quoted Robertson's words nearly verbatim to a public meeting of the Australian Aborigines Protection Society.

> The Richmond police, in 1827, killed fourteen of the natives, who had got upon a hill, and threw stones upon them. The police expended all their ammunition, and then charged with the bayonet.[12]

Nevertheless, after 1838 it vanished from written records for 110 years, although it stayed indelibly in local memory. A much later narrative, written by a Sorell resident and published in 1948 in a little-known and now-forgotten book, independently verified what Robertson told the Aborigines Committee, showed that he was indeed referring to a Kikatapula/Laing clash, and demonstrated the extraordinary fact that the killings were remembered around Sorell and the Pitt Water region 122 years afterwards. The book, Roy Bridges' *That Yesterday Was Home*, includes this electrifying paragraph:

> Black Tom and his force of natives, after a succession of outrages through the Richmond Police District and beyond, were chased by Chief District Constable Lang [sic] and his men up the Sorell Valley, overtaken, and destroyed near the head-waters of the rivulet.[13]

That cannot possibly refer to anything but Kikatapula's capture at Bank Head Farm because the two principal antagonists are named and Bank Head Farm was the only time their paths crossed violently. The location too is corroborative. Bank Head Farm is near the head of Sorell Valley (now Pawleena Valley) and the headwaters of both Orielton Rivulet and Sorell Rivulet.

Bridges' version is worded so differently from Robertson's and Robinson's, neither of which mentioned Laing, that it is most unlikely he was familiar with either man's testimony or with Laing's unpublished 1867 memoir, none of which it resembles. As Bridges narrated the story it sounds very much like oral history. So his words are startling. They attest that knowledge of the killings was general around Sorell and survived for the 122 years until Bridges wrote his book. The events must have been in some way extraordinary, then. They must have been much more memorable than merely the peaceful capture of a handful of unarmed and passive Palawa; a nonviolent capture is not something people would remember and talk about for more than a century. That is confirmed by Bridges' use of the word *destroy* to describe what Laing's party did to Kikatapula's mob. Bridges, a respected journalist on major newspapers, an internationally successful novelist, and a founder of the Australian Journalists' Association, would hardly have used such a powerfully emotive word to describe a peaceful rounding-up of nine or 10 sleep-addled Palawa. *Destroy* confirms something violent happened at Bank Head Farm.

A descendant of some of Pitt Water's earliest pioneers, Bridges (1885–1952) had strong lifelong connections to the region. He was a frequent sojourner there during his youth, a resident for the last two decades of his life, and a keen student of its history. He cherished his grandparents' stories of their pioneering days there. 'My mother, as a girl, heard from her grandmother, Mrs John Wood [*née* Sally Nash, a Pitt Water resident from 1814], the stories of the early days which were handed down to us', he wrote.[14] As Robertson and Robinson must have hoped, knowledge of what happened at Bank Head Farm survived despite an official cover-up in Tasmania and official indifference in Britain.

Other evidence pointing to Palawa being slain at Bank Head Farm, although circumstantial and sometimes allusive, can be read from Chief District Constable Laing's deteriorating career in the wake of Kikatapula's apprehension and the constable's attempts in his late-life memoir to distance himself from it. Further evidence can be seen in what happened to Kikatapula after capture. The two former matters, which are not directly relevant to Kikatapula's life, are discussed in Appendix 3: Alexander Laing: Cover-up and Downfall, which recounts how Laing's career, far from being given the fillip he might have expected after his capture of Tasmania's most wanted man, subsequently went abruptly and irreversibly downhill. In response to Laing's efforts at Bank Head Farm the gentlemen of the colonial administration squeezed the convict – Laing seems never to have been officially pardoned – out of the powerful office of Chief District Constable and into a lowlier position where he could be supervised by someone sound: Gilbert Robertson, another gentleman even though black.

For five Britons armed with clumsy single-shot weapons, which even trained soldiers took at least 20 or 30 seconds to reload, to kill 14 people they must indeed have used their bayonets, as Robertson reported. And for five Britons to have bayoneted any Palawa at all suggests a surprise attack in which some victims, perhaps including women and children, were slain either as they slept or in the befuddled moments of first waking, for Palawa were famously adept at scattering and vanishing when attacked.

So a credible case exists for 14 Palawa having been killed at Bank Head Farm. Equally credible evidence exists that the killings were covered up – and evidence of a cover-up is proof something happened that was nefarious enough to need concealing. No killings were mentioned in the *Colonial Times*'s report of the incident or in Gordon's official report to the Lieutenant Governor, written the day Kikatapula was captured.

> I beg to report to Your Excellency that Information being received by the Police at Sorell yesterday evening of a Number of the black Natives being in the Neighbourhood of the Little Plains [Runnymede] the Constables accompanied by the Military proceeded to the Place where they succeeded in Surprizing a Party of Nine – viz, 6 men and 3 women, one of whom has an infant, and amongst the men, Black Tom is of that number. They had been to the hut of a man named Grimes, who had been so intimidated by their language and manners that he was obliged to kill a sheep for them ... [15]

Murders of Palawa, although not rare in Tasmania, were never punished. It was against the law, which stated the guilty would be hanged, but there was tacit agreement within colonial society that a blind eye would be turned if the slayings were not officially reported. That there were massacres that were covered up is widely acknowledged by historians. '[C]olonists ignored Arthur's edicts to treat Aborigines humanely and ... he often did not hear of mass killings', writes one.[16] Another observes that 'a conspiracy of silence by the settlers to shield each other meant that, in practice, Aborigines were hanged, but no whites'.[17] A third pertinently points out that 'If indeed such a massacre did take place, no police magistrate would feel "obliged to report it", since the Colonial Office [London] would certainly demand the police be tried for murder'.[18]

After Kikatapula and the other survivors were marched from the scene of the slaughter to Sorell, they were confined in the jail there. With his experience of the British and his knowledge of the fate of Musquito and his own three Oyster Bay brethren convicted of killing whites, he must have expected a quick trial and execution. For about two weeks he and the other captives remained crammed in the little jail's single cell. Then 'Colonel Arthur the Governor, came to Sorell to see them', Laing wrote, 'and held a long consultation with ... Tom ... His Excellency ordered them to be removed to the Richmond Gaol, where they would be turned out for exercise under the care of the constables and javelin men'.[19] So around Christmas the 10 survivors were transferred to the larger Richmond jail, where they remained through the rest of December and into January, but nothing further was done about them. Kikatapula was not taken to Hobart for trial, although Arthur and Gordon had a private conversation about him, being careful to commit to paper nothing incriminating.

The matter remained in stasis until 5 January 1827, four weeks after Bank Head Farm, when Gordon sent Arthur a written reminder that the captives were still incarcerated and had not even been charged. Astonishingly, Gordon recommended their release. Even more astonishingly, the original suggestion to release them came from Arthur himself, as Gordon was careful to note in his letter.

> I beg to draw the Attention of His Excellency to the Black Natives now in Confinement in His Majesty's Gaol at Richmond. In a Conversation the

other day *His Excellency suggested the Propriety of releasing them as there is no Charge against them of any Outrage committed* [emphasis added]; with which I fully concur; but at the same time I beg leave to offer my Opinion that should they be liberated without a moderate Supply of Provisions they will be prowling about the Settlers Houses by which they will be in Danger of being shot; also by giving them a few days Provisions on their being liberated will tend to conciliate them, as I fear they feel not a little sore at their Confinement. As I intend to be present at their Liberation I shall recommend Tom to return to Hobart Town where I think he will find a home with his old Mistress [Sarah Hodgson]. I am under engagement to meet the Magistrates in the Coal River District at Richmond on Monday next; if therefore His Excellency will communicate his Pleasure to me on the Subject [it] shall be particularly attended to.[20]

It was an extraordinary statement – a blatant piece of official obfuscation. That neither Gordon nor Arthur was unaware that Kikatapula was wanted for murder is inconceivable. That the Lieutenant Governor did not know of Kikatapula's attacks on settlers, reported to him by local magistrates and publicised in Hobart's newspapers, is simply not credible. When the Executive Council met in late November 1826, just days before Bank Head Farm, its members 'read anguished messages from officials and settlers' about Palawa attacks.[21] Gordon's having spoken with Arthur about Kikatapula means he had certainly told the Lieutenant Governor in confidence the full story of the capture and that both men were aware of their consequent dilemma. Resolving it became Arthur's responsibility, and he was dilatory until Gordon prompted him, telling him, in effect, that he (Gordon) would need written gubernatorial ratification of Arthur's extraordinary assertion that 'there is no Charge against them of any Outrage committed'. He would also need Arthur's written permission to release Kikatapula without trial. Once he had that, he would personally see the captives off the premises, so to speak, for it is not difficult to infer what he meant by 'I intend to be present at their Liberation'. Eventually, to protect Laing, Arthur confirmed that no action need be taken; the captives were to be freed unpunished. 'Colonel Arthur sent instructions to the Police Magistrate to furnish them with an ample supply of blankets and provisions and turn them out at large in the bush', Laing wrote, strangely without a hint of rancour that his capture of a feared killer was wasted.

In his conversation with Arthur, Gordon may have cited a common view that the law now permitted violence to be used against Palawa in specific circumstances, a belief engendered by Arthur's proclamation of 29 November 1826. Stressing 'the need to capture certain natives who, making use of what they had learnt in previous intercourse with Europeans, were said to be directing the attacks upon the settlers', it tellingly declared: '[I]f the offenders cannot otherwise be taken, the officer and his assistants will be justified in resorting to force.'[22]

The proclamation was published in the *Hobart Town Gazette* on 2 December, a week before Bank Head Farm, and Laing may have believed it gave him *carte blanche* to kill. The government, however, shocked at the number of slain Palawa, hid the facts to protect the guilty. Although Arthur had his most wanted man behind bars, he had a tiger by the tail and a serious headache: how to deal with Kikatapula without publicising the bloody circumstances of his capture, thereby incriminating Laing. If Kikatapula were put on trial the whole story would come out under oath because he spoke English and had been baptised, so he could swear on the Bible that he was telling the truth. Moreover, Sarah Hodgson would have ensured his representation by legal counsel, boosting likelihood that the killings would be revealed. Arthur would then be forced to bring a murder charge against Laing, whose defence would be that he had acted in accordance with Arthur's own proclamation and its licence to kill – catch-22. So the government, to shield Laing from prosecution, had to do the same for Kikatapula. It would simply pretend that no violence had been committed by either man. No charge against Kikatapula meant no charge against Laing.

Consequently, on or about Monday 9 January 1827, at the Lieutenant Governor's own suggestion and with his full approval, Tasmania's most feared guerrilla leader, whose personal culpability in the killings of Matthew Osborne and John Guinea had been publicised in the *Hobart Town Gazette*, was freed, untried and unpunished, with his surviving followers because 'there is no Charge against them of any Outrage committed'. The decision, which unequivocally proves the government was hiding something abhorrent, quickly cost more British lives, for if Arthur believed the destruction of so many Palawa at Bank Head Farm would deter Kikatapula from further hostilities, it was a futile hope, as the *Colonial Times* observed within days of his unannounced release.

> A few days ago, about eleven Natives were taken by a party of Soldiers, and imprisoned at the Coal River, for having committed some trifling depredation. They have since been liberated, but appear to manifest a strong feeling against the whites, on account of the execution of Tom [*sic:* correctly Jack] and Dick, two of their sable brethren, who suffered for the murder of Mr. Hart's stock-keeper.[23]

For as he was turned loose in Coal River Valley, Kikatapula was not chastened or conciliated or cowed. He was livid.

11

'Beset by these black furies'

At the beginning of 1827 Kikatapula alone stood between his people and cultural annihilation. Two full years into the Black War, no other Palawa leader had emerged to stand with him or take his place. As a result, peace reigned everywhere during his month-long incarceration in Sorell and Richmond jails; not a single attack on colonists can be identified anywhere in Oyster Bay or Big River country in that period. Clearly, he was both the progenitor and the leader of Palawa resistance.

The rare period of tranquillity moved the *Hobart Town Gazette* on 30 December 1826 to proclaim that hostilities were over. A fortnight later it followed up by observing that Palawa were now completely tranquil throughout the colony.[1] Published within days of Kikatapula's release, the observation was naïvely optimistic. But the *Colonial Times* saw things more clearly. Mulling early in the new year over events in the old, it commented that Palawa outrages had kept colonists in a continual state of alarm; then it took aim at the *Gazette*'s complacency, saying 'the enormities have *not* ceased'.[2] Three weeks and several Palawa attacks later the *Times* further hardened its attitude, urging that all Palawa be exiled offshore because 'they declare, that they will exterminate every white man on the Island'.[3] The editorial voiced a common sentiment. Many colonists believed that ethnic cleansing, to use a 20th-century term, by exile or even extirpation was the only way to ensure the usurpers could enjoy undisturbed the fruits of their seizure.

Hostilities were dormant only while Kikatapula was in jail; as soon as he was freed, attacks resumed. What Palawa had lacked during his incarceration was a leader, and his release during the second week of

January was quickly followed by renewed attacks on a familiar target: George Thomson's farm on the Shannon. The message was unmistakable: Kikatapula had taken up the spear again. Although he was not identified by name in any attack before April, after his release he headed straight for the Clyde/Shannon region. There, on 21 January, two Britons were slain at Thomson's in a familiar occurrence: a post-liberation reprisal attack. Thomson's shepherd George Roberts disappeared, believed slain, and a stockkeeper was fatally wounded with three spears, one of which, 4.3 metres long, pierced his side and emerged near his spine.[4] By June the *Hobart Town Gazette* could report that Kikatapula was leading a mob of 100 Palawa – a sizeable proportion of all those left – in depredations around the Clyde/Shannon region.[5]

The renewed hostilities began a bad year for colonists, quickly causing the *Hobart Town Gazette* to rescind its optimism and admit that Palawa were indeed still troublesome, with several stockkeepers missing, believed killed.[6] Before November, when Kikatapula was apprehended for the third time, there were 39 recorded incidents (including four undated ones) likely to have involved him, although he was identified by name only in six. In the 10 months between his release from jail and his subsequent recapture Palawa slew 21 colonists and another five were listed as missing, believed killed, in country he is known or was very likely to have frequented. Three of the undated incidents were only thefts or harassment, but a sawyer and a shepherd were wounded at Kittys Corner (Eastern Marshes).

The next attack after January's raid on Thomson's was on 6 February at Avoca. Palawa speared two stockkeepers, one so badly that he was not expected to live.[7] From Avoca to Swansea is only about 50 kilometres across country, and on an unrecorded date in March Palawa plundered Thomas Buxton's house at the latter place. On 16 March, at Great Lake, they set fire to Spyers Dodson's thatched roof, razing his house and destroying its contents.

An attack at Jericho early in April was by 'a tribe, with Black Tom at their head'.[8] Professing friendliness, they approached Romney's stock hut, which housed James Johnson and two other men. After the Palawa lit and smoked their pipes, chatting amicably with the three stockkeepers, Kikatapula asked Johnson to go outside with him because he had something to show him. A short distance from the hut he suddenly spun around and belaboured Johnson with a waddy. When they heard his cries the other stockkeepers fled, leaving the hut for the Palawa to plunder of booty that included two muskets and some ammunition.[9] Kikatapula's release was costing colonists dearly.

After attacking Romney's the Palawa moved northward in the Midlands, where Kikatapula led a series of raids. On 12 April his guerrillas robbed several huts at Green Hills, about 10 kilometres from Campbell Town, then attacked Walter Davidson's stock hut and slew two stockkeepers, Thomas Rollands (or Rawlings) and Edward Green, whose bodies were found on the same day in a mangled state with spears protruding from them.[10]

Next they wheeled south again, rifling two huts as they travelled. Four local settlers armed themselves and with a small party of soldiers went in pursuit. They caught up with the attackers about 16 kilometres south in a gully opposite David Murray's farm near Mount Augusta, just west of today's Midland Highway between Campbell Town and Ross. The clash, most likely during the penultimate week of April, was historic because 'for the first time ... trusting to their numbers, [Palawa] contended a field of battle against European arms and discipline'.[11] The Britons split into two groups, one to attack, the other to hide in reserve. As the first party took cover behind trees the Palawa assailed them, showering them with spears and stones. Despite defensive gunfire the Palawa fiercely pressed their attack, unaware of the reserve party, but when they too entered the fight the attackers retreated, leaving behind many spears and waddies as well as loot from various raids. One abandoned item was a carving knife that had belonged to old Reynolds, Gillies's shepherd, slain by Kikatapula's mob the previous November.[12]

Although at first the *Colonial Times* did not mention any Palawa fatalities – its following issue claimed 30 – the *Hobart Town Gazette* trumpeted a most important scalp.

THE BLACK NATIVES. – The atrocities of these ignorant and misguided people, it is to be hoped, are now at an end, if it be true that Black Tom, the man who has been the main instrument of their late attacks upon the stockkeepers met his death last week, in a skirmish under the western

Table mountain ... We have not been able to learn the exact particulars,
but it is ascertained that Black Tom the ringleader has fallen, from persons
who have seen the body and recognised his features, particularly a
remarkable scar on his forehead.[13]

The *Colonial Times* caught up with the good news in its next issue,
hailing the demise of 'the notoriously treacherous and infamous leader',
calling him 'implacable' and 'perfidious' and a 'despicable creature'.[14] But
a correspondent who claimed to have thoroughly searched the scene
of battle found neither bodies nor blood. He opined that not a single
Palawa had been killed and also belittled another correspondent's belief
that Kikatapula's death would put an end to Palawa attacks. 'I augur,' he
declared, 'he would find Black Tom's spirit revived in the heart of every
savage in the island.'[15] Regardless, Kikatapula was still very much alive,
although the *Gazette* did not acknowledge it until 23 June, the *Times* six
days later.

About a week after the fight, around the end of April, the same Palawa
attacked two sawyers in the Elizabeth River area near Campbell Town.
The men barricaded themselves in their hut, but during the night one
managed to sneak away to fetch ammunition, and the Palawa were driven
off by gunfire when they attacked next morning, supposedly leaving a few
bodies behind.[16]

The east coast was next to suffer. After Palawa attacked Silas
Gatehouse's Grindstone Bay run in May, stockkeeper Richard Addey was
found to have disappeared, believed killed. In another attack that month
sawyers Patrick Lapham and James Ruebottom were splitting shingles
about 14 kilometres from Lake River, south of Cressy, when Palawa
ambushed them. Ruebottom succeeded in escaping with three spears
in his body but was mortally wounded.[17] Lapham's body was a mass of
wounds, his head smashed to pieces.[18]

When Kikatapula was identified leading the next two attacks, colonists
had to accept that reports of his death were false. The *Hobart Town
Gazette* prefaced its news of the first attack by noting his resurgence.
Black Tom was still alive, it said, and responsible for leading the various
recent raids. In the first of them, on a wet 15 June, he led a mob of about
100 Palawa that surprised two employees of J.A. Eddie splitting rails near

Michael Howes Marsh, south-west of Tunbridge. The Palawa concealed themselves and waited until Eddie's men stowed their firearms inside a hut out of the rain. Then they struck. The splitters attempted to flee, but not before one of them, Samuel May, who had been 'many years in the service of Mr. Hodgson', recognised Kikatapula. Despite nine spear wounds in his back, May survived.[19] The ferocity of the attack and the extent of his wounds suggest he and Kikatapula had not been friends when co-workers. The other splitter, John Flood, died from a spear thrust through his chest.

Pushing northward, Kikatapula's warriors ambushed two men next day who were working in a sawpit at Michael Lackey's farm in the Tunbridge area. One sawyer managed to escape despite many spear wounds in his back. The other was found next morning, still alive but so badly battered by waddy blows that his survival was thought unlikely. A strong force consisting of Chief District Constable Bennett, Lieutenant Travers, some soldiers, and several civilians pursued the attackers and surprised them only three kilometres from the sawpit. The Palawa instantly dispersed and disappeared, leaving behind only some spears and about 200 waddies.[20]

Chief District Constable Bennett's victory was ephemeral, however. Four months later he too became a victim of Kikatapula's spears.

An unexpected peace now settled on the south, the Midlands, and the east. Although settlers and their stockkeepers remained tense and fearful, loath to venture out unarmed or travel alone, for five peaceful weeks there was neither sight nor news of Kikatapula or of any hostile Palawa in his usual stamping ground. The wily resistance leader, moving with his usual speed and cunning, had nonplussed his pursuers by moving his raids to the Central North, about 80 kilometres north-west of his last attack at Tunbridge and well outside Oyster Bay people's country. His presence was announced by a sudden burst of violence around Quamby Bluff two days after he fled Lackey's. On 18 June an estimated 200 Palawa assailed Thomas Baker at the Western Marshes (now Dairy Plains, between Mole Creek and Deloraine). Baker managed to escape, killing one Palawa as he did.[21] At Glenore, near Quamby Bluff (between Deloraine and Great Lake), on 29 June, a frigid day of snow and torrential rain, a mob of about 200 Palawa killed Herbert Chapman's stockkeeper and plundered his hut.[22]

Around the same date, Palawa slew an unnamed stockkeeper on William Field's farm near Quamby Bluff.

The northern bloodshed continued into July. On the first day of that month Palawa raided a hut at Quamby Bluff and slew two shepherds. Another man, hearing their cries, grabbed a firearm and ran to help. He managed to drive off some of the attackers but others plundered the hut while he was doing so.[23] In the same area that week Palawa killed an old man employed by magistrate Thomas Simpson, beating his head flat with waddies and transfixing him with a spear.[24] A military party chased the attackers but captured only spears, waddies, muskets, and blankets. In another attack that week, two men working for Captain Thomas at nearby Great Western Lagoon (Norfolk Plains) vanished, believed slain.[25]

Angry settlers retaliated. A newspaper reported that a party of soldiers and civilians, bent on avenging Simpson's stockkeeper, surprised a Palawa mob sitting around their fires and began shooting at them from 30 metres away, supposedly killing or wounding about 60 of them and capturing muskets, ammunition, tomahawks, and sheep shears (which Palawa valued as weapons). The report also expressed a growing conviction.

> We are thunderstruck when we consider these murders, at the supineness of the Government, in not instantly removing the blacks. We repeat what we have said ten times before, there will never be an end of such transactions till the natives are removed – *removed*, REMOVED, REMOVED.[26]

Because settlers in the Central North did not know Kikatapula by sight, he was not named in any of those attacks. Yet he was no stranger to the region, having killed John Guinea there only a few months earlier, and there are other pointers to his culpability, namely that the east and south suffered no Palawa attacks at all during the time the north was under siege, but as soon as the assaults around Quamby Bluff stopped, hostilities were resumed in the south, including some in which Kikatapula was a named participant. After switching battlegrounds from south to Central North to bedevil pursuers, he had suddenly whirled south again. Soon after the northern attacks ended – the last was in the first week of July – the south was rudely reawakened by the renewed rash of raids. They were the only ones anywhere in Tasmania at the time except for a couple around Launceston, meaning the resumed southern attacks effectively comprised all Palawa resistance during the period. They began near Bothwell on 20 July and ended in Derwent Valley on 13 November – the day Kikatapula's luck ran out.

A plundered hut at Norwood, about eight kilometres north of Bothwell, signalled Kikatapula's return to the south. Nearby next day, on the Abyssinia Tier, a horseman named Holmes 'was beset by these black furies' who pursued him all day, although he managed to escape despite frequently having to dismount so he could lead his horse through thick bush. A newspaper report of his escape expressed alarm at the number of hostile Palawa seen around the Clyde and the Shannon, noting that they 'express the most determined vengeance against every white who happens to fall in their power'.[27] Large mobs were involved – 'about 50', 'about 60', '150 natives'. Other reports noted they were 'very numerous' or 'in considerable numbers'.

A rash of attacks in late July were reported by a newspaper.

> The Natives.– These black savages have been committing further devastation and outrages. Last week, two of Captain Wilson's men, while splitting palings, on his farm at Salt-pan Plains [near Tunbridge], were attacked by the natives, who speared them both. One of the men has been brought to town, and the other is supposed to have been murdered, not having since been heard of.– On Monday last, Mr. Wilkinson's stock hut was attacked and robbed by a tribe. Another Settler was robbed at the Hunting-grounds [about 7 km west of Kempton]; and a shepherd, in the employ of Mr. Wilson, of Salt-pan Plains, was wounded, and chased by about 50. He only escaped by taking refuge in the tent of Mr. Scott, the Surveyor. A man named Field, was last week attacked at the Broad Marsh by another tribe, who robbed him of his fire arms, and nearly murdered him.[28]

August, the dead of winter, was mainly quiet, but in September Palawa again struck Nant, near Bothwell, where Kikatapula's mob had killed two men the previous October. This time they wounded William Lewis with a spear.[29] Several more attacks between 9 and 14 September reported a likely Kikatapula connection. At J.A. Eddie's Tunbridge farm Palawa surrounded two men working in a paddock, but with some difficulty the

Britons escaped to the safety of their hut. A newspaper reported the attackers were the Palawa who had fatally attacked Flood and May some weeks earlier: Kikatapula's mob.[30] Next the attackers proceeded to G.C. Clark's sawpits in the Ross area, where they split into two groups. One decoyed two workmen away while the other stripped their hut. The fate of the two men is unknown.[31]

On 3 October Palawa beset two of Alexander Macpherson's sawyers near Ouse, plundered their hut, and set alight all their sawn timber. A few days later they struck in the Midlands near Antill Ponds in a raid that newspapers reported was 'headed by that notorious fellow, Black Tom'.[32]

Little more than a week later 50 Palawa targeted William Presnell's house six kilometres from Sorell Springs. James McLannachan, Captain Clark from Salt Pan Plains, and Chief District Constable Bennett were outside when the Palawa appeared. Clark, a mariner, declared he was very experienced at dealing with native people worldwide and would have no difficulty making friends with them. Although Bennett tried to dissuade him, Clark was undeterred. He approached the Palawa while Bennett briefly hesitated before joining him. Clark was attempting to converse with the Palawa when one cried out 'kangaroo, kangaroo'. When Clark turned to look, a spear was thrust into his shoulder. He broke it off, knocked his assailant down, and ran for the house. Bennett ran too but was impaled by a spear in his back. More spears were hurled at them as McLannachan helped the two wounded men into the house, which was now surrounded by Palawa. McLannachan kept them at bay by pointing his musket at any who approached, while his wife pointed a stick at the nearest attacker 'in the manner of a firelock'. The threat was enough to deter them until, tiring of the impasse, they disappeared as suddenly as they had appeared. Clark was not badly wounded but Bennett died a day later, the only policeman known to have died at Palawa hands.[33]

Kikatapula's guerrillas next speared a man at Lake Dulverton, near Oatlands.[34] Back in the Antill Ponds region about 24 October they approached magistrate Robert Harrison's Woodbury house under cover of darkness. The residents were alerted by the arrival of a strange dog, soon followed by a few Palawa, but the intruders vanished into the night at the sight of Harrison and his men. Some of the employees stayed on watch, and about 2 am the Palawa returned. When the Britons fired shots into the darkness they heard a yell of pain. At daylight they tracked the intruders to a nearby mountain, but whatever ensued is unrecorded.[35]

It can be seen that Kikatapula's tactics were usually simple: small targets, surprise, hit and run. Men living or working alone or in twos or threes were ideal targets. After careful reconnoitring, waiting until the Britons' work took them away from their hut or wherever they had deposited their firearms, he attacked, with some warriors positioning themselves between the victims and their firearms or hut. 'They have now arrived at so desperate a pitch', a newspaper observed, 'that they are no longer to be intimidated easily, and they know very well that a white man without his gun, is an easy prey for them, and in such a case they never fail to make sure of their victim'.[36]

He also employed cunning. With just a few of his people he might smilingly approach a settler, claiming in English to be tame and asking for food or tobacco. As the no-doubt-relieved Briton was complying, he would suddenly be attacked (as Matthew Osborne had been), perhaps after his firearm had been quietly removed while he was distracted.

Kikatapula also used guile in another way, for however wary stock-keepers were, theirs was a lonely existence and sex an irresistible bait.

> Another plan [Palawa] have of discovering the strength of men there are in any hut, how many muskets they have, &c. is by sending a number of their women, who they call 'Gins,' to the stock-keepers, and other huts, where they go with the greatest familiarity and good-will, perhaps remain the whole night with the men, by which time they obtain a complete knowledge of every thing in the hut, which they acquaint their sable husbands with on their return ...[37]

The attackers would quickly disappear afterwards, sometimes travelling a surprising distance in a short time. Mobility, speed, and endurance were crucial to their survival, and Kikatapula was demonstrably fleet and elusive.

Nevertheless, he was willing to risk another pitched battle with armed Britons if the odds were favourable. It was very likely he who did so in early November when Palawa assailed Field Police George Charman, Charles

Carter, and John Rogers. The three had been dispatched from Richmond to search for a stolen horse reportedly seen at Brown Mountain, between Runnymede and Coal River Valley. In unusually dry spring weather they proceeded there via Lemon Springs and Eastern Marshes. But what they encountered at Brown Mountain on 10 or 11 November were 150 hostile Palawa, who immediately attacked them with stones, striking Rogers in the head. The police responded with a fusillade, 17 shots in all, without hitting their assailants or even deterring them. Overwhelmingly outnumbered, the constables were now in mortal peril, handicapped by slow-to-load weapons and limited ammunition. In desperation they fixed bayonets and charged their attackers, and the tactic worked. The Palawa scattered and fled, perhaps with memories of cold-steel carnage at Bank Head Farm the previous year.[38] Given the date of this skirmish, its location, and the number of Palawa, it is probable that Kikatapula was their leader. He, more than any other, would have recalled recent bayonets and Bank Head Farm, which was neither geographically nor psychologically far away that day.

But Kikatapula's career was about to take an unexpected turn. On 12 November he led 60 Palawa in attacking Edward Abbott's farm in Derwent Valley near New Norfolk. Reports of what followed are conflicting, but it seems Abbott's shepherd dropped a bundle he was carrying and ran for his life to George Stokell's neighbouring farm, Bryn Estyn, about three kilometres north-west of New Norfolk.[39] His attackers pursued him to Bryn Estyn, which had a long frontage to River Derwent, and he was never seen again.[40]

When Hobart's Superintendent of Police Adolarius Humphrey learnt of Kikatapula's presence at Bryn Estyn, he dispatched constables Scott and Sherwood to the scene. Next morning, 13 November, they managed to creep close enough to the Palawa before being spotted for Scott to seize Kikatapula. Sherwood too grabbed a man but he broke free and in the ensuing confusion he and the others plunged into the Derwent and escaped. Kikatapula, however, remained securely in Scott's grasp. The constables took him to the New Norfolk jail where, 'With the hope of meeting favour, he has been very communicative, and has described several murders as having been committed, which was before doubtful'.[41]

The New Norfolk jail was actually part of the Valleyfield homestead, which was once licensed as the King's Head Inn, so it was neither purpose-built nor secure. Charged with murder, Kikatapula was quickly transferred to the Hobart jail to await trial. For the third time Tasmania's most feared man was in British custody, and this time could expect no mercy.

12

'He has aided in many murders'

For colonists the second half of 1827 had been bloodier than ever, but if they expected Kikatapula's imprisonment to halt all Palawa hostilities, as his 1826 confinement in Sorell and Richmond jails had, they were profoundly disappointed. Arthur admitted as much in a report to London, saying Palawa hostility had intensified during the last six months of 1827 and settlers had demanded action.[1]

His first response, on 29 November, was to issue a proclamation. Pointing out that attacks against settlers had been renewed with greater violence, he enjoined colonists to cooperate in driving all the Palawa from the settled districts 'as they cannot by conciliatory means be induced to retire from them'. Every district was to be given enough troops for civilians to confidently comply.[2] Expelling Palawa from their own land was now 'a measure of indispensable necessity' to allow Britons to occupy it undisturbed. Ethnic cleansing had become official policy.

As to what he should do with his infamous prisoner, Arthur was again in a quandary. Hanging Musquito and Black Jack in 1825 had proved seriously counter-productive, having inflamed Palawa hostility, and the executions of Jack and Black Dick the following year had sparked the vicious attacks on the Clyde/Shannon and the subsequent trail of blood along the Macquarie. Moreover, the constraints that prevented Kikatapula's prosecution after his capture at Bank Head Farm had not disappeared, and liberating him unpunished had also backfired, so Arthur was again on the horns of a dilemma, forcing him to contemplate a different policy. Kikatapula was the most respected resistance leader, a man Palawa would listen to, and he spoke more than one of their languages or dialects. If he could be persuaded to change sides and mediate with his countrymen, they might be convinced of the futility of resistance and the benefits of peaceful submission, after which they could be confined or exiled. He put the proposal to Kikatapula, who was willing. Arthur then explained his reasoning to the Executive Council, assuring its members that Kikatapula 'was desirous of being so employed and undertook to export himself in the endeavour promising at all events not to rejoin his own or any other tribe in case the attempt failed'.[3]

Kikatapula was undoubtedly eager to oblige. By the time the Executive Council met he had been in jail for a month without a foreseeable future except a murder trial with an inevitable result. He was terrifyingly reminded of that likelihood during his first month of confinement when 10 fellow prisoners were taken out in one day and executed on the gallows in the prison yard. So he clutched at Arthur's proffered lifeline, but Arthur procrastinated. He neither freed his prisoner nor sent him for trial.

Meanwhile, Palawa resistance was intensifying. The first four months of 1828, as Kikatapula languished in jail, were far more violent than the same period of the previous year: 11 incidents in that part of 1827 but 48 in 1828, including 16 settlers killed and 12 wounded.[4] In the eight months from November 1827, when Kikatapula was captured, to July 1828, when he finally faced court, the frontier became a war zone. At least 73 attacks on settlers resulted in 24 British deaths and many more woundings.[5] As Kikatapula endured his fifth month in the shadow of the scaffold, waiting for the proffered parole, Arthur admitted the necessity of adopting harsher measures against Palawa to suppress 'their increasing predatory incursions' and their 'frequent barbarous murders'.[6] After several days of deliberation and discussion in the Executive Council he notified London that he was convinced it would be necessary to remove the Palawa from the settled districts altogether, although admitting the British were undoubtedly the first aggressors and that escaped convicts had committed the worst outrages.[7] That did not matter. The Palawa had to go.

But the war went on and the casualties mounted. Hamstrung, Arthur again contemplated mediation. On 10 April he ordered his notorious prisoner be taken from jail for questioning by the Executive Council. Under interrogation Kikatapula reaffirmed his willingness to defect to and cooperate with the British, convincing the councillors that using him as an intermediary would be desirable and possibly beneficial.[8] Hope renewed, he was escorted back to jail to await parole.

But Arthur remained irresolute. Five days later he issued a proclamation that eventually led to the deployment of armed parties combing the countryside for Palawa to round up.[9] His proclamation had divided Tasmania into settled districts and unsettled districts, the former for Britons, the latter for Palawa. To enforce this geographical apartheid Arthur placed troops at district borders to prevent Palawa from passing through unless their leaders had a pass, available only (and ludicrously) on direct application to him. The plan was absurdly impracticable. Kikatapula thought it was risible, especially the idea of his eternally nomadic people needing passports to traverse their own country. 'You been a make a *proclamation*, ha! ha! ha!' he said to Arthur. 'I never see [anything] dat foolish. When [Palawa] see dat? He can't read, who tell him?'[10]

But that was later. For now he remained a prisoner awaiting trial for murder. The threat of slowly strangling to death at rope's end did not go away.

Although the fighting on the frontier was fiercer than ever, Kikatapula's own mob were now harassing colonists only in a leaderlessly half-hearted way. In late December 1827, at Bark Hut Plains a few kilometres north of Bothwell, Captain William Clark and one of his servants were returning home when Clark noticed a Palawa woman trailing him. She asked for bread, which Clark agreed to give her, whereupon she shouted and a dozen Palawa appeared from behind trees. They followed him home but went away after being given the promised provisions. Next morning Clark's shepherd was attending to his flock when he was surprised by several Palawa debouching from a thicket. He stopped to wait for their approach, expecting them to be friendly because of the previous day's largesse. But when they rushed at him he fled under a volley of flung waddies. Clark and his men immediately scoured the area and found the attackers' campsite, but they had vanished. That night the same Palawa, 'known by the name of the Hobart Town Tribe', approached Clark's house, only to disappear when the alarm was raised.[11]

Another incident in one of their haunts early the following month confirmed how demoralised they were. When a stockkeeper unexpectedly encountered them near Four Square Gallows, between Apsley and Bothwell, he was allowed to proceed unmolested. A newspaper reported that it was the first and only appearance of Palawa in that and the adjacent districts for three months.[12]

The summer of 1828 cedes to autumn and autumn to winter but in Hobart jail little changes except the degree of discomfort. The small two-storey building, badly constructed on damp ground, is clammy, squalid, notoriously overcrowded, and now hibernally frigid. The food is bad, the bedding vermin-infested, and there is frequent unrest in the packed cells holding prisoners awaiting trial or execution. Petty oral or physical violence is a constant threat for a black killer of whites crammed in with the lowest stratum of them. Perhaps as protection, he is given clerical duties to perform, for despite his infamy he is charismatic and clever and rarely lacks friends at every level of white society. He makes a new acquaintance, a violent lifer named Thomas Arthur whose release he is later able to facilitate.[13]

Far more significant is a prison visitor who is about to play a crucial role in his life: George Augustus Robinson, the London builder who witnessed the execution of Musquito and Black Jack. Actively involved with several Christian and benevolent associations, Robinson sometimes visits the jail to proselytise to prisoners and comfort the condemned. He takes an interest in the engaging Palawa who speaks English, is familiar with Christianity, and appears ripe for evangelising. Sensing the young man's despondency, he offers him hope of a different kind. To Kikatapula, helpless in the grip of his enemies despite his long battle against them, it must seem the white man's god is as powerful as Robinson claims and worth at least an each-way bet now the age-old certainties are vanishing. Subsequent events suggest Robinson's jail visits have a crucial but previously unnoticed influence on Kikatapula well before the historically recognised beginning of their association 18 months later.

On the frontier, meantime, Britons were fighting back, overtly and covertly. Throughout 1828 attacks on colonists were increasingly countered, avenged, or pre-empted by vigilante groups' ambushing Palawa camps. Palawa were rarely surprised by day, but after dark their campfires became beacons, and hundreds were said to have been shot as a result.[14] Tukalunginta, from Kikatapula's natal Paytirami band, recalled how his fires had drawn Britons to his camp in such a surprise attack. They clubbed to death three women and shot dead two men, he said. Another shot wounded Tukalunginta so devastatingly that his arm had to be crudely amputated by another Palawa, who cauterised the stump with fire.[15]

The old Hobart jail, where Kikatapula spent a year as prisoner and clerk.
To the right of the gate the scaffold is just visible. Drawing by Henry Melville.
(Courtesy Libraries Tasmania)

Meanwhile, in the dank limbo between proffered parole and possible execution, Kikatapula continues to mark time, helplessly awaiting the hoped-for liberation. But nothing happens. No matter how promising the Lieutenant Governor's mediation offers seem, the towering scaffold in the prison yard, higher than the jail walls, is a constant baleful reminder of his own situation, one cruelly reinforced whenever fellow prisoners are taken out to be hanged. Two more are dispatched in January, two in March, six in May. Their clamorous execution-eve prayers and lamentations echoing through the jail's dark confines are chilling reminders of the precariousness of his position.

In mid-winter it suddenly became even more precarious. When a Hobart sitting of the Criminal Court was scheduled for late June, the Police Magistrate at Ross Bridge was ordered to obtain from James Rush a statement about John Guinea's slaying. On 22 June Rush deposed that he had seen Kikatapula fatally spear his colleague in 1826 and that Guinea had sworn a deathbed oath identifying Kikatapula as his killer. The statement, enough to send Kikatapula to the scaffold, was duly dispatched to the Attorney-General in Hobart.

The ink was hardly dry when ominous news flashed through the prison: the Criminal Court had begun its sitting. Over three weeks Kikatapula and more than two dozen other accused men and women were shepherded across Murray Street from the jail to the Supreme Court for trial and sentencing. Most were convicted as charged. Four were sentenced to death, two others had death sentences recorded against them, and a score more were punished with savage penalties ranging from public flogging to life imprisonment. But when Kikatapula's day in court came on 17 July, the final day of the session, the outcome shocked the colony. Despite Rush's damning testimony being in the Attorney-General's hands, no prosecution witnesses came forward to testify and no evidence was presented, so he was not tried but discharged by proclamation, free to take up the spear again.[16]

This extraordinary result had been triggered a few days earlier by a letter from his friend Gilbert Robertson. Seeking a lucrative government post because he was again in financial difficulties, Robertson had written to the Lieutenant Governor on 6 July offering to lead a party of armed Britons to round up Palawa for ejection from the settled districts. He would need a dozen men, he told Arthur, and Kikatapula to guide them.[17] So the 'despicable creature', as one newspaper characterised Kikatapula, was released untried and unpunished.

The news outraged colonists who had been awaiting his conviction and execution. George Hobler, an Evandale farmer, fumed that 'only last week Black Tom – a civilised native black was discharged at the goal [*sic*] by proclamation tho' it is well known he has aided in many murders. I suppose he must take many more lives before he loses his own, unless one stock keeper in self defence has the luck to shoot him …'[18]

And when a newspaper subsequently reported that 'Black Tom is at large, and is threatening to make white man pay for his imprisonment', Hobler's fears seemed all too well founded.

13

'Murder shakes her bloody spear'

It's springtime,
The birds is whistling,
The spring is come
The clouds are all sunny,
The fuchsia is out at the top,
The birds are whistling,
Everything is dancing,
Because it's springtime,
Everything is dancing,
Because it's springtime.

(Palawa spring song[1])

In 1828, however, settlers and stockkeepers were anything but joyous at the advent of spring. Spring was when Palawa attacks usually resumed, although even winter had brought no respite that year. Sporadic raids through June and July suddenly erupted with a savage new desperation in August and continued unabated in September. Even as warming days heralded the new season, icy fear gripped the frontier. Settlers' apprehension was voiced in the *Hobart Town Courier* by a correspondent signing himself 'Paul Harrowtine'.

> Spring approaches with rapid strides, and nature wears her most delightful garb ... and might tempt you to quit the desk and quill; but

remain in safety where you are, the sun has already warmed the natives into life and mischief, and judging of the future by the past, we are filled with apprehension. How unlike the season at home ... which we have been accustomed to see introduced by the singing of birds and the blooming of flowers, but here – murder shakes her bloody spear, and ushers in the spring.[2]

A fortnight later, on 27 September, the same newspaper published the first post-prison news of Kikatapula. Written by a Campbell Town settler named Taylor, the report confirmed colonists' worst fears.[3]

The natives have been on my farm several times last month. As soon as the floods subside, I anticipate a renewal of their attacks. A report exists that Black Tom is at large, and is threatening to make white man [sic] pay for his imprisonment.[4]

The familiar threat gave Taylor particular cause for alarm because Kikatapula's warriors had slain his brother George nearly two years earlier. Nevertheless, the report was wrong, as the *Colonial Advocate* noted nine days later.

It may not be generally known that Black Tom, the Aboriginal Native, who so long headed the sable tribes, and has for a considerable time past been confined to the Gaol at Hobart Town, acts as Clerk in the prison, and also as Chaplain's clerk, at Divine Service, in the Floating Chapel, in Sullivan's Cove [Hobart], on Sundays. It was lately reported without any foundation, that this black was at large in the neighbourhood of Macquarie Harbour [sic].[5]

Hobler's misgivings and Taylor's fears were clearly baseless. Kikatapula had not resumed his war on Britons and he was not marauding on the Macquarie. He had not fled Hobart, had not even left the prison. The Sheriff, Dudley Fereday, notified Colonial Secretary John Burnett of that startling turn of events the day after the prisoner's discharge.

I have the honour of informing you that the 4th Session of the Criminal Court finished yesterday, when Black Tom (a native Black) was discharged by proclamation, but voluntarily returned to the Gaol with the Under

Sherriff [*sic*]. I have therefore to request His Excellency's instructions as to his disposal.[6]

Although pacified and demoralised, Kikatapula remained a potential threat, at least until Robertson was ready to employ him to guide his roving party, so Arthur tried another tack. He drafted a reply to Fereday on 21 July.

> I should like the Sheriff to ascertain whether Black Tom would voluntarily go to N.S. Wales – if so, the Governor [of NSW] I have no doubt will place him in a situation to obtain his livelihood – I will order him to be forwarded by the Mermaid ...[7]

The *Mermaid* was loading in Hobart ready to sail for Sydney, which it belatedly did on 14 August. Perhaps impatient with Robertson's tardiness in taking Kikatapula off his hands (which did not happen until November), Arthur wanted the troublesome Palawa to sail with it. But Kikatapula was not amused at, much less interested in, this blatant attempt to exile him, as Fereday reported on 23 July.

> In reply to your Letter of yesterday's Date relative to 'Black Tom' I beg to state for the information of His Excellency that this individual refuses to go to New South Wales, but he will go to England or live with a Master in Hobart Town.[8]

Palawa thought that after death they went to a distant island of the dead that some believed was England, so Kikatapula, who was no stranger to British machinations, was perhaps declaring he would rather be dead than exiled for political expediency.[9] He might have been saying, even more pointedly, 'Why only New South Wales? Why not send me even farther away, to England?' But since he was by far the most intelligent and imaginative Palawa war leader of whom we have substantive record, his motive might instead have been a desire to broaden his knowledge of the victors and improve his chances of finding a place for himself in the new order. Going to England would also wholly remove him from the battleground Tasmania had become and absolve him of having to keep his promise to betray his own people. Moreover, he would have been warned that discharge by proclamation was not exoneration and did not preclude his being tried at some future time for killing Guinea if the government saw fit. So the threat of execution remained ever present. Perhaps he thought going to England would remove that possibility.

You apprehend his feeling of defeat and sense the uncertainty it all engendered. He was at liberty once more, free either to resume the fight against British usurpation or to lose himself peacefully in whatever remained of traditional life in the bush far away from colonialism's greedy grasp and the lingering threat of trial and execution, but he did neither. To save his own life and dodge the hangman he had promised to abandon resistance and betray his people (and he would keep his word, more or less), but he remained in the jail's stink and stew, unwilling to leave it or Hobart, reluctant to decide which way to jump. In jail he was safe from avenging whites who resented his release and Palawa who might resent his defection, and staying put also buttressed him from having to decide who and what he had to be from now on. Prison duties cocooned him, a riven black man unsure of his place in a now overwhelmingly white world. They allowed him to survive day by day while he awaited Fate's next throw of the dice. Best to stay safely at the jail until required to keep his promise to collaborate. The soundness of that decision was confirmed on 1 August by a familiar harrowing spectacle in the jail: the execution of Abraham Aaron who, like him, had fronted the Criminal Court in July.

Perhaps, in his uncertainty, Kikatapula the inchoate Christian derived some solace, some comforting rationalisation for his apostasy, from his assisting with services in the floating chapel in Sullivans Cove, 200 metres down Murray Street from the jail. The chapel was a project of the Van Diemen's Land Seaman's Friend and Bethel Union Society, which George Augustus Robinson had helped establish. Robinson, who was secretary of the society, conducted the chapel's Sunday services and had invited Kikatapula to assist with them.

Their paths thus having crossed, their lives thenceforth would intertwine.

Taylor's false report in September of Kikatapula's renewed hostilities had spawned a frisson of frontier disquiet. The following month he was blamed for an attack on a tailor named William Troop at Hollow Tree Bottom. Troop was chased by a warrior 'who spoke the English language well' and called out to him, 'Stop you white bugger or I will spear you through the shoulder.' From Troop's description the assailant was 'supposed to be Black Tom', but magistrate Thomas Anstey scathingly dismissed the tailor's testimony. 'I do not believe there is any truth in the story', he wrote.[10] It was not to be the last report that Kikatapula had resumed hostilities. Some shade of his notoriety had imprinted itself on the colony's collective subconscious and was mysteriously to linger there long after the man and his deeds were buried and forgotten.

For the scourge of British settlers 1828 was a watershed year, a pivot point when, in the final rupturing of his life and soul, he changed sides in the war he had been instrumental in fomenting. He had broken his spear. He had promised never again to wage war against Britons. From now on he would help them capture and subdue his own people.

Or so he said.

Part Two

The Spear Broken

14

'Now I like catch all dat black un'

Kikatapula's incarceration was a transformative experience. His unsettling eight-month stay in the scaffold's shadow had not broken his spirit, but it had given him ample time to contemplate his limited choices. The futility of active resistance was obvious; the overwhelming population imbalance and the obvious permanence of the colony's spreading settlements showed that. As the shrinking number of Palawa men sought wives from among the even fewer women left, the invaders' ships continued to dock, the streams of convicts, colonists, and military continued to be disgorged, the hundreds of thousands of sheep and cattle to displace native herbivores. With their generation-long experience of aggression and dispossession the surviving Palawa, now numbering a few hundred at most, must have understood they were doomed, although the bloodiest years of the war were yet to be fought. While Kikatapula did change sides to save himself, he surely believed that by accommodating British aims he could help protect and preserve from annihilation the remnants of his race and culture.

How much his transformation might have been influenced by Robinson's and others' Christian proselytising is impossible to say, but while he was in jail he and the other inmates were subjected to frequent visits from clergymen and missionaries eager to lead the wicked to righteousness. The Birches and probably Knopwood had seeded Christianity in the youthful Kikatapula; compulsory Sunday services in the jail and the ministering of visiting evangelists seem to have brought it to fruition and may have influenced his decision to defect and collaborate. In coming years Robinson would several times record

Kikatapula's public avowal of Christian tenets, something never reported before his months in jail.

War-weary, re-Christianised, and bound by his promise not to reoffend, the leader of Palawa resistance was effectively neutralised. Yet some Britons doubted the wisdom of attempting a peaceful settlement of hostilities. Roderic O'Connor, referring by name to Kikatapula, wondered 'is it possible to conciliate those who have become more brutal in proportion to the kindness shown?'.[1]

For Kikatapula the answer was *yes*. He would never take up the spear again. He would keep his word and serve the British. He would be a turncoat, a quisling who would help his new masters locate for capture and subdual those he had incited to resistance in the first place.

At least, that was the impression he would give.

The alarming upsurge in hostilities in August and September 1828 had continued unabated throughout October. Two of that month's 18 attacks especially shocked the colony because they inaugurated a savage new desperation in the war: Palawa were no longer sparing women and children. In one of those attacks, on the Gough family near Oatlands, two women and a four-year-old girl were killed and an infant and a girl of seven wounded; the other, on the Langford family at Kempton, resulted in the death of a 14-year-old boy and the spearing of his mother and younger sister. Terrified shepherds on the frontier were deserting their flocks.[2]

Palawa had now slain an estimated 369 colonists, and every measure intended to curb attacks had come to naught.[3] Arthur's proclamation a year earlier had ordered all magistrates to take effective measures to stop the attacks, but the response had been general indifference. Only Oatlands magistrate Thomas Anstey took the time even to reply, telling Arthur that no one in his district was willing to incur the danger of attempting conciliatory communications with the Palawa.[4] Arthur's subsequent proclamation of 15 April 1828 had divided the colony into settled districts (for colonists) and unsettled districts (for Palawa) with the borders separating them policed by military posts. But the Palawa, if they somehow learnt of and understood the proclamation, naturally ignored it. Kikatapula, as noted, thought it was hilariously impracticable.

So in late spring 1828 the authorities formed armed parties of police, military, and trustworthy convicts with the aim of capturing and permanently removing all Palawa from the settled districts. To strengthen their hand Arthur proclaimed martial law on 1 November, ordering 'the Chief District, Division, Field Police, and Special Constables … to act up with the vigour and vigilance' in accordance with his proclamation of 15 April in 'effecting the retirement or expulsion of the Aborigines from the settled districts of this territory'. He commanded all Palawa 'immediately to retire and depart from, and for no reason or on no pretence … re-enter such settled districts'.[5] Already dispossessed of their country, Palawa were now to be expelled from it altogether. And expulsion was only one option. The overall objective, as one roving-party leader admitted, was 'capturing or *destroying* the Natives [emphasis added]'.[6]

One way or another, exile or genocide, *lutruwita* would be purged of its traditional owners.

By the beginning of November 1828 Gilbert Robertson had his desired government contract and Kikatapula as his guide. Newly appointed as Chief District Constable of Richmond, Robertson was to lead his roving party of Palawa-hunters throughout the Richmond police district, a vast area that extended in the north-west from just south of Kempton along a line extending roughly east to Prosser River at Prossers Bay, then in a generally south direction down the coast to East Bay Neck, whence it followed the shoreline up through Pitt Water as far as Richmond, then down the shoreline to South Arm and Opossum Bay and up the western shore of Derwent River to Bridgewater, and finally in a north-westerly direction from there through Brighton and Pontville and along Jordan River to the point of commencement at Hunting Ground (Abyssinia). Robertson eventually ranged even farther afield, from the Eastern Marshes near Andover to Ross and Campbell Town and the east coast at Oyster Bay and beyond that to Fingal and Avoca and St Patricks Head, west almost as far as Frenchmans Cap, and north-west to Great Lake and Lake Echo.

The task of the black rangers, as roving parties were sometimes called, proved exhausting and onerous. Their forays usually lasted from 12 to 18 days, but despite the ruggedness of the terrain and the immense area they had to cover they were forced to travel on foot. Although their task called for the speed, mobility, and endurance of cavalry, a scarcity of horses forced them to be infantry and supply train in one, for they did not know how to live off the land and had to carry on their backs all their food, camping equipment, spare clothing, weapons, and ammunition. Consequently they were never able to match their quarry's speed and mobility. The rocky terrain quickly demolished their boots, which had to be repaired or replaced often.[7] Further, complained one soldier attached to a party, they were expected to march from 48 to 64 kilometres in a day on rations that were 'not enough to support a hearty man on the fatiguing and harrowing duty of "Black Hunting"'.[8] An anonymous correspondent to the *Hobart Town Courier* noted another impediment. Palawa 'have some extraordinary method of concealing themselves', he wrote,

> for nothing is so difficult as to overtake them. They run over the wildest passes on all fours, almost as fleet as dogs, and conceal themselves in holes and trunks of trees, or behind stones, and though you may see them at a short distance and run up to the place where they are, not a vestige of them will be found.[9]

Robertson's party, initially comprising Kikatapula, his former cellmate Thomas Arthur, and six soldiers, left Richmond on their first sortie on 5 November 1828.[10] They soon encountered the Lieutenant Governor and his entourage who had set out from Hobart a day later to go to Maria Island and Oyster Bay.[11] That night Arthur invited Kikatapula to his tent to confer. Their dialogue was recorded by a witness and given to the journalist Henry Melville for publishing, but his rendering of Kikatapula's speech as a sort of facetious pidgin is racist and objectionable by today's standards (although undoubtedly in accord with contemporary expectations). More to the point, it's wrong. Kikatapula spoke English correctly. Sarah Hodgson testified to that, and Alexander Laing, who once held Kikatapula in his jail, affirmed his prisoner's English fluency. Corroborating both are several examples of Kikatapula's speech reported by Mary Osborne, Robert Grimes, and Robert Jones, all of whom had survived hostile close encounters with him, while examples quoted in George Augustus Robinson's journals – see Chapter 16 *et seq.* below – are especially substantiating. Robinson had a good ear for recording speech with verisimilitude, and a comparison of how he recorded Kikatapula's with his rendering of any other Palawa man's is conclusive. When Kikatapula speaks, his superior command of English demonstrates that it is unmistakably he who is speaking. Yet although Melville's published version of Kikatapula's idiolect is demeaningly blackface, the young warrior's dialogue with the Lieutenant Governor is worth quoting in full because it provides a compelling example of his opinions, intelligence, feisty spirit, and sense of humour.

> The Lieutenant Governor being desirous to make use of Tom, as a negociator [sic] with the savages questioned him very particularly, on the cause of the hostility of the aborigines against the whites. The following dialogue took place, as reported by a by-stander: –
>
> Tom. – 'An't your stock-keeper been a kill plenty black fellow?'
>
> Governor. – 'But your countrymen kill people that never did them any harm – they even kill women and children.'
>
> Tom. – 'Well, an't dat all same's white un? An't he kill plenty black un, a woman, and little picaninny too?'
>
> Governor. – 'But you know, Tom, I want to be friendly and kind to them, yet they would spear me if they met me.'
>
> Tom (laughing). – 'How he tell you make a friend along him? An't he all same a white'un? 'Pose black un kill white fellow, an't you send all your soldier, all your constable after him? You say, dat black a devil kill a nurra white man, go – catch it – kill it – an't he then kill all black fellow he see, all *picaninny* too? An't dat all same black fellow – an't you been a take him own kangaroo ground? How den he like?'
>
> Tom laughed most immoderately on hearing the proclamation read, particularly at the idea of the tribes applying for passports to travel through the settled districts.
>
> Tom says – 'You been a make a *proflamation* [sic], ha! ha! ha! I never see dat foolish – (meaning I never saw anything so foolish.) When he see dat? He can't read, who tell him?'
>
> Governor. – 'Can't you tell him, Tom?'
>
> Tom. – 'No! me like see *you* tell him *yourself*, he very soon *spear me*' …
>
> Governor. – 'Well, Tom, do you think you will be able to find your countrymen, and persuade them to come in?'

Tom. – 'Can't tell Mata Guberna, I try. 'Pose I see track, den I find him, and party catch it – den I bring him Hobart Town.'

Governor. – 'Very well Tom, you must do your best, and if you bring them in, I will reward you handsomely – besides giving you the whale boat which I promised you.' (It may be worthy of remark that Tom never got his boat.) [In fact he did.][12]

Tom. – 'Dat very good, Mata Guberna! 'Pose I catch dat black un, what you do wid him?'

Governor. – 'I will make friends with them, Tom, and tell them that I have given all this part of the country (pointing out a line on a map), to themselves, where no white man will go near them; and if they want to go to the east coast, the magistrates will give them a pass, so that no white man will trouble them, and I will give them food and blankets.'

Tom. – 'Aye, Dat very good, Mata Guberna, you take it all, him kangaroo ground yourself, give him nurra mob kangaroo ground. 'Pose he walk dere, a'nt nurra mob make fight, you call it war, and kill him right out. You give him blanket, bread, tell him walk about. Dat very good – by and by, pose he see you, den he spear you. I tell you dat black un nebber make a friend along a you, he nebber take dat word from you … Dat way nebber do.'

Governor. – 'Well, Tom, I will send them to Maria Island.'

Here Tom burst out into a loud laugh. ''Riah Island! I like a hear you talk dat b——y foolish – ha! ha! ha! A'nt he go dere himself come back again, often he like. I tell you dat, his own Wallaby ground – he make't catamaran, come back so soon as yourself. Dat way nebber do, Mata Guberna.'

Governor. – 'Well, Tom, I will put them in prison, and keep them there.'

Tom here looked unutterable things. 'Put him in a gaol, Mata Guberna! You take it him own country, take it him black woman, kill 't right out, all him litta child – den you put him in your gaol. Ah, Mata Guberna, dat a very good way. 'Pose you like that way – 'pose all same dat black un! I nebber like dat way. You better kill it right out.'

Governor. – 'Well, Tom, I will send them to one of the islands in Bass's Straits, and keep them there.' Tom enquired the distance from the main land, and whether there was game on the island, being satisfied of this, he continued. – 'You send him dat hyland, and take't all him own country – what you give him for him own country?'

Governor. – 'I will give them food and blankets, and teach them to work.'

Tom. – (Laughing) 'You make't black un work! I nebber see dat, Mata Guberna.' Here Tom pointed to a fly that was on the table. 'You see dat man, Mata Guberna?'

Governor. – 'Yes, Tom, I see a fly.'

Tom. – ''Pose you tell dat man work – you tink he work for you?'

Governor. – 'No, Tom, I do not think he would.'

Tom. – 'Well, black un all same; he nebber see work, you nebber make dat black un work, he too d – m lazy.'

Governor. – 'Well, Tom, he can go and hunt, and come back when he likes, to get food and blankets, and I will send people to take care of the children, and teach them to work.'

Tom. – 'Aye, dat very good way, litta one work by and by. I like dat way. Now I like catch all dat black un.'[13]

Robertson's party moved on next morning, their immediate goal being to capture the Palawa responsible for recent killings on the east coast opposite Maria Island.[14] A few days later they had a major success.[15] Kikatapula told Robertson that after a raid Palawa usually sought sanctuary in the interior, and that when they had used or lost their spears the two bands from that region went for fresh supplies of spear-making wood to a place called Blue Hills Bluff. So from somewhere near Sandspit River in the Three Thumbs region (a noted Palawa stronghold near Spring Bay) Robertson's party hiked past Maloneys Sugar Loaf, Blue Hills Bluff, and the lower end of the Eastern Marshes.[16] At James Hobbs's farm at Macgills Marsh they learnt that a man had been speared at Maloneys Sugarloaf and that Palawa had been seen near the junction of Little Swanport River and Eastern Marshes River. Accompanied for some distance by Hobbs's overseer, they proceeded in that direction on 12 November, only to become lost in a place Kikatapula claimed to be unfamiliar with. Yet he was no stranger there. Robertson's party was in the heart of Oyster Bay people's country, and the Eastern Marshes were recognised as their best hunting ground.[17] (Passing through there with Kikatapula three years later, George Augustus Robinson noted how familiar with it all his Palawa guides, including Kikatapula, were.)[18] So this was the first known instance – there were to be many more – of Kikatapula's sabotaging British aims by feigning ignorance of his own country's geography. By surreptitiously refusing to betray his people he could continue to resist the British while keeping his promise not to retrogress.

Uncertainty notwithstanding, Robertson proceeded. About 4 pm next day, at *mellareremertitter* (probably Black Johnnys Marsh near Little Swanport), they heard a shout that stopped them in their tracks.[19] Recognising it as a Palawa cry, Kikatapula ordered the party to 'Stop! – lie down – dat a black un, he been a hundin''. The rest of the party waited while Robertson and Kikatapula crept forward to reconnoitre. They soon spied several Palawa, one of whom Kikatapula recognised as a chief, sitting around a small fire. He and Robertson then retreated a safe distance to wait for daylight. About 9 pm, when rain began to fall, they could hear the Palawa chopping bark off trees to build a shelter.

Through a cool spring dawn next day, 14 November, Robertson's party (now numbering nine with the addition of Robert Lee) set out to attack the Palawa camp, but Kikatapula appeared to lose his way in the dark, forcing them to wade about two kilometres through knee-deep marsh.[20] When they finally gained dry ground only 100 metres from the fire they silently formed up to surround it. In the centre were Robertson, Kikatapula, Lee, and Arthur, and three soldiers from the 40th Regiment were on each flank some distance away. Then they advanced, perfectly executing a surrounding manoeuvre, but when they reached the fire they found no Palawa there. It was a decoy, something Kikatapula would have expected. Spying another fire about 100 metres away to the right, they ran toward it. Robertson, outrunning the others, was first to reach the back of a bark hut there that he had not noticed in the dark, but five furious dogs suddenly set upon him. The commotion sent Palawa tumbling out of the back of the hut right where he stood. He fired his musket at one, hoping the shot would frighten them all, but those still inside ran the other way, toward where the rest of his men were coming up. Someone else fired a shot, and Robertson saw the man he had fired at fall into the scrub. The Chief Constable then seized a boy who was scrambling through the bark and dragged him back into the hut, where he found Arthur, Lee, and Kikatapula with a man and a woman they had captured. Robertson's young captive then indicated a sheet of bark, under which they found a stout Palawa man whom they also took prisoner.

By now the six soldiers had reached the scene. They had lain down in the scrub when the shots were fired, then jumped up to pursue the fleeing Palawa. A soldier named Clark found the wounded man lying at the base of a tree and broke his musket over his head, inflicting a serious injury to compound the bullet wound. The ball had struck bone at the back of his ear and passed upwards, leaving a very deep flesh wound, but had not entered the skull or broken any bone.

After tearing up several of the 36 pairs of blankets they found in the hut, Robertson's men used the strips to secure their captives. The five expected to be shot immediately, which Kikatapula urged as the best way to dispose of them because at least two of them were Tayarinutipana, traditional Paytirami enemies. He described them as a very bad mob that had killed many of his people.[21] When the five understood they were not going to be slain they asked for bread and sugar, then ate a hearty meal including all the provisions Robertson's party had brought and some kangaroo meat from the hut. While they were eating, Kikatapula questioned them and gave Robertson details of each one. The wounded man was a chief of the Tayarinutipana or Stoney Creek band of the North Midlands people. His name was Eumarrah or Umarrah, which Kikatapula explained was not his Palawa name – they were Multiyalakina and Kahnneherlargenner – but one he had borrowed from a former employer, a settler named Hugh Murray.[22] Umarrah was said to have been responsible for several raids on colonists in the Campbell Town region, so he was an important capture.

Three other captives bore English names: Jack (Cowertenninner), a youth from Little Swanport; Jemmy (whom Robertson described as a chief); and Umarrah's wife Dolly (Laoninneloonner). The stout man, Parewareatar, was lame, having broken his thigh as a boy in a fall from a tree, and had no English name.[23] Also a Tayarinutipana, he was a man Kikatapula had once tried to kill.[24] (See page 62.) Kikatapula explained that Parewareatar's lameness made him useless as a hunter or warrior but 'He very good a lawyer – he eat all a urra fellow catch'. Kikatapula knew of lawyers' reputations from his months in prison, where it was a common saying among thieves that the lawyers who defended them got all the proceeds of their crimes. Parewareatar was thereafter known as The Lawyer.

At full daylight Robertson's rangers found they were still in unfamiliar territory and Kikatapula was still claiming not to know where they were, but again his claim is spurious. Travelling with him through the same area three years later, George Augustus Robinson recorded further evidence that Kikatapula had known precisely where they were, describing it in his journal as 'the place where Tom had first taken UMARRAH ... MEL. LARE.RE.MERTIT.TER is the name of the place ... '[25] *Mellareremertitter* is in the heart of Oyster Bay country, and since Robertson's Tayarinutipana captives, from the Campbell Town region of the northern Midlands, knew where they were despite being far from their country, it is hardly credible that Kikatapula in his own country did not. The captives had to point out the way before the party could move off.

As well as the usual knives and blankets, Robertson had found in the Palawa camp what was described as Umarrah's royal insignia. Laoninneloonner's only covering, it consisted of four wreaths of beautiful shells and a highly polished skull.[26] After destroying about 100 spears and twice as many waddies, Robertson took the trophy with him and marched his captives to Dudgeon's stock hut at Maloneys Sugar Loaf, where Umarrah had speared the overseer the previous day. From Dudgeon's Robertson herded his captives into Richmond, writing from there to the Lieutenant Governor on 17 November to report his success. He especially commended Kikatapula, 'of whom I cannot speak with enough praise'. Then he took the five prisoners to Hobart, where the *Hobart Town Courier* lauded his success, also noting Umarrah's great indignation at being captured. He considered it his patriotic duty, the *Courier* stated, to destroy all the whites he possibly could. It noted too that 'The conduct of Black Tom, and two prisoners, Thos. Arthur and Robert Lee ... is highly spoken of'.[27]

Next day the Executive Council summoned Robertson to thank him. Kikatapula and the prisoners were also present, their nakedness suitably covered by European clothing. Laoninneloonner's was 'a gown of the Cameronian tartan, which Mrs. Bradley of Oatlands had bestowed upon her, she had altered it into a most complicated and curious drapery'.[28] Because the Lieutenant Governor intended to put the captives on trial for their lives, Robertson found himself having to defend them, arguing that they should be treated as prisoners of war rather than criminals. He then withdrew while the captives were interrogated. They denied spearing any Britons, instead blaming the Port Dalrymple people.[29] When Robertson was called back all the Palawa were squatting on the floor except Kikatapula, who was acting as interpreter and master of ceremonies. The Lieutenant Governor told Robertson he had decided not to prosecute Umarrah. He and the other captives were to be treated as prisoners of war and would be incarcerated without trial in Richmond jail. The Executive Council duly noted Kikatapula's contribution to their capture and the fact that he was continuing to express a desire to be employed as a guide.[30]

On 21 November the Lieutenant Governor sent Kikatapula and the convicts Arthur and Lee back to Richmond with orders that they be victualled at the jail. He instructed magistrate Thomas Lascelles to confine in the jail all the captives except Cowertenninner, who was to reside with Robertson in the hope he might be persuaded to assist the roving parties.[31] But Cowertenninner did not live up to Arthur's expectations. Although he, like Kikatapula and later Umarrah, subsequently acted as a roving-party guide and all were reported to have proved faithful and useful in that role, their fidelity was honoured more in the breach than in the observance.[32] Kikatapula's apparently enthusiastic service during Robertson's first sortie was to show he had kept his word and demonstrate his fealty. And it was prudent for him to appear to keep doing so, knowing Umarrah was now a prisoner in Richmond jail, which Kikatapula, with bitter memories of durance there and in Sorell and Hobart jails, had no desire to be. But he would continue to subvert whenever possible, and he would sway Cowertenninner and other guides to emulate him. Their resistance would continue.

Preparing for his second sortie, Robertson spent the first week of 1829 in Hobart waiting for all his men to arrive, but on 8 January he was back in Richmond where he found his stores were incomplete. While he kept busy writing urgent requests for more, he put his black rangers to work making such essential items as ammunition pouches.

Robertson's party, comprising Kikatapula, Cowertenninner, a convict

constable named William Grant, and about a dozen convicts including
Thomas Arthur, left Richmond on 12 January, camping late that night in
a makeshift hut at White Marsh, Prossers Plains. Their following night's
bivouac was in a valley between Prossers Plains and Blue Hills where
'After supper we had the opportunity of observing one of the superstitions
of the Aboriginal Natives', Robertson wrote in his journal.

> An Owl one of the species called by the Colonists: – More Pork [a southern
> boobook or mopoke] – having perch'd upon a Tree near to our Break
> wind began to hoot his evening Note, – The two Blacks attached to the
> party started up and began an earnest conversation principally addressed
> to the Bird who occasionally hooted his response[,] on hearing which
> they shouted with the most extravagant demonstrations of Joy[;] when
> the unmusical conversation ceased Tom explained to us that the Bird
> (which he called Cocolo diana) was capable of giving any information he
> required concerning his wandering Countrymen[.] Tom interpreted to us
> the Conversation by which we had just been amused but as we did not
> place much faith in Mr. Cocolos information it is not worth recording what
> his votaries informed us he had communicated to them.[33]

Next morning the party proceeded north-west to Dusky Glen where they
camped for the night, much fatigued after tramping heavily laden over
hilly terrain in withering summer heat. The country they traversed –
carefully observed, evaluated, and recorded by Robertson, who hoped to
be rewarded with land grants – was reputedly favoured by Palawa, but the
party saw no sign of them. On 15 January, after passing Crown Lagoon,
about 25 kilometres east of Oatlands, they spent the night at R.W. Loane's
farm in the Eastern Marshes where they were told that a Palawa fire had
been sighted a few days earlier about nine kilometres away on Eastern
Marsh River. Next day they proceeded down the river to that location but
were unable to find any tracks.

After another fruitless day's march in which their only encounter was
with a herd of wild horses, they reached Glen Shee (location unknown),
where they spent the following day while some of the party caught up
with washing and baking and others unsuccessfully scouted nearby
for Palawa. With Richmond little more than a week behind them they
were already so low on provisions that they were living on bread and

water. Two days later even their scanty flour supply was nearly gone. Increasingly fatigued after constant exertion on such meagre rations, they trudged past several old campsites and huts but saw no Palawa. Cowertenninner, who clearly knew the country well, warned Robertson to be sparing with the remaining flour because it would be many days before they came to another settler's hut where they could replenish supplies. The news disturbed the famished black rangers. Although game was plentiful, they had so far refrained from shooting any because gunshots would announce their presence. But when they suddenly chanced on a mob of kangaroos that morning, hunger conquered caution. Several of the party immediately fired, bringing down one boomer, which in a few minutes was stewing over a campfire. The effect was tonic. 'No mob of Natives could be more noisy or sincere than our party on making sure of this seasonable supply', Robertson recorded next day, noting 'it also had a cheering effect on our spirits'.[34]

Full stomachs and boosted morale, however, did not compensate for their being lost, with Kikatapula and Cowertenninner again professing ignorance of their location. Again the claim is spurious, for they were able to tell Robertson the name of the hill where they had killed the kangaroo (although he thought the name, which he wrote down as 'Dually lualinga lea', might literally mean 'a Hill abounding with Kangaroo'). Moreover, Cowertenninner was able to inform Robertson that on the far side of a nearby hill there was a white man's house where he and his mob had often stolen potatoes, so he knew precisely where they were. Grant deduced that he was referring to John de Courcy Harte's farm, which was on Wye River west of Moulting Lagoon and close to Great Swan Port – country assuredly as familiar to Kikatapula as it was to Cowertenninner, who again demonstrated his topographical knowledge by subsequently warning Robertson that no drinking water would be found in a tier they were about to cross. But Cowertenninner's initial helpfulness, sparked here by the need for self-preservation, did not last. He later confessed to Jorgen Jorgenson that he had stopped cooperating after Robertson beat him for some misdemeanour. As a result, he said, he was often on the trail of his countrymen but would not track them, which Jorgenson later reported to Anstey.[35] But other evidence, discussed below, indicates that the trigger for the younger man's subsequent non-cooperation was Kikatapula.

On 21 January the party visited Harte's farm before moving on to Adam Amos's Glen Gala and another replenishment of their supplies. After resting there for a day they set out again on the 23rd, their destination St Patricks Head, about 80 kilometres farther northward. Trekking along the coast they passed many shell middens where Palawa had immemorially feasted on abalone and oysters, but such signs served only to drive home the frustrating absence of the Palawa themselves.

Within a few days of leaving Glen Gala a familiar problem resurfaced: they had eaten all their meat and other food supplies were low. But as they approached St Patricks Head on 28 January they saw some cattle and took the opportunity to slaughter one. Later they sighted Palawa fires about 40 kilometres away and diverted toward them, passing through marsh country on the 29th, then crossing a hilly region where Robertson tellingly noted that finding water would have been difficult were it not for Cowertenninner 'who appears to know every spring and Stream in the Island'. Late in the day they saw a fresh fire in the direction of a conical hill, which they named Mt Hope for the optimism it engendered. It appeared to be about eight kilometres away – little more than two hours' determined march – so before dawn next day they struck out toward it. Through the warming forenoon and the enervating afternoon heat they dragged themselves over barren near-perpendicular hills, but by nightfall they appeared to be no closer.

When they resumed their trek at sunrise it was with less spring in their step. They reached Mt Hope and its fires before midday, but elation and expectation quickly evaporated. All they found were Palawa tracks that led toward Break o' Day Plains, where fresh fires were tantalisingly visible. Muttering imprecations, they reslung their packs and weapons and set off in that direction, but after slogging all day 'over burning Hills, [we] could see no recent Places where the Natives had stopt or slept'. Low on supplies once again, they were forced to seek out settlers' huts to procure food. They failed to get any at Daniel Stansfield's at Fingal and had to trudge a few kilometres farther west to William Talbot's Malahide.

As well as supplies they were given conflicting intelligence about Palawa sightings: five had been seen nearby in the last few weeks, while others had appeared in considerable numbers a few days earlier at St Pauls Plains. Faced with uncertainty, Robertson decided to leave a detachment under Constable Grant, with Cowertenninner as guide, to search there. But Talbot was scathing about both Robertson's Palawa guides and 'in the presence of Jack and Tom', Robertson reported, 'Disapproved of showing any mercy to those who should fall into our power[,] even recommending that Jack and Tom should be shot – I observed with regret that his words were marked by the two natives and excited much apparent uneasiness in their minds'.[36] Fearing for his life, Cowertenninner absconded before dawn next day. Robertson's men conducted a wide search for him but even Kikatapula could not find his tracks.[37]

Grant and his contingent split from Robertson at Malahide on 2 February. Kikatapula later implied that he had gone with them, but he is not mentioned in the journal Grant kept from 2 February to 13 March, the day he returned to Richmond to rejoin Robertson.[38] Since Kikatapula featured several times in Robertson's own journal during that period, the first only four days after the two groups parted and the last on the day before Robertson's returned to Richmond, it is clear he did not go with Grant on that occasion.

Robertson's group left Malahide on the same day and made for Major Gray's run at Avoca, where they were further provisioned. From there they proceeded easterly next day to a place called No Where Else and then south-west to Kearneys Bogs, investigating any fire they saw as they travelled. No Palawa were seen. Robertson, despite his experience at Black Johnnys Marsh (and like George Augustus Robinson after him), never understood Palawa use of decoy fires, and Kikatapula did not enlighten them.

Soon they were hampered by dense fog, torrential rain, and bewildering terrain. On 5 February, having no map or compass, they found themselves wandering in concentric circles of high rocky hills they could not extricate themselves from and had to sleep 'on the top of a Rocky Hill with Iron Stones for our Beds – Without any shelter and unable to get a Drink of Water'.[39]

Next day they suffered badly in the heat as they tramped over more barren hills and through thick scrub, eventually descending a steep hill into a deep gully where they found a creek. After quenching their thirst and refilling their flasks they followed the creek for some time but could not find egress. Thick overhead scrub made it impossible for them even to see daylight, and the opposite side of the gully was so steep and thickly matted with scrub that they could not climb out. Kikatapula continued to proclaim ignorance of their location. 'After many fruitless attempts to make our way to Campbell Town', Robertson wrote, 'Tom whose knowledge of the Country we had on every other occasion found equal to any Compass was as much at a loss as any of us/We were obliged to return to St. Pauls [sic] plains ... and slept in the Bed of a rocky Creek on the stones[,] being unable to find any other place where we could stretch ourselves – we had a most miserable night and nothing to eat'.[40]

Starting out at first light next day they found their way to James Stynes's hut a little south-east of Campbell Town, where they were fed a meagre meal but refused provisions. Too weak and weary to attempt the hills again, they sought an easier route and at 11 o'clock that night staggered into Campbell Town footsore, sunburned, dehydrated, and weak from hunger. Some of the party were barely able to walk, forcing them all to recuperate there for two days.

Strength restored, on 10 February they left Campbell Town's comforts to hike the 20 kilometres to Windfall Marsh, north-west of Lake Leake, where they based themselves for a few days, splitting into two groups to search the hills. At midday on the 15th they headed toward Stockers Bottom, north-west of Tooms Lake, attracted by smoke seen rising there the previous day. They had no sooner arrived than fresh smoke began to billow up about five kilometres behind them on the route they had just taken, as though watching Palawa were taunting them. Cursing in frustration, they retraced their steps and found tracks leading toward Maloneys Sugarloaf. Kikatapula opined that those who made them must have gone through Stockers Bottom toward Glen Shee, but he soon lost their trail, so he said.

The party spent the next day scouring the hills in the direction of Stockers Bottom, calling at Dudgeon's hut for information. They were told no Palawa had been seen there since Kikatapula and Robertson had captured Umarrah nearby three months earlier.

On 17 February the party moved on toward Glen Shee, but a day's searching there revealed only a cleverly concealed bushranger's hut. The following day brought much the same: heat, dust, flies, thirst, aching muscles, sore feet, frustration. Never any Palawa.

From James Robertson's farm at Kittys Rivulet on 21 February they traipsed toward a fire sighted near Government Run. On the way they encountered Thomas Anstey's shepherd, who told Robertson that Palawa had speared a man there the previous day.[41] The rangers searched all day but the culprits had vanished, and it was long after dark when they finally trudged into the convict station at Ross.

Robertson's plan for the following day was to meet up at Maloneys Sugarloaf with Jemmy, one of the Tayarinutipana captured with Umarrah. He had arranged for Jemmy to be escorted there, planning to leave him and a small detachment of his party at Dudgeon's stock hut in case Palawa appeared before Grant arrived there in obedience to Robertson's orders. His own plan was 'to Travel with Black Tom and a sufficient number of the party through the Eastern Marshes and by the Forest between the Jericho Lagoon [Lake Tiberias] and Jerusalem [Colebrook] where it was probable we might meet with the Natives', he wrote.[42] A constable from Oatlands scotched that plan when he arrived next morning with the news that Jemmy had escaped his escort and disappeared. The constable also brought a note from magistrate Thomas Lascelles ordering Robertson back to Richmond to testify in court. He decided to take the whole party with him to refresh, and with high hopes they set out toward the Blue Hills on a route often used by Palawa, but they saw none.

Still heading for Richmond, they stayed overnight on 24 February at the hut near Lake Dulverton where four months earlier Palawa had slain Patrick Gough's wife, his four-year-old daughter, and a neighbour as well as wounding two Gough children. Next day the party marched toward Prossers Plains, looped back, saw no Palawa, but encountered many abandoned huts. Robertson noted that although the oldest appeared big enough to hold 200 people, newer huts became gradually smaller, while the most recent – dating, he thought, from the previous winter – had a capacity of no more than 30 people. The camps' extent had also shrunk commensurately.[43] A quarter-century after the first Britons arrived to stay, Palawa numbers had dwindled so dramatically that it was obvious even to such a recent arrival as Robertson.

Hiking toward Richmond through blazing February heat next day, a parched Robertson mused about Kikatapula, who was being headstrong and uncooperative. In his cogitation the Chief Constable unwittingly recorded proof that his guide's knowledge of the countryside was far better than he let on.

> [W]e trusted to Tom as our guide who[,] on this occasion as on several others when he was fatigued and wishing to bring his Journey to a close[,] taking advantage of our Ignorance of the Country [to] lead us in the direction of the nearest habitation[,] but in his anxiety to reach Jerusalem by the direct line he led us into a Scrub on the Banks of the Coal River which in this place is composed of perpendicular rocks ...[44]

Yet Robertson was very dependent on Kikatapula. After pausing that day to eat berries, hoping they would quench his raging thirst, he found himself separated from his guide and the rest of the party, who had not waited for him. After failing to find them or attract their attention by shouting and firing his musket, he spent most of the day lost, fearful of 'Perishing by Hunger or Thirst or by the Hands of the Savages in an unknown wilderness'. He wandered for hours in increasing desperation before finally recognising some landscape that enabled him to find his way at dusk to John Aldridge's hut (between Richmond and Runnymede). Next morning, 27 February, he walked into his Richmond home well ahead of Kikatapula and the others, who did not arrive until 10 o'clock that night. Despite nearly seven gruelling summer weeks' tramping hither and yon over a very large area, Robertson's second sortie had been unsuccessful. He had taken no Palawa, had not even sighted any.[45] Kikatapula's resistance had been maintained without a spear being thrown or a waddy wielded.

Robertson was soon busy attending court while members of his party were employed in police duties and in exercising Palawa prisoners in Richmond jail. He supposedly remained in the town all through March, kept there by police and court duties, although, as he claimed in a report, he made occasional forays during that time to parts of the Richmond district that Palawa were known to frequent.[46] He was not specific.

If he were dilatory about returning to the field, others were not. In the Bothwell area alone, he noted, no fewer than 12 parties were now hunting Palawa.[47] On 27 March, while still attending to duty in Richmond, he ordered Grant's detachment out to search the Clyde/Shannon region, but only on 20 April 1829 did Robertson finally join the hunt. By then, as his procrastination implies, his enthusiasm had waned. During the following eight months of purported Palawa-hunting he was active only sporadically, sometimes remaining in or near Richmond and claiming to be too physically indisposed to be afield. He failed to keep the required journal of his activities, and although the Colonial Secretary wrote to demand he submit regular reports, Robertson did not comply.[48]

Only in early spring 1830 did he finally produce a retrospective third-sortie report covering the entire April–December period of 1829, but it was, at best, an abridgement, a bare listing of some of the places his party went and when they went there, and it was largely devoid of the details of incident and landscape that enlivened his earlier reports. It also failed to mention that his party was sometimes in Richmond when it should have been afield, at which times he incurred official wrath by putting his rangers to work on his own farm. The report rarely referred to Kikatapula by name, although his whereabouts can sometimes be deduced.

Robertson began this sortie by joining up near Bothwell with Grant, who reported that he had sighted no Palawa during a month of scouring the region between the Ouse and the Derwent. On 27 April Robertson's rangers crossed the Derwent, where he divided them into three detachments, which he was to do frequently for the rest of the year, to search between New Norfolk and Broadmarsh. Grant led one detachment with Cowertenninner as guide, and Kikatapula was guide for the other, which was in charge of a convict named James Crawn who had also been part of Robertson's January–February patrol. The detachments searched between New Norfolk and Broadmarsh without reported incident. Until 17 May they searched Macguires Marsh, Bashan Plains, and Lake Echo, all without success, then Hells Corners, the Shannon, the Quoin, and Michael Howes Marsh with the same result, reaching Oatlands on 22 May. A newspaper reported that during those four weeks Robertson had travelled almost to Frenchmans Cap, a mountain in the wilderness about 140 kilometres west of Richmond. 'He was frequently close upon the natives, and in one part came upon a small village of their huts which had been built about 4 Weeks', the report went on,

but did not capture any of them. As a strong proof of the rapid decrease
of this benighted race, their temporary villages which a few years ago
consisted sometimes of from 30 to 40 wigwams or huts, (each containing
on an average 4 or 5 inmates), are now seldom found to consist of more
than 4 or 5 huts.[49]

Supplies replenished, Robertson's party left Oatlands on 23 May in
response to reports that Palawa had attacked and killed settlers at
Prossers Plains on 14 May, when James Olding's and John Morgan's huts
had been besieged and two stockkeepers had disappeared, believed slain.
After the black rangers had combed the Eastern Marshes, the Blue Hills,
and Kittys Corners without success, Robertson divided them again. He
sent Grant with a detachment to maintain patrols between Campbell
Town, St Pauls Plains, and Oyster Bay with orders to station themselves
near Kearneys Bogs. Robertson himself, with his remaining men, passed
through Stockers Bottom and by Maloneys Sugarloaf and Kittys Corners
as he headed back toward the Eastern Marshes, the Blue Hills, Brown
Mountain, and Brushy Plains in fine dry autumn weather. No Palawa were
reported seen.

In early June Kikatapula's continuing sabotage was briefly
highlighted when, from a patrol across frost-cloaked country near
Oatlands, Robertson responded to an incident east of the town, where
John Ruith had been chased by seven or eight Palawa and their pack
of ferocious dogs. Robertson's men went in pursuit, setting Kikatapula
to tracking Ruith's assailants.[50] But despite the compelling evidence
of numerous Palawa fires reported nearby, the attackers were never
located. Ruith's employer, Captain George Robson, a former cavalryman,
joined Robertson's party in their futile search and was so angered by
Kikatapula's obstructive efforts that he wrote a letter of complaint
about him to Anstey.[51] Robertson's skimpy third-sortie report, however,
mentioned neither his guide's obstinacy nor even his party's participation
in this action.

From then until December 1829 Kikatapula is again seen only by
inference – present, even if rarely mentioned by name – as a member of
Robertson's party or of Crawn's detachment whenever they separated.
Crawn, although literate, did not lodge any written reports of his

activities, so details of Kikatapula's life for most of the final two-thirds of 1829 are scarce. Robertson's undertakings, and Crawn's whenever his detachment operated independently, are often all that indicate where Kikatapula was. His continuing subversion can be assumed, however, for neither Robertson nor Crawn made any captures.

On 21 June, Robertson's party found Palawa tracks near the Blue Hills and followed them toward Brushy Plains but concluded that those they were tracking had gone toward Swan Port Tier. Still on their trail, by early July the party was low enough on supplies for Robertson to order Crawn's detachment to detour to Sorell for provisions. In the town Crawn sought out Alexander Laing, who had charge of Sorell's commissary store, to obtain the required victuals, but Laing refused to recognise Robertson's written authority because it was not an official requisition form and was nearly three weeks old.[52] Crawn and his men were forced to hike back to Richmond for supplies before restarting their long trek toward Swan Port Tier.[53]

On 12 August 1829, while Robertson and his party were at Prossers Plains in pursuit of marauding Palawa, he was informed that his quarry had been seen at Pitt Water two days earlier. He ordered his men (including Crawn and Kikatapula) to Carlton in pursuit while he went back to Richmond to report. When news reached him that Palawa had robbed two stock huts at the back of Mt Mangalore, Robertson immediately joined a posse responding to that raid, taking Umarrah from Richmond jail to be his guide.

After the Carlton detachment returned empty-handed on 18 August, Kikatapula was ordered back to Hobart for a meeting at the jail with his missionary friend George Augustus Robinson.[54] Now in charge of the Aboriginal ration station on Bruny Island, Robinson was in town to confer with the Lieutenant Governor. Arthur had approved his offer to lead an expedition to conciliate peaceful Palawa in the unexplored south and south-west, but now, two months later, the Lieutenant Governor had raised a reprehending eyebrow because he had not yet set out. So Robinson, who had been impressed with Kikatapula's intelligence and linguistic skill during their prison acquaintance and subsequent colleagueship at the Floating Chapel, met with the charismatic Palawa to sound him out about joining the expedition as guide, hunter, and interpreter. Kikatapula was willing, but Robinson's departure was still some months away, so Kikatapula rejoined Crawn and Robertson in the field.

Crawn's detachment was soon in action again. On 22 August Robertson reported from his Richmond home to Thomas Lascelles that Crawn had fallen in with the natives 'in the direction from which I sent him from Prossers Plains'. Yet two days later, when Crawn and the rest of the party had rejoined him, Robertson recorded nothing of that supposed encounter, implying another failure.

Sources other than Robertson's retrospective report, however, show his party did sometimes locate Palawa. In August his rangers were in a bungled skirmish that he did not report, although the *Hobart Town Courier* did on 29 August.

> The blacks ... again appeared in the neighbourhood of the Coal river last week, and were surprised by Mr. Robertson's party, leaving a number of spears, besides various articles which they have stolen from the huts[,] behind them.

Soon afterwards, in the same area, Robertson had an even more promising encounter that was also unmentioned in his report.

> Last week ... a party of the blacks was overtaken by Mr. Robertson's party in the neighbourhood of Jerusalem [Colebrook]. They had however placed themselves in a thick and almost impenetrable scrub, and it was necessary to wait until day in order to attempt their capture, and in the meantime unfortunately a gun in the hands of one of the party ... accidentally went off and gave the alarm, by which means the blacks escaped.[55]

Clearly there were Palawa in the areas Robertson traversed and clearly he did sometimes encounter them, yet in the eight months of his third sortie neither his main party nor any of the three detachments reported any captures. We are left to wonder whether this silence, this ostensible unsuccess, hid something more sinister. Robertson was a Palawa sympathiser, unlikely to condone unnecessary killings, but that does not mean none took place or that they would have been reported if they had, and Arthur's proclamation of 29 November 1826 with its blanket licence to kill – '[I]f the offenders cannot otherwise be taken, the officer and his assistants will be justified in resorting to force' – still applied. The 'Mr. Robertson's party' mentioned in newspaper stories might in fact have been only one of the detachments rather than the entire group with Robertson present; besides, as we have seen, he was often absent. Possibly his rangers sometimes killed Palawa when he was not present, or one of his detachments, when operating independently of him, might have slain Palawa from ambush or as they were fleeing an encounter. A newspaper had reported Grant's detachment slaying five Palawa during the second sortie, although his official report did not mention killings.[56] Since another roving-party leader, John Batman, asserted that their objective was 'capturing or *destroying* the natives', and that historian John West claimed the parties killed more Palawa than they captured, it is possible that Kikatapula witnessed killings of his own people by Robertson's rangers or Crawn's detachment.[57]

Little is known about James Crawn. Although a freeborn Norfolk Islander with a small farm near New Norfolk, he had criminal charges of arson and assault and battery on his record, and when he joined Robertson he was serving a seven-year sentence for stealing pigs. Sentencing Crawn and his brother in 1827, the trial judge commented that they were such bad characters that he 'regretted he could not pass a harsher sentence upon them'.[58] None of this proves Crawn participated in or condoned any slaughter of Palawa or indeed that any killings took place, but the possibility must be aired. And if Kikatapula were present when Palawa were slain, it would have hardened his resolve not to betray any more of his people. It would also help to explain a growing despondency at what he had wrought.

On 22 September, again writing from his home at Richmond, Robertson reported to Anstey that after receiving a note from Crawn the previous evening he had attempted to join him at Brown Mountain 'but I am not yet equal to the task. My Rheumatism [is] still continuing to affect me tho[ugh] I hope it is going off – I have also suffered most severely from an excruciating attack of the Piles … I sent a messenger to the Brown Mountain to order Crawn *not* to proceed to the Eastern Marshes but to confine himself to the back of Pitt Water until I meet him …' He and Crawn's detachment must have reunited soon afterward because although he complained to Anstey that his pain 'was almost amounting to torture' he was quick to respond a few days later when Palawa speared two men, one fatally, in Coal River Valley near Brown Mountain. Two of Crawn's detachment went with him.

Ten days later, on 7 October, Robertson's party responded to reports of Palawa near Bothwell. Acting under instructions from the local Police Magistrate, Crawn's group, including Kikatapula and Umarrah, stayed in the area while Robertson hurried back to Colebrook where Palawa were reported, but by the time Crawn's men joined him there on 19 October it was too dark to follow their trail. Heavy rain during the night had washed out all the Palawa tracks from two days before, but Robertson was confident his party could find them because his trusted guides Kikatapula and Umarrah were now back with him.[59] Despite their efforts, or because of them, no Palawa were located.

Kikatapula took this opportunity to register a complaint on behalf of his incarcerated countrymen, which Robertson duly reported to Anstey. 'The Blacks in Richmond Jail have been complaining to Tom that they can only get Salt Meat which I know they cannot eat ...'[60] Kikatapula also pleaded the case of a former enemy who was being harshly treated in the jail, so Robertson put both grievances in a deposition he made before Richmond magistrate J.H. Butcher.

Last week an Aboriginal Native called Black Tom joined me at Jerusalem – he complained that the Aborigines at present confined in the Richmond Gaol were not supplied with fresh meat and their allowance of food was not Sufficient ... Tom also complained that the gaoler had confined the Native calld the Lawyer [Parewareatar], handcuffed in a Cell, and requested me to lay the matter before the Governor, which I did through Mr Anstey, the Police Magistrate at Oatlands ...[61]

Kikatapula's intercession was successful. Arthur ordered better treatment for the prisoners.[62]

With his two Palawa guides back and his whole party at Colebrook, Robertson split them into detachments and sent them out on 20 October to search in different directions. Concluding there were no Palawa anywhere in the Richmond district, they then set out by three different routes for Oatlands, hunting Palawa all the way. The result was the same.

November's sallies, despite several Palawa attacks in the southern Midlands and on the Clyde that month, were reportedly as unproductive as October's. Robertson's party arrived empty-handed in Bagdad on the 13th and, after a conference with Division Constable George Armytage, advanced a further 10 kilometres to protect settlers at Broadmarsh. Next day they bungled another ambush. Palawa had attacked a hut at Constitution Hill, so Robertson's party, including Crawn's detachment, devised a plan to retaliate. Robertson and a handful of men were to be decoys in a hut at neighbouring Kempton while a large body of local settlers and police hid nearby. Trap set, all waited nervously, fingers on triggers, eager for blood. But they revealed themselves too soon and 'All the natives escaped', Robertson fumed, 'and no one could tell how, though they were in a manner surrounded by upwards of thirty people, each one more anxious than another to capture or destroy them'.[63] That word *destroy* again. Even the sympathetic Robertson was perhaps willing by then to see Palawa slain if they could not be captured.

The rangers stayed in the area, Robertson noting five days after his arrival that Crawn and his men would remain under Armytage's orders although he himself was leaving. No Palawa were reported captured, shot, or even seen. Robertson's party had now been afield for seven months on their third sortie without a single capture.

Other roving parties were also finding their quarry elusive. While the black rangers criss-crossed familiar and unfamiliar country on foot and heavily encumbered, the fast-moving Palawa travelled light and lived off the land. Lack of bushcraft hindered the rangers. They made so much noise talking and blundering heavy-footed over dead wood and bark, opined a correspondent to a newspaper, that Palawa heard them coming long before they saw them.[64] Those and other factors undoubtedly contributed to the parties' failure, but by mid-1829 the colonial authorities had come to understand the primary reason: their Palawa guides were consistently leading the parties astray. Kikatapula and his fellow guides knew all the ploys and stratagems Palawa used to evade pursuers, and those like him who had raided far and wide knew every topographical hiding place and scrubby sanctuary the countryside afforded, but they were determined not to betray any of their race.

Eventually their chicanery became so obvious that Jorgen Jorgensen, leader of an Oatlands-based roving party, could confirm that the main impediment to success was 'Black Tom and the other Blacks accompanying the expedition not being willing to bring the parties to where the natives would very likely to be. – I have this from general opinion chiefly', to which Colonial Secretary Burnett added a marginal note: 'I think this extremely probable.'[65] James Bonwick recalled Jorgenson's telling him 'I have not found one [Palawa guide] that I could recommend, or seem fit to be a negotiator between us and his countrymen. Eumarra, Black Tom, and Black Jack [Cowertenninner] ... possess much cunning, but little manly sense, and they are otherwise corrupted'.[66] William Grant made the same observation about Cowertenninner. After spotting a Palawa in the bush one evening, he reported, his party set out at first light next day (4 July) to track him but were stymied by their guide.[67] A comment Anstey scrawled in the margin of Grant's report confirmed that Cowertenninner was emulating Kikatapula. 'This conduct in Black Jack corresponded with the supposed conduct of Black Tom', he wrote, 'as related to me by Letter by Captn. Robson, a new Settler on the Upper Macquarie River'.[68]

Hampered by those counteractions and his own ebbing enthusiasm, Robertson recorded no captures at all in 1829. Yet during the eight months of his unsuccessful third sortie, in the very areas he and his men were fruitlessly combing, Palawa slew at least 19 Britons, wounded 38 more, and made 23 other raids on settlers.[69] Kikatapula's passive resistance had been notably effective.

As the dry spring gave way to a wet early summer, Kikatapula's year as a black ranger was coming to an end (as was Robertson's, the government having decided not to renew his contract). On 1 December the Colonial Secretary ordered Anstey to have Kikatapula report for service with George Augustus Robinson's forthcoming mission to Port Davey.[70] But Kikatapula was in the field with Crawn's detachment, and it was not until they rendezvoused with Robertson at Brown Mountain on 22 December that the order reached him. Robertson acknowledged his compliance in a letter that Kikatapula himself probably delivered next day to the Colonial Secretary.

I send Tom to Town in obedience to your order[.] I should have sent 'Eumarra' with him in case you might approve of his going to visit the establishment at Brune [which Robertson had suggested to Arthur on 9 June 1829] – But on my arrival here I heard of the natives being at Pitt Water and divided my party to go in different directions in quest of them. The detachment with which 'Eumarra' went has not returned and I expect that he must have found the track of the natives[.] I would not detain Tom for his return lest I should incur your displeasure by the delay.[71]

How Kikatapula felt about his new assignment can only be surmised. If he had been party or witness to any slaughter of Palawa by the black rangers he would have been glad to escape the possibility of more, and he would not have forgotten William Talbot's suggestion only a few months before that he and Cowertenninner should be shot. He might have been glad too to get away from a frontier constantly traversed by bands of armed Britons intent on capturing or killing Palawa. The protection of a different Briton in a peaceful expedition to parts of *lutruwita* away from the frontier, away from the war, away from vengeful Palawa and Britons with guns, might have seemed prudent and desirable by then.

Regardless, Kikatapula farewelled Robertson that day and set out to walk the 40 or so kilometres to Hobart to join Robinson, in whose service he would spend the rest of his short life – and whose mission he would also sabotage when possible.

15

'I entertain great hopes of the assistance of Tom'

Kikatapula's new master was born in the East End of London in 1791, the son of a bricklayer and builder. After leaving home aged about 11, Robinson too became a bricklayer. He married Mary Amelia Evens (or Evans) in 1814, and they had five children by 1823. That year he was involved in a financial scandal to do with a religious institution, for which its members may have hounded him out of London. He went to Leith, Scotland, via a short sojourn in Surrey. After contemplating immigrating to Nicaragua he decided Australia offered better prospects and sailed in the *Triton* on 7 September, only 12 days after reaching Leith. He had not been able to contact Mary, who was still in London with their children, in time for her to join him, but they would eventually follow him to Australia.

The *Triton* reached Hobart on 20 January 1824. Robinson, who had arrived with only four shillings in his pocket, was soon working as a builder. By year's end he had several employees and, he claimed, capital of £400, but despite this apparent prosperity he could not persuade Mary to join him until April 1826. Meanwhile, he involved himself in Hobart with various Christian organisations, visited prisoners in the jail, and helped found the Mechanics' Institute. But according to his biographer he was accused of sharp practice and double-dealing, some of his business interests failed because of an economic depression in 1826, and by 1829 he was said to be close to insolvent, although the claims have been disputed.[1] On 7 March that year he saw in a newspaper a government advertisement for a man to live on Bruny Island, establish good relations with local Palawa, and take charge of the ration station there.[2] He applied, and on 21 March was notified of his appointment. His intention was to

George Augustus Robinson, leader of the Friendly Mission.
(Courtesy Libraries Tasmania)

make the Bruny Island station a model settlement complete with a school and a church so Palawa could be taught to live in houses, grow crops, and behave like Britons. Although there were few Nununi, Bruny Island's original inhabitants, left by that time, the Lieutenant Governor intended any Palawa captured by the roving parties to be exiled there with them.

When Robinson reached the island on 30 March he found only 19 Palawa left; six years earlier there had been 160.[3] Fed low-protein convict rations, dressed in European clothes, and housed in huts, many islanders had sickened and died. Those left included Nelson, Musquito's one-armed former companion (who, however, died on 2 July that year); a woman named Pagerly or Tuererningher (thought to be Nelson's sister) and her future husband Mangana; Mangana's daughter Trukanini; and a Ninene woman from Port Davey named Draymuric. In July nine Ninene had crossed by catamaran from Recherche Bay to visit Bruny, but only three of them survived to return to their country.[4] Although the *Hobart Town Courier* reported all was well, 10 of the 19 surviving inhabitants had died by 22 September.[5] Faced with the imminent collapse of the project, Robinson grasped at an idea the same newspaper had floated three months earlier: that he, with his conciliated Palawa, should mount an expedition to make friendly overtures to the Ninene around Port Davey and gain the goodwill of other Palawa along the way.[6] The notion appealed to him. If he began by befriending the Port Davey people, he thought, he might eventually conciliate all the Palawa remaining in Tasmania and exile them on Bruny Island, where he could civilise and Christianise them, thus allowing the British undisturbed possession of all mainland Tasmania. The force of reason rather than the force of arms, he believed, would ensure his success.[7] His expedition consequently came to be called the Friendly Mission.

He approached the Lieutenant Governor, who had received a similar proposal from Gilbert Robertson. Arthur was agreeable to the idea but Robertson was now out of favour, so on 23 June 1829 Robinson was appointed to lead an expedition to Port Davey, in south-western Tasmania.[8] But he was slow to start, making excuses about the unsuitability of the winter weather and the number of Bruny Island Palawa who were too ill for him to leave. As summer approached, the Colonial Secretary gave Robinson permission to take with him five Britons, Kikatapula from Gilbert Robertson's party, and Trepanner, a man then in hospital in Hobart.[9] Although Robertson seems to have been in two minds about Kikatapula's subversive efforts, he sent his guide to Hobart with a generous encomium. 'I find that "Tom" will be able to communicate with the Port Davey Tribe as some of them have been in the habit of visiting his Tribe,' he told the Colonial Secretary.

> I believe Tom to be perfectly sincere in his wish to further the views of Government toward his countrymen and that he fully appreciates the benefits they would receive by embracing the proffered protection of His Excellency – I mention this because I know that reports of the controversy [about Palawa guides' fealty] have been industriously propagated not only with regards to 'Tom' but also with regards to 'Jack' and 'Eumarrah'.

And the poor creatures appear much hurt when they hear the slightest suspicion of their Fidelity.[10]

After walking to Hobart from Brown Mountain, Kikatapula joined Robinson at the Aboriginal asylum adjacent to his house on 23 December 1829, followed next day by Umarrah. Three days later Robinson took them and Trepanner to Bruny Island in a whaleboat, noting in his journal that the three amused themselves on Bruny by throwing spears at one another. He admired the skill and dexterity with which each caught spears thrown at him.[11]

Kikatapula was no stranger to G.A. Robinson's Hobart home.
(Courtesy Libraries Tasmania)

Next day he issued them with clothing. Kikatapula, whom Robinson had promised land and a boat for participating in the mission, received a jacket, a waistcoat, trousers, a handkerchief, stockings, and a shirt. Umarrah was given a jacket, trousers, a handkerchief, and stockings, Trepanner a handkerchief, stockings, and a jacket. A day later Robinson took them, dressed in their new apparel, back to Hobart in the whaleboat, and on New Year's Day 1830 Kikatapula accompanied him to Richmond with two convicts, Alexander McGeary and Alexander McKay, who were to join the mission. They returned to Hobart on 4 January, taking with them the captive Palawa from Richmond jail. When Kikatapula and the other Palawa were sent to church the following Sunday Robinson praised their decorous conduct throughout the service and lauded their submission to anything religious. He found they were enraptured by the music, although less rapt in the Wesleyan service they were sent to next day.[12] His renewed acquaintance with Kikatapula was a source of enthusiasm. 'I entertain great hopes of the assistance of the aboriginal Tom who has hither to been very respectful and compliant', he noted in his journal on 11 January 1830. 'If I can succeed in influencing his ideas so as to unite them with my own as regards the welfare of his aboriginal countrymen, much good may result to my endeavours. He is a famous interpreter and this is the stronghold on which I build my chief hopes.'[13]

On Sunday 17 January, after issuing clothing to the Palawa women, Robinson sent them with the men to St David's church. Their conduct was again decorous, due, he thought, to the grandeur of the edifice, the highly respectable congregation, and the sacred music. He hoped it would all have an abiding place in their memory.[14]

As preparations for the mission were nearing completion, supplies that included provisions for 10 weeks were being loaded aboard the schooner *Swallow* which, with the whaleboat from Bruny Island, would transport the party to Port Davey and then support their overland trek by following them around the coast. A former ship's longboat displacing about eight tonnes, the *Swallow* was not a particularly suitable vessel, as Robinson noted, having 'been lengthened at the stern instead of amidships, which made her very crank [unstable], and had also been rose upon; and was withal an old vessel'.[15] *Swallow* carried three crew, the whaleboat six. All the trusted convicts to comprise the escort party had been selected: McGeary (leader), McKay, Thomas Macklow, Joseph Platt, John Simpson, and William Stansfield, each of whom hoped to receive a ticket of leave for participating. Robinson's son Charles also went. The 12 Palawa guides were:

- Kikatapula
- Umarrah, from Robertson's roving party
- Parewareatar, from Richmond jail
- Trepanner, from Hobart hospital
- Wurati, a Nununi man from Bruny Island
- Trukanini, a Nununi, Wurati's wife (but not his sons' mother)
- Myyungge (David Bruny), a boy, son of Wurati
- Droyyerloinne (Peter Bruny), a boy, son of Wurati
- Malapuwinarana (Timmy?), a young male thought to have been a native of the north-east coast
- Robert (Palawa name and natal band unknown), raised from childhood by colonists
- Draymuric , a young Ninene woman
- Pagerly, a young Nununi widow

Most of the Palawa were keen to make the journey, especially the Bruny Islanders, who had no desire to remain around the mission station with its lingering miasma of sickness and death, and Draymuric wanted to return to her own people at Port Davey. Umarrah was overjoyed to have his freedom after being imprisoned and then accommodated in the jail at Richmond for more than a year.

On 27 January 1830 Britons and Palawa boarded the *Swallow*. Unfavourable winds delayed sailing until the following afternoon, when the expedition finally set out. Kikatapula, the greatest and most feared Palawa guerrilla leader, was embarking on the final phase of his life – as a not necessarily wholehearted guide, hunter, and interpreter for a government campaign to ethnically cleanse Tasmania of the last remnants of the people whose home it had been for more than 35 millennia.

16

'Mountain tiers as far as the eye could reach'

Kikatapula would spend scarcely a day apart from his new master for the rest of his life, and because his role in Robinson's mission would be crucial he features frequently and sometimes prominently (if not always favourably) in Robinson's journals. They are virtually the only record of the final 28 months of his life, but they are one Briton's subjective observations, so Kikatapula's motive for this action or that mostly has to be inferred or guessed. Only rarely do we hear his speaking for himself, but his moods – playful, defiant, sullen, fearful, subversive – are sometimes clear.

Robinson himself remains a controversial figure 150 years after his death. He has been vilified by some and praised by others, but any reader of the 900-plus pages of his remarkable journals must be impressed by some of his personal qualities: his courage, self-assurance, and endurance; his apparently genuine desire to help the Palawa; his religious faith; his steely determination. Although he intended his mission to better himself financially and socially – he was an ardent and unashamed self-promoter – it does not overshadow the personal qualities that saw him through the years of the Friendly Mission. His hold over the mission's Palawa and those he rounded up for island exile was noteworthy and has been called mesmeric. But 'He was guided, fed, sheltered and, in all likelihood, managed by his Aboriginal companions. It was they, and not God, who "led him in paths which he knew not"'– two sentences that spotlight one of the great tragic ironies of the lives of all the mission Palawa, none more so than Kikatapula.[1]

The first leg of the mission took Robinson's party through the ruggedly hostile terrain of southernmost Tasmania, from Recherche Bay in the far south-east to Port Davey in the far south-west – a region little inhabited even today and now largely included in the state's near-pristine World Heritage Area – and then northward along the west coast. The area had not attracted settlers for good reasons. One was the climate, which has been succinctly described as *vile*, 'a land of strong winds, squalls, storms, rain, sleet, snow and a kind of saturating dampness that penetrates into the very core of your being, especially in winter'.[2] The terrain in some places is difficult to the point of near-impassability: hills and gullies thickly tressed with dark, dank rainforest riven by icy, fast-flowing rivers, dense canopy, deep gorges, great tree ferns dripping moisture, boggy ground, and constant impediments of rock and fallen timber made treacherous by moss. Even worse were the great wide thickets of western Tasmania's notorious horizontal scrub, a small tree whose slender trunk grows upwards for as much as 10 metres until its own weight as it thickens makes it topple over, where it continues to spread, now horizontally, further thickening into an impenetrable, ever-widening tangle by sending up new stems that themselves grow vertically until they too topple to the horizontal under their own weight, starting the ongoing process of spreading upwards and outwards all over again. Since it is impossible to pass through horizontal scrub, it is necessary either to walk around it or to climb across the top of it, a perilous exercise because it forms vast raised platforms metres high.[3] Robinson's expedition was to make history by successfully traversing the unmapped region with its cloud-mantled mountains, an area at that time unexplored by Europeans, then trekking northward along the wild west coast and emerging in the less demanding north-west, which was just being opened up by the Van Diemen's Land Company. But that emergence was many punishing and hazardous weeks away.

After leaving Hobart, a stop at Bruny Island, and an overnight camp on Huon River, Robinson's party reached Recherche Bay on 1 February 1830. Two days of adverse winds and the reluctance of the schooner's commander and the whaleboat's coxswain to chance their vessels in the prevailing conditions forced Robinson to strike out on foot for Port Davey by following the coastline, which he did on 3 February with Kikatapula and Umarrah, eight other Palawa, and five Britons. He calculated the distance at 100 kilometres, which he estimated would take three days to walk, through country previously untraversed by any European and considered to be impassable.

From the outset the going proved arduous. 'The first part of this day's journey we travelled through swamps, half way up our legs in mud and in some places up to our knees', Robinson wrote in his journal.[4] Next day they followed a *markenner*, a Palawa route, but it proved no easier. Instead, they had 'a fatiguing day's journey, having to pass through dense forests, crawl through holes on knees and hands and anon having to scramble over trees covered with moss', Robinson wrote. 'Once the party had to descend a cliff so steep that I felt apprehensive for the safety of the men who were bearing burdens, as it was with extreme caution that I myself descended.'[5]

The following day was even tougher.

Ascended a steep and lofty mountain [the Ironbound Range], the greatest in altitude of any I had yet travelled over. After travelling over thick scrub for a quarter of a mile [400 m], the mountain became barren and very difficult of ascent. It was composed of white and variegated marble. Obliged to travel with extreme caution: to have looked down would have endangered the life of one not accustomed to such elevations. When again descending we had to proceed with extreme caution and stop our speed by clinging hold of tufts of grass and small shrubs. Passed over a chasm, in which the water gushing down the rocks reverberated with a hollow sound, and ascended a much steeper and higher barren mountain, up which I was obliged to pull myself by laying hold of the rushes and grass ...[6]

From its summit, however, they could see the schooner and the whaleboat waiting in Louisa Bay about 10 kilometres away. The sight was very welcome. The party had already consumed most of their food, game had proved to be scarce and the rivers to be devoid of fish, and Robinson feared they might yet have four days' walking ahead of them. After crossing a plain about eight kilometres wide and then wading through Louisa River they reached the boats late in the afternoon. Even the Palawa guides were exhausted by then. Robinson was surprised at Kikatapula's fatigue, believing him to have been well conditioned to hard travelling after spending the previous 14 months tramping the countryside with roving parties. But Kikatapula explained that 'the ground up the country was clear and level and that they did not travel so fast', for, as Robinson boasted in his journal, 'we travelled as fast as some people travel on the road'.[7]

On 10 February the expedition reached Cox Bight, where the guides butchered a seal for food. Trekking westward next day they encountered more difficulties. 'Travelled over an extensive marsh, which the recent rains had greatly flooded', the now-ailing Robinson recorded. 'Was very fatigued; at one step ankle deep, the next up to the knee and frequently up to the middle in water'.[8] The following day, after a 32-kilometre hike that included scaling a high tier and crossing another marsh and a river, they camped for the night on the eastern shore of Port Davey.

The weather remained miserably wet and windy. After crossing Hannants Inlet on a hastily built native catamaran on 15 February the exhausted Robinson reached the mouth of Bathurst Channel and camped nearby. Two of the convicts were completely spent and very ill, and the expedition was again short of food. A hunting party went out but returned empty-handed after searching all day. On the 17th Robinson was forced to send McKay and Stansfield back overland to bring provisions from the *Swallow*. The foul weather persisted.

Next day the guide Robert absconded. 'Supposed he had gone to the schooner', Robinson mused, 'and concluded that he would perish in the attempt from his extreme weakness and his natural inertness'. Having been raised since childhood by colonists, Robert, who was about 21, had little knowledge of bushcraft, so his decamping in some of the most inhospitable country in Tasmania made his early demise seem inevitable. During the day Robinson climbed several times to the top of a high hill to look for the approach of one of the boats, but in his ailing state such efforts made him nauseous and giddy.

Although the weather began to improve on 19 February, McKay returned that day with shattering news: the *Swallow* had broken its anchor cables and gone aground in Louisa Bay six days earlier, seriously holing its hull. The crew had managed to save most of the provisions except the potatoes.

> [McKay] stated that he and Stansfield and two of the boat's crew had started that morning, but that they had stopped halfway unable to proceed further; that judging of my situation he strove to get to me. When this man arrived with the provision I had been eight days subsisting upon mutton fish [abalone] and a few crawfish, mussels, roots and berries, such as the natives could procure. The mussels was very bad and made the men sick. I felt a swimming in the head and sick at the stomach. Two of the men made sure that they should die and [were] tormented much that they were sent [on the expedition].[9]

The damage to the *Swallow* was a devastating blow to Robinson's plans. Although his weakened and exhausted people made frequent hikes to the vessel and back, provisioning the overland party was now and would continue to be very difficult without seaborne supplies. Robinson stayed in the area for about three weeks, eventually deciding to have all the provisions carried across country to him from the schooner. He kept one man with him and sent the others back to Louisa Bay for more supplies. Still unwell and much vexed by mosquito bites, he was now lame from boils on his legs.

On the evening of 22 February the men returning to the camp toting supplies from the *Swallow* reported that the vessel was definitely unsalvageable. Robinson ordered them to return to Louisa Bay next morning and bring back all the remaining supplies. When they returned two days later insisting the schooner was beyond repair, he decided to see for himself. Despite his lameness he set out on the morning of the 26th to walk to Louisa Bay, taking Kikatapula and the other guides with him. After following a different route across the Bathurst Range they reached the vessel a painful nine hours later. In spite of the substantial damage to the *Swallow* and its overall unseaworthy condition, Robinson ordered it repaired, then rested for a night before returning to his camp.

In Hobart, meanwhile, on 25 February, the government issued an order offering bounties of £5 for every adult Palawa captured and £2 for every child. The news did not reach Robinson until five months later, but when it did the Friendly Mission became somewhat less so.

Robinson's health continued to worsen, yet he was not daunted. His journal even at this time records acts of remarkable personal stamina and determination. While waiting for the refloated *Swallow* to catch up with his party he explored waterways in the whaleboat and continued to search for the Port Davey people, of whom the only signs were dozens of uninhabited huts. And he had sighted none of the Lowreenne of Cox Bight, the other band of the South-West people whose country he had passed through. As he familiarised himself with the lie of the land he was constantly reminded how formidable was the task he had undertaken.

> The country round Port Davey viewed from the water presents a very cheerless aspect, lofty barren mountains as far as the eye can discern, which seem as if they had been thrown together by some convulsion of nature into a confused mass, presenting a surface so rugged that it would seem almost impossible to travel.[10]

Two days after writing that, he was even more wretchedly unwell 'with a violent pain in the bowels occasioned, I think, by eating oysters ... Thought it was the dysentery as some of the men had been affected with the same ... This detention is much to be lamented – I feel most anxious to proceed ... '[11]

Proceed he did, his health still precarious. With Kikatapula, five other Palawa, and five convicts, he resumed his explorations on 10 March, crossing a wide plain and ascending the Norold Range. That night, after climbing to the top of an adjoining mountain, he camped on the side of a deep ravine.

> There I had an extensive view of the country, mountain tiers as far as the eye could reach, covered some of them to the very summit with dense forest, and the valleys between [with] impenetrable thickets. Returned much fatigued, descending a steep cliff to where my people was stopping. Here nature appeared in all her pristine forms; perpendicular cliffs, immense chasms through which the water was heard to gush with frightful roar, mountain tops hid in the clouds, and anon the piercing wind gushing up the ravines rendered our situation truly uncomfortable. I continued still very unwell. Yet there was no alternative; to decline was useless. No

medical assistant, no friend near to soothe or to offer consolation. The night excessive cold.

On 11 March the expedition reached the Arthur Range and crossed a deep and thickly forested ravine. Robinson became separated from the rest of the party and found himself in difficulties, which Kikatapula and the other guides managed to extricate him from. But his woes continued. That night 'the fire caught hold of my clothes and nearly destroyed them. I suddenly awoke and had I not extinguished the fire should have been severely injured'. He noted again that he was 'excessively ill'.

In fine weather next day the party resumed their trek. For once the mountaintops were clear of cloud and mist, so despite his weakened state Robinson decided to climb one to get an unimpeded view of the surrounding terrain. Kikatapula insisted on going with him.

> Travelled across the marsh and proceeded up the mountain, Black Tom and a white man keeping by me, each carrying a jug of water which I repeatedly drank to allay my thirst. At short intervals stopped for rest. Tom has since told me that the reason of his being anxious to accompany me up the mountain was that he was sure I should die that night ...[12]

A 20th-century Port Davey resident called the expedition's progress to this point a notable feat. 'Even today with modern camping equipment this would not be a trip that would be taken lightly', he wrote. 'The difficulties of this undertaking cannot be fully appreciated by anyone who has not been through this country and experienced the type of weather that prevails in these parts. The mountains and hills are deeply intersected with very steep gullies and gorges running in all directions and mostly clothed with very thick scrub or forest'.[13]

By 13 March, his fever finally broken and his strength returning, Robinson moved on with renewed vigour. 'Proceeded to reach the high mountain. Came to another lagoon sunk in the mountain ... Then to two other lagoons ... In the waters of the second were to be seen small islands and from the shore ran out points with white sandy beaches. The aborigine Tom called them "boat harbours" and said he would take his farm on one of the islands' – a reference to the land Robinson had promised him for joining the expedition.

Kikatapula's comment is puzzling. He was in one of the most inhospitable parts of Tasmania, far from his own temperate country, so his remark might have meant nothing more than 'that looks like a nice place to live compared to what we've been through'. Or perhaps his enthusiasm had to do with the area's remoteness from trigger-happy Britons and the scaffold at Hobart jail. Perhaps he really did have some notion – a fallback position – of settling down to be a farmer. His use of the term 'boat harbours' is interesting because he had no known nautical experience other than a few days with Robinson. Perhaps his using it hints at some unrecorded time spent with whalers or sealers before he went to Hobart in 1819 or during his years with the ship-owning Birches.

On 16 March, near Macquarie Harbour, Robinson's party had a sobering reminder of the perils prevailing in that harsh and isolated region when they discovered the skeletal remains of three convicts who had absconded from the penal settlement and perished in the bush. But a more positive

Nununi man Wurati, Kikatapula's fellow Friendly Mission guide.
Portrait by Thomas Bock. (Courtesy British Museum)

sighting followed. As they were moving their camp to a site near Kelly Basin the expeditioners spotted smoke from Ninene fires close to where they were intending to erect Robinson's tent. But when they approached the fires the Ninene scattered, igniting the brush to alert others as they fled. After ordering Wurati, Trukanini, Pagerly, and Draymuric to strip off their European clothing, Robinson sent them forward to negotiate. Early in the evening three of them returned – Draymuric had stayed behind after finding her brother with the Ninene – and confirmed they were the Port Davey people. They also brought word that the Ninene were willing to talk with Robinson next morning, although they had cautiously camped five kilometres away.

Next day Draymuric rejoined the expedition, bringing with her two young Ninene women. At mid-morning Robinson took Kikatapula, seven other mission Palawa, and three Britons to meet the Ninene at the foot of a high hill. But the Port Davey people, still wary, did not appear. Several hours' searching by Kikatapula and the other guides found no trace of them. Reasoning that the size of his party might be intimidating, Robinson returned to his tent, leaving only Trukanini (who could speak the Ninene dialect), Kikatapula, and Wurati at the meeting place to negotiate a parley. But when the three returned to camp the following day they reported that the Ninene had not appeared. Robinson decided to search for them himself, taking Wurati, Draymuric, and the two young Ninene women with him. They tracked the Ninene over hills and through thick bush for about 14 kilometres before finally locating them and persuading them to come out of hiding. In all, 25 men, women, and children came to his campfire and accepted small gifts. By morning, however, all but Draymuric, three other women, and an infant had vanished into the bush.

For the next few days members of Robinson's party tracked the Ninene without success. They were 'fleeing before my approach as the clouds fly before the tempest', Robinson wrote in frustration. On 22 March, with seven mission Palawa and the Port Davey women, he set off to look for them himself, followed by four Britons whom he ordered to keep out of sight. They camped for the night by the coast, and early next morning spotted Robert coming toward them. Having earlier rejoined the party in unrecorded circumstances, he had been sent to bring flour and ask for instructions.

As the mission trailed the elusive Ninene up the west coast, the countryside improved. Travelling became easier. At Mulcahy River Robinson noted its 'romantic appearance, with hills rising on each side covered with beautiful shrubs of variegated hue, between which the water was seen to meander on its way to the great ocean'.[14] Near Low Rocky Point on 25 March they saw smoke from Palawa fires, but as they crossed a plain to a headland between Mulcahy River and Giblin River they found most of the plain ablaze. The guides called out to Robinson that they could see the Ninene but they were running away. Wurati dashed up a hill and signalled to Robinson to go around the other side. Near the top they were met by two tall well-built Ninene men, Tawtara and Neennevuther, armed with waddies. Kikatapula and the other guides went forward and found more Ninene hiding in the bush, and soon the whole band was gathered. The confidence of the Port Davey people had been restored, Robinson noted. He gave permission for some of the mission Palawa to go off with them to hunt. Later that day the mission stopped at a place Palawa called *nomeme*, possibly the north end of Nye Bay, where the Ninene had a village. Robinson noted with interest that their hut construction was very different from those of eastern Palawa.

> A large hut was erected … about ten by ten [3 m x 3 m] and seven feet [2.15 m] in height. This hut, like many others I saw, was in the form of a circular dome and was stuck full of duck or cockatoo feathers [for insulation]. The door or entrance was a small hole about a foot [30 cm] wide by two feet high. These villages are always near to fresh water and close to some fishing rocks, and at them are in general to be found the native fig.[15]

After the hunters returned with a kangaroo 'The evening was spent with great conviviality, singing and dancing until a late hour, making the woods to echo with their song'. The image is haunting.

Next morning Robinson had Kikatapula cut the Port Davey people's hair, which seemed to please them. He proposed now to cross the river because the Ninene wanted to go to Low Rocky Point and he intended to go with them. But Wurati, who hated the Ninene and had been secretly fuelling their apprehension about Robinson's intentions, said they were planning to abscond. The Ninene women controverted, however, saying they did not intend to run away. Robinson responded by telling them:

I came not to injure them, I came to do them good. If they wished to accompany me they were welcome, if not they could stop [there] and I would proceed on. They one and all said they wished to go with me. Whether they went with me or stayed was a matter of no consideration, but to conciliate and tranquilise and to adjust their grievances was the object for which I came amongst them.

Wurati continued to sabotage. He pecked away at Kikatapula's peace of mind, telling him 'the [Port Davey] natives were savage people and would by and by spear us', Robinson noted, 'and Tom, who is mortally timorous, listened to it and also said what he could to keep me back'.[16] The 'mortally timorous' comment seems odd. Kikatapula had amply proved his mettle over more than four years as a guerrilla and another year as a guide for Gilbert Robertson. He might have been concerned about the possibility of armed conflict because he was unarmed and Robinson kept his firearms out of sight in a knapsack where they would have been useless in the event of a surprise attack. Moreover, as the best-known resistance leader Kikatapula continued to fear reprisals by Palawa who had learnt of his defection and collaboration. Or perhaps he was simply leery of trying to cross the river, although he could swim, as Robinson's journal later recorded. Umarrah certainly dreaded the water, Robinson observed. He himself could not swim, but he climbed onto the catamaran and was propelled across by four Palawa women.

It has been suggested that Wurati's attempted undermining of the mission at this time was because Robinson had been copulating with Trukanini, his wife, but the matter is inconclusive. Kikatapula was later to take a strong and active fancy to Trukanini, although at an unrecorded point in these early stages of the Friendly Mission he had taken the recently widowed Pagerly to wife.

Very little is certain about Kikatapula's wife or wives. The wording of a newspaper report of the death on 12 July 1827 of Black Kit (or Black Trish), 'queen of the tribe which used to have Black Tom at its head' (so probably a survivor of Bank Head Farm), suggests she might have been his wife. He certainly would have had at least one during his guerrilla years, but nothing else is known of her or of her relationship with Kikatapula.[17] As to Pagerly, she was a young woman already widowed by July 1829, after which, like her friend Trukanini, she spent time consorting with whalers based at Bruny Island's Adventure Bay.[18] In October 1829 she was wooed by the Nununi man Mangana, Trukanini's father, whom she resisted for some days before marrying him. But the union was brief: Mangana died on Bruny Island three months later.[19] So by the time Robinson's mission reached Recherche Bay on the first leg of their journey Pagerly was again a widow and free to unite with Kikatapula, which she did in March or April. She was to be his last wife, although she was far from being his last romantic interest. Nevertheless, he had no known offspring.

While the expedition rested on 28 March, a Sunday, Robinson conversed with the Ninene, who wanted to feel his arms, legs, and hands. Kikatapula explained that it was to see if he had bones. That night Robinson recorded his first misgivings about what he thought should be Kikatapula's proper subservience to him, although without noting the cause. 'Black Tom's conduct today was very improper; he appeared to act independently of me', he wrote. 'The man is innately wicked'. Occasional tension between the two, both strong personalities, was to become more pronounced as the mission progressed. Although Kikatapula was a proven leader, Robinson was usually able to assert his authority, but their relationship was to vacillate periodically, and sometimes dramatically, for the rest of Kikatapula's life.

At 3 am two days later Robinson heard the Ninene quietly decamping. Draymuric told him they were frightened of the mission Palawa because they had learnt Kikatapula and Umarrah had previously been attached to a roving party. They referred to the mission guides as *num*, 'white people', perhaps because they wore European clothes.

For another week or so the expedition stayed in the region around Low Rocky Point and Elliott Bay. On 6 April Robinson pushed ahead with Umarrah and Dray but ordered Kikatapula and the others to remain at Low Rocky Point. Ten days were to pass before the two parties were reunited.

Kikatapula might have been out of sight but he was rarely out of the minds of embattled colonists in the east. On 17 April a Hobart newspaper reported he had resumed hostilities in the settled districts.

We regret to learn, that Black Tom, the native, who has for some time acted as a guide to Mr. Robertson's party, has absconded from his companions and joined the incursive tribes. Several of the out-stock huts about Swan port and Prosser's plains have been robbed, we fear, in consequence of being led on by him.[20]

A fortnight later the *Tasmanian* made a similar claim.

It is understood that a man was killed by a party of natives at Jerusalem [Colebrook] last week. Black Tom is with them, and has taught them to skin and dress a sheep in the European way. They now look out for sheep flocks wherever they go.[21]

The reports must have chilled settlers' blood, but Kikatapula was not the culprit. Robinson's journal for 6 April, 18 April, and 9 May prove he remained with the mission, so he had not sneaked away for a lightning trip to the far distant east for some quick hit-and-run raids. He was blamed because he was the best-known and most feared leader of hostile Palawa and the public was not aware of his new role on the other side of the island, a great and difficult distance from Swansea and Prossers Plains and Colebrook.

A week after making its erroneous report the *Tasmanian* corrected itself.

BLACK TOM. – We are authorized to state that [reports of] Black Tom, the Aborigine, being at large with his native brethren, is untrue. He is now with Mr. Robinson, the Superintendent of the Aboriginal establishment at Bruni, having married one of the women there.[22]

After Robinson left Kikatapula behind at Low Rocky Point his attempts to befriend and conciliate local Palawa continued to have mixed results. None of those he contacted stayed with him for long before vanishing into the bush; others ran away at first sight of him. But he claimed he had no particular wish they remain with him, only that they introduce him to other Palawa in the area. When a local family came to his camp at the mouth of Hibbs River on 18 April 'Woorrady, Tom and the other natives, finding they meant to leave, urged me to capture them and was very annoyed at my intention to leave [without the newcomers]'.[23]

Robinson was in poor shape by then. When he reconnected with Kikatapula's portion of the mission on 16 April his eyes were infected, his body was pustular, his clothes were in tatters, and his only footwear was a bag bound onto each foot with kurrajong bark. Nevertheless, he pressed on.

On 24 April the party reached the penal settlement at Macquarie Harbour, where they rested for a week while replenishing their provisions. Robinson took the opportunity to send word of his progress to Hobart by sea, and it was reported in a newspaper the following month.

> We rejoice to learn, that Mr. G. A. Robinson who has been for some time on his excursion, has succeeded in holding a friendly intercourse with several tribes, of the blacks in the neighbourhood of Port Davey, and it is fondly anticipated, that so propitious a beginning may lead to the pacification and the ultimate civilization of the other tribes throughout the island.[24]

After a subsequent sojourn at either the heads or Birches Rocks the mission resumed their trek northward along the coast on 7 May. But more cracks were appearing in their fabric. At Trial Harbour on the 12th Umarrah, Parewareatar, and another Palawa man – presumably Trepanner – absconded, taking their dogs with them. The three boys, Malapuwinarana, Myyungge, and Droyyerloinne, had already been sent from Port Davey back to Hobart with the schooner, and Draymuric had stayed behind with the Ninene, so only Kikatapula, Pagerly, Wurati, Trukanini, and probably Robert were left as Robinson's guides, interpreters, hunters, and envoys.

The reduced mission reached Pieman River about 16 May and stayed in the area for several days. In the intervening period Kikatapula rated only one mention in Robinson's journal: 'Sent Hopkins to the heads blind [speculatively] with Tom and Pagerly.'[25]

On 22 May, after a night of heavy rain, Robinson ordered Kikatapula and Wurati out to scout for *Toogee*, as Palawa from that part of Tasmania were called. They soon returned with news they had seen three men walking along a small sandy beach a long way off, and a day of hide-and-seek followed without contact being made. When the search resumed next morning Robinson noted with irritation another sign of his guides' subversion: 'Had the greatest difficulty in keeping my natives quiet;

frequently put my hand over their mouths to stop the sound of their voice.'[26] Despite such broadcast warnings they eventually chanced upon a large group of well-armed Palawa who dispersed at Robinson's approach, abandoning kangaroo skins, abalone, crayfish, baskets, and waddies. Robinson's guides wanted to take the fish but he would not allow it. Instead, he left gifts of handkerchiefs, beads, knives, scissors, and blankets, at which Kikatapula commented sourly that 'some people would break all their things and throw them away'.[27] Although these Palawa from the North-West people continued to avoid contact, they shadowed the mission for about three weeks, all the way to Cape Grim.

Late autumn was upon them and several days of strong wind, heavy rain, and biting cold slowed progress before the weather improved on 30 May. Two more days passed uneventfully as they followed the coastline north. Then, on 1 June, slightly south of Sandy Cape, Kikatapula signalled to Robinson that he saw Palawa.

> Tom said that there was three men and that they had run away upon their hands and knees. Each had a spear. On turning round where I stood [I] saw a black man walking along close to where the knapsacks was left. I called to him KAG.GER, come. He was a fine young man and carried a spear at the back part of his neck, laying hold of it with both his hands. I opened my knapsack in order to get bread &c and while I was thus employed he quitted behind a small sandhill and run away on his hands and knees. I told WOORRADY and Tom not to run after the TOO.GEE as they had frightened them.

Next day Kikatapula, Wurati, and McKay returned from hunting to say they had seen two large huts and a Palawa man who had two spears. But when Robinson went to investigate, the huts had been abandoned.

Once again the expedition was short of provisions; nothing was left except 18 kilograms of flour. They were a long way from the only two possible replenishment sources: about 130 kilometres north of the Macquarie Harbour penal settlement, Robinson estimated, and 80 kilometres south of the Van Diemen's Land Company's pastoral holdings at Cape Grim. So in renewed bad weather the mission turned south-east, away from the coast and into the bush, to hunt. Day after day the weather stayed wet and the cold intense. They saw Palawa tracks and occasional huts but no *Toogee*. Their flour supply dwindled. On 6 June, after having camped near Mt Norfolk, they retraced their route toward the coast at Sandy Cape. Late on 8 June, somewhere coastal between Richardson Point and Sandown Point, Kikatapula had a fearful experience, which an amused Robinson recorded.

> Near to where I stopped for the night one of the natives observed a smoke rising out of a thick forest of tea-tree. Went to where the natives was to listen if they was in conversation. Black Tom proceeded on about a hundred yards and then on a sudden shrunk back and would not go any further, calling out that it was RAEGGEOWRAPPER [the devil or evil spirit]. Tom showed it to me, when I told him it was only a honeysuckle tree, but he would not be persuaded to go on.

Kikatapula salvaged his pride next day. With everyone exhausted and weak from hunger, he killed a kangaroo, the first since their turn inland six days earlier. The fresh meat was a blessing in the bitter cold. Subsequently, Robinson recorded Kikatapula's medicinal use of a kangaroo bone. 'Tom this morning took the leg bone of a kangaroo, heated the marrow and poured it on his belly. He said he had the bellyache and it would cure it.'[28]

Early on 12 June the guides found fresh tracks, but the Palawa who had made them fled at the mission's approach. From the vantage point of a hill Robinson watched their retreat, estimating that there were about 40 of them.

Next day he ascended Mt Cameron West, 'the whole covered with grass and large gum and peppermint trees, an open forest with clear walking. From the top was seen broad extensive plains covered with grass and small grassy hills, and small belts of open forest interspersed throughout'. In 19 backbreaking weeks the mission had traversed some of the most difficult and dangerous terrain in Tasmania, finally arriving at the green and pastoral north-western tip of the island, which the Van Diemen's Land Company, with an initial grant of 101,250 hectares (1012 km²) of Palawa land, had begun in late 1826 to open up for wool production.

The following day the party reached Cape Grim, where they were victualled and accommodated by Joseph Fossey, a VDL Company official.

Fossey told Robinson that although Cape Grim itself was peaceful, Palawa had recently attacked some of the company's employees elsewhere on Woolnorth, as its huge grant was named. During an 11-day stay Robinson again sent news of his progress back to Hobart by sea, and again it was reported in the *Hobart Town Courier*.

> We have great satisfaction at stating that very favourable accounts have been received of the success of the expedition sent by government under Mr. Robinson to conciliate the native tribes. The news has reached us by the way of the Van Diemen's land company's establishment at Circular head. Mr. Robinson, it appears, after making his way from Port Davey to Macquarie harbour ... had arrived within 30 miles [50 km] of Circular head. During this course he had frequent intercourse with several tribes, all of them of the most friendly nature. On one or two occasions he passed several days and nights alone amongst them, finding it prudent to send his companions apart to avoid a little jealousy which some of them appeared to have when several whites were collected together ... [29]

Any good news about the Palawa was welcome in the east, for the war there was being waged with unprecedented ferocity. In the 188 days between Robinson's arrival at Recherche Bay and the day the report was published there were about 100 Palawa raids on colonists, resulting in at least 18 British deaths and numerous woundings.[30]

While at Woolnorth Robinson explored nearby islands in his boat to visit sealers living there. One group had living with them six Palawa women. They included a sister of Robinson's absconded guide Parewareatar and a youth aged about 18 named Tanaminawayt or Piway, a member of the Parperloihener band of Robbins Island. Robinson explained his mission and told the sealers they would have to give up their women, which they refused to do, although they approved Piway's joining the mission.

Shortly before setting off again, Robinson repaid Fossey's hospitality by inviting him to dinner with the mission's two senior guides.

In compliment to Mr Fossey for his kind hospitality during my stay here, I gave him an invitation to dine with me in my tent. On the occasion WOORRADY and KICK.ER.TER.POL.LER was dressed in their red coats with white trousers, and looked remarkable well.[31]

The mission resumed their trek on 25 June, leaving Stansfield to look for Robert who had absconded again. They had now been afield for five months, and seven more were to pass before they returned to Hobart, to be followed by two more missions that Kikatapula would participate in with waxing opposition and waning enthusiasm.

17

'They are desperate people and will spear us'

For the first few days after leaving Fossey Robinson camped by Welcome River collecting Palawa words for his vocabulary and writing in his journal. On 28 June he sent two of his guides, presumably Kikatapula and Wurati – Piway and Robert were now the only other males with the mission – off to hunt. Less than an hour later they returned with four kangaroos.

Taking the Palawa and two other men, on 30 June Robinson crossed to Robbins Island where he persuaded two more Parperloihener – Piway's brother Pintawtawa and a woman called Narrucker – to join the mission. Subsequent visits to the island and to Perkins Island over the next few days failed to locate others.

The mission proceeded on 9 July, arriving at Circular Head on the 12th. Two days later, when the melancholy news reached Robinson of his infant son's death in Hobart months earlier, he was racked with grief. But things brightened when he learnt about the government order of 25 February offering cash bounties for captured Palawa, provoking an instant reaction from him. 'Having been informed of the offering reward for the apprehension of the aborigines, I this day despatched my boat to Robbins Island in quest of the aborigines there.'

He had immediately seen the potential for making greater rewards from what he was already being paid to do. But merely befriending wandering Palawa before allowing them to vanish into the bush would gain him no cash. Chicanery or coercion would need to supplement conciliation. No blacks, no bonuses.

On 24 July the mission left Circular Head, destination *pinmatik* (Rocky Cape). During the next few days Robinson described the difficulties of the topography and mused about the apparent absence of Palawa despite ample evidence of their recent presence. 'The country is very rugged,' he noted on 26 July,

> the mountains covered with scrub and terminating in steep rocky cliffs ...
> [S]aw traces of the natives, where they had had their fires, and where they
> had been eating roots, fresh done. They are therefore not defunct. Am of
> an opinion that there are some inland tribes who never visit the coast ...
> and who are not known to the other tribes. I interrogated the natives
> [about them] but could not learn anything ... Saw a native hut which had
> been recently made ...

Kikatapula is not mentioned in the journal for about four weeks after they farewelled Fossey, and it was to be six months before a testy Robinson again recorded an instance of his guide's blatant recalcitrance. In general, Kikatapula was being a very effective saboteur, feigning sufficient cooperation to escape censure and not attracting attention to his subversion.

On 27 July the mission had just forded Inglis River when Robinson's boat appeared, bringing two more captive Palawa. One was a club-footed runaway from the VDL Co named Nikaminik; the other man, Linermerrinnecer, had been enticed into the boat by the coxswain. After shipping Pintawtawa, Narrucker, and Linermerrinnecer to Emu Bay in the boat, Robinson sent Nikaminik and Piway in search of more Palawa, more cash bounties, but by nightfall neither man had returned. Next morning he dispatched Kikatapula and Wurati to look for them while he proceeded toward Emu Bay. The two guides caught up with him later in the day but claimed they had seen no sign of the missing men, although at an unrecorded time in the next few days Nikaminik and Piway did return, but without new captives.

On 28 July the mission reached Emu Bay, giving Kikatapula his first sight of the tiny British toehold where 21 months later he would breathe his last. From there Robinson, eyes firmly on the prize, arranged for Nikaminik, Pintawtawa, Linermerrinnecer, and Narrucker to be sent in the *Friendship* to Launceston, whence they would be shipped to Hobart so he could claim the bounties on them – £20 in all.

When he left Emu Bay for Hampshire Hills on 6 August he took with

Robinson's sketch of the Friendly Mission trekking through snow in the Black Bluff Range, August 1830. The leader is at far left, and Kikatapula is probably the tall man in the lead facing him. (Courtesy State Library of NSW)

him Kikatapula, Pagerly, Wurati, Trukanini, Robert, and two convict servants, with Piway as guide. Bitter winter weather soon hampered their progress. 'The climate of the Surrey Hills is exceeding cold and wet and I have known but one fine day since leaving Emu Bay', Robinson wrote on 17 August as they travelled beyond Hampshire Hills, where he noted trees festooned with icicles 30 centimetres long. Next day he recorded 'The natives playing at snowballs', and a day later 'It will scarcely be believed that this country for so many miles should be covered with snow. The shepherds say the sheep could overcome snow, but the heavy rain which continues for a fortnight together they cannot endure'. The mission soon faltered in the brutal conditions. Pagerly and Robert complained of being ill on the 22nd, so Robinson sent Kikatapula and Joseph Platt to take them over an easier way to Vale of Belvoir while he and the others took a different route. By the time Kikatapula, Platt, and the two invalids rejoined them on 26 August, Pagerly had improved but Robert was worse.

'Sent McKay and the invalid natives and Tom by the road to Emu Bay', Robinson noted on 2 September. Three days after they arrived Robinson was also at Emu Bay, nursing an injured knee. He was angered when he received news that three of the four Palawa he had shipped to Hobart via Launceston for the bounties had been allowed to return to Circular Head and had subsequently vanished into the bush; only Nikaminik had reached Hobart. Denied £15 of the expected £20, a furious Robinson fulminated at length against the perfidious government, 'those wiseacres at their parlour fireside at Hobart Town'.[1]

By 13 September his knee had improved enough for the mission to set out toward Launceston. Three days later they followed fresh Palawa footprints near Mersey River but lost them next day near Port Sorell. Early on the 18th Robinson sent Kikatapula, Pagerly, and Stansfield back toward Northdown Plain to 'track the natives and to endeavour to find them out, and to return with the boat on Monday'. Kikatapula, he felt, 'would speak their language and probably would know them should he fall in with them'. When they rejoined him on 21 September they brought supplies but no captives. If there were Palawa tracks to be found, Kikatapula had not pointed them out to Stansfield.

On the following day Robinson 'went in the boat up to the head of Port Sorell [Rubicon] River, and proceeded in a southern direction through the forest to Avenue Plains' with Kikatapula, Pagerly, Robert, Trukanini, McKay, and Joseph Maclaine, a Tahitian convict known as Black Joe. The stage was uneventful; light-heartedness prevailed. At night the mission guides 'amused themselves ... in spearing trees', Robinson wrote. The following night 'the natives amused themselves by singing'. A night later the men went out to hunt possums while the females made baskets, 'which is generally their employment when they stop at night'. Life was peaceful and pleasant when you were in the bush and able to avoid betraying your people.

In the settled south and east, however, the Black War raged on, leading a desperate government to plan a massive military operation intended to put a stop to all Palawa hostilities. Robinson first read about it at Westbury on 24 September in proclamations announcing the forthcoming campaign. Dubbed the Black Line, it was an ill-conceived (and expensive) venture in which a vast human chain of field police, soldiers, and armed colonists would traverse the settled districts in a generally south-easterly pincer movement and sweep all remaining members of the hostile Oyster Bay and Big River peoples across East Bay Neck at Dunalley, forcing them onto Tasman and Forestier peninsulas for internment in a reserve there. Involving 2200 men with 30,000 rounds of ammunition and 300 pairs of handcuffs, the Black Line was the greatest military operation ever mounted in Australia against Aboriginal people.

As the Line's participants were setting out for their assembly points in the east and south-east, the mission pressed on in the north. On 1 October they completed the second stage of their remarkable trek, travelling by boat down *kanamaluka* (Tamar River) from George Town to Launceston. But if Robinson expected a hero's welcome in the northern settlement he was disappointed. The imminent Line was the subject of enthusiastic general discussion; all the talk was of shooting Palawa, not conciliating them, and he had some difficulty protecting his people from physical and verbal assault until a humane man named George Whitcomb offered them sanctuary at his home.[2] When Robinson found that Piway and two other Palawa who had absconded from the mission on 22 September were now in Launceston jail, he decided to cement the others' dependence on him by intimidation.

> Told my natives how PEE.VAY was in gaol. They cried then and said the commandant was no good, and seemed much alarmed when I told them the commandant was going to put them in gaol. I told them not to fear, they were safe with me.[3]

But with the prevailing mood of hostility in Launceston and the Black Line due to begin on 7 October, Robinson was unsure about continuing, although he wanted to extend his mission eastward.[4] Lacking orders from the Lieutenant Governor, he consulted the commandant, who was unable to help, so he decided to confer personally with Arthur who was about 70 kilometres away in Campbell Town overseeing preparations for the Line.[5] Robinson rode there on a borrowed horse, then continued on to Ross, a dozen kilometres farther south, after finding Arthur had moved on.

Initially the Lieutenant Governor was eager for Robinson and his party to join the Black Line, but Robinson argued instead in favour of continuing with his mission, pointing out that the prevailing hostility would put his Palawa guides at great risk from trigger-happy colonists and military. Arthur was amenable, agreeing too that Swan Island was where Robinson might temporarily place any captives until the Tasman Peninsula reserve was ready. He wanted Robinson to explore other Bass Strait islands to find a permanent place of exile for all those yet to be rounded up. So from Ross on 6 October Robinson wrote to his wife to tell her he was ordered to proceed immediately to Cape Portland, in the north-east, and then to Tasman Peninsula, nearly 400 kilometres away in the south-east. Two days later he wrote to her again, this time from Launceston, saying Arthur had ordered him to proceed immediately to the east.[6] His first aim was to rescue Palawa sex slaves from the sealers on various Bass Strait islands. They would become wives for his guides, which would boost morale and enhance his prestige with the black men, inclining them to assist him to track and capture other Palawa. He arranged for Piway and the other two prisoners to join the mission, then left Launceston by boat on 9 October.

The mission reached George Town at 2 am next day. In the afternoon, after a convict servant reported being attacked by Palawa at Cimitiere Plains, Robinson and his party followed an armed posse setting out in pursuit and soon found the attackers' footprints, but the mission guides quickly identified them as white men's tracks. 'Tom said plenty white man put charcoal on their faces and robbed people and then said it was the black man that did it', Robinson noted (something verified in his journal on 13 January 1831). The story of the attack proved to be false. The mission moved on.

On 12 October they crossed Piper River and early next morning Robinson took Kikatapula, seven other Palawa, Stansfield, and Black Joe along the coast to Double Sandy Cape. When they discovered next day that Black Joe was missing, Robinson sent Kikatapula to look for him. He soon located the Tahitian, who had been walking in the wrong direction, and guided him back to Robinson.

Near *wukalina* (Mt William) on 18 October they saw several dogs on a tract of burnt ground. Kikatapula and Wurati said they were wild dogs and wanted to catch them, but Robinson was displeased, saying 'it was blacks I wanted, not dogs'. Captured blacks meant cash bonuses; dogs did not. Travelling on, he noted with wonder the abundance of Palawa food sources in the vicinity: crayfish, mussels, oysters, abalone, ducks, pelicans, swans, and an 'immense number of paroquets'. On the coast near Cape Naturaliste he counted more than 100 swans' nests. 'I never saw so many before', he commented. 'My natives swam to the nests and obtained near a hundred eggs. I ate some of them, which were very good'.[7] Next day, 21 October, he and Kikatapula set out alone to search for Palawa sign. He described the country they trekked through as delightful 'with little grassy hills and extensive plains where the young kangaroo grass was shooting up on the burnt ground, forming a beautiful carpet of green pasture, and the plains was studded with a yellow flower … altogether the finest country I have seen … The kangaroo bounded before us in every direction'. Then he had a memorable experience, one that must have been familiar to Kikatapula.

> Whilst I was walking along the coast on some hills [I] descried an immense quantity of mutton birds flying in a NW direction and for a full hour and [a] half they had not passed. The sea was darkened with them and they continued flying along in one continuous stream. I never before witnessed such a sight.

They came across Palawa tracks but no other sign of a reputedly 700-strong mob said to be in the area. When the two weary men returned to camp that evening Robinson estimated their day's walk at not less than 40 kilometres.

For several days afterwards the mission proceeded southward along the coast past Eddystone Point and *larapuna* (Bay of Fires) and King Georges Point. They saw no Palawa although 'All the coast is strewed with shells which have been burnt by the natives', Robinson wrote on 30 October near St Helens Point. 'Some years since [ago] they must have been numerous, but from George Town on the north to Georges River on the east there is no indications except at Cape Portland of natives having been, not the least track, no bush burnt'.

In frustration he turned the mission inland next day, heading north-north-west. As they crossed a tier of hills they saw smoke from Palawa fires in the distance and struck out toward it. But at dusk, after a 20-kilometre hike, they were still some distance away. Everyone was tired, so Robinson decided to halt there until morning, although he went forward with two guides to reconnoitre. They found the bush ablaze for a considerable distance, but those who had fired it were not to be seen.

Chill torrents fell next morning, 1 November, quickly liquefying tracks they were following. In frustration Robinson resumed his north-north-west heading, a decision that proved sound. Soon afterwards, probably in the Anson River valley, they discovered recently debarked trees, beyond which were a native hut and fire. But they had been spotted, and their quarry fled. Robinson urged Kikatapula, Wurati, and Bullrub, a former sealer's woman, forward to look for the fleers, but Wurati ran back in panic when he saw some of them had spears.[8] Kikatapula and Bullrub hesitated, uncertain, but Bullrub called out to those hiding and they answered her. Robinson then went forward to join them. When a man emerged from concealment Kikatapula and Bullrub explained to him why the mission was there, and Robinson gave him a few trinkets. While they parleyed, another man emerged, and eventually a woman and four men (probably including a leading north-eastern warrior named Manalakina) came out to join him, although another man and a woman remained hidden in the bush.[9]

To scare the five newcomers into attaching themselves to the mission Robinson graphically described to them the Black Line and its purpose, exaggerating the details to frighten them. 'I ...informed them', he wrote, 'that the mighty enemy who were at that time engaged in capturing their countrymen to the southward would shortly appear in formidable array in front of their own territory ... I proposed to them to accompany me to Swan Island as a place of security ...'[10] That night he confided to his journal, 'I had told them previously such a story of the soldiers killing the blacks that they would not stop on any account and all said they would accompany me'. He had also told them,

> the sooner we got away the better as the soldiers was coming ... I had the extreme satisfaction to feel that I was on my way to the boat and accompanied by five fresh aborigines ... As we walked along the fresh natives sang a song ... To see fourteen blacks following me a stranger whither they knew not, no guns, no tying of hands, no shooting of men ... afforded me much satisfaction.

Next day the man and the woman who had stayed in the bush came out to join Robinson, who noted they seemed dejected. Toward evening he and some of the mission reached their base camp on the coast just north of Cape Naturaliste; the others straggled in later. Kikatapula told Robinson the woman and two men would not come on but had stopped in the bush and made a fire. 'Tom said he told the man Mr Robinson would be angry if he did not go with him and the man said he knew that, but he might go on and he should come by and by.'

After issuing clothing to the five Palawa next morning Robinson observed that 'Trousers is excellent things and confines their legs so that they cannot run'. Around campfires that evening they told him the names of all the remaining Palawa they said were still at large in the bush – 72 men and three women. Robinson wrote all the names down. Including the three women already with the mission, it meant there were only six women to more than 70 men in the north-east, a graphic illustration of the gender imbalance now terminally afflicting the Palawa. No children were named.

On 4 November Robinson ordered all the Palawa into the boat for passage to Swan Island, about eight kilometres offshore. They were reluctant but he was persuasive. 'It was astonishing to me with what readiness my orders was complied with', he wrote. 'I said come and they came, go and they went.' But Swan Island was not a salubrious place. Less than two kilometres in circumference, it was flat and low and almost devoid of trees. The soil was so poor that little vegetation grew there; consequently, there was little animal life except mutton birds. There was no running water, and when wells were sunk the water found was brackish.[11] Nevertheless, they set up camp and for the next few days Kikatapula remained there with the others while Robinson investigated nine different islands, confronting sealers living there and freeing three more Palawa women. On Preservation Island on 13 November he learnt the much-vaunted Black Line had failed, having captured only two Palawa and killed two others, while an unknown number had broken through the Line, slain two whites, and wounded nine more.[12] No Palawa had been driven into the Tasman Peninsula trap.[13]

Six more came to the coast during Robinson's absence and made smoke signals to those on Swan Island, who signalled back. Concerned that one of the armed parties from the Black Line might arrive and attack the newcomers, Kikatapula, Wurati, Pagerly, Piway, and Tanalipunya (a former sealer's woman) crossed to the mainland early on 15 November to meet them. Although the new arrivals immediately hid, their hiding place was soon discovered, prompting a woman named Luggenemenener to come forward. Captured after John Batman's roving party had attacked and slain many of her band, she had once been at Robinson's Aboriginal asylum in Hobart and consequently knew Kikatapula, who told her they had come across in Robinson's boat while Robinson was on Swan Island. She 'wept for joy', according to Robinson, who returned to Swan Island the same day, 'and immediately called the rest of her mob to come to her'. They were five young men, including one named Tillarbunner (or Jack) who had been with Batman's roving party and spoke English. The six newcomers were taken to join the others on Swan Island. But Luggenemenener brought bad news for Bullrub: her brothers had been shot. 'This information was the occasion of general lamentation and there was not one aborigine but wept bitterly', Robinson wrote. 'My feelings was overcome. I could not suppress them: the involuntary lachryme [sic] burst forth and I sorrowed for them.'

When Luggenemenener tried to convince him there were only five or six Palawa left in the bush, Robinson read out the 75 names on his list, and she had to agree it was correct. He then pensively noted that they were 'all that remained of their tribes, and comprise all the aborigines in a line from the Tamar to the Derwent [that is, much of eastern Tasmania]. There are parts of different nations, some of Prossers Plains, Ben Lomond, Oyster Bay, Piper River, Cape Portland, &c'.

For the next two days the Palawa on Swan Island amused themselves dancing and singing, but on 17 November Robinson observed they all seemed dejected. Inquiries revealed that sealers who were aggrieved at the prospect of losing their sex slaves had been spreading stories that a boat was bringing soldiers from Launceston to shoot all the Palawa or put them in fetters and jail them. Robinson had to rely on his own good reputation to scotch the rumours. 'I appealed to the woman LUG. GE.NE.MENE.NER', he wrote, 'who had stopped a long time at my house in Hobart Town and asked them when it was they heard of my injuring a black man. KICKERTERPOLLER and several others joined me in this appeal'.

In Hobart, news of Robinson's success where the expensive and now-disbanded Black Line had failed was well received. He was praised by a newspaper.

Mr G.A. Robinson has we are happy to say completely succeeded in his attempt under the directions of His Excellency, and in addition to the ten friendly Blacks (if there are any such) whom he had before with him, has captured and removed 13 others of the hostile tribe near George's river, and placed them in security on Swan Island, where he now is with them, in all 23 in number.[14]

For some time Kikatapula was again absent from Robinson's journal, although as a proven hunter he was likely one of the three men who on 18 November were sent with their dogs to mainland Tasmania to look for game. They returned two days later with two wallabies and a kangaroo.

Smoke from the mainland was signalling the return to the coast of more Palawa from Ben Lomond and Penny Royal Creek bands, so on 22 November Robinson proposed that Kikatapula and Pagerly try to persuade them to join the others on Swan Island, but nothing happened. A day later, as the Palawa were away procuring mutton birds and their eggs, Robinson admitted he was finding it difficult to maintain their good spirits, so to keep them occupied he had them move their huts to a new site. Daily he sent them to fetch mutton birds and eggs, sometimes from a smaller island nearby, but they soon tired of the activity. On 23 November they spent the day 'throwing rushes as spears'. Three days later 'all the aborigines tattooed themselves, the shoulder of some and back and belly of others was completely scarified. After the operation is performed they rub in the incision powdered charcoal and red ochre mixed with grease'.[15] Ennui unassuaged, six days after that they spent the daylight hours painting themselves.

Fresh signal smoke began to balloon up from the coast, but when Robinson proposed crossing to investigate, Kikatapula balked. He 'was very much alarmed at going to meet the natives on the main[land]; says that they are desperate people and that they will spear us', Robinson wrote in his journal, apparently satisfied with that.

Nevertheless, on 3 December he took Kikatapula and five other Palawa across to the mainland with him and another man to search for the signallers. They trekked for several days in beautiful weather through an attractive landscape but saw no Palawa, only country they had burnt. On 7 December they spotted two signal smokes about 16 kilometres away, but it was too late in the day to act. Although a night's sleep renewed their optimism, the dawn sky next day was frustratingly smoke-free. After another aimless day's searching the party returned to Swan Island on 9 December. En route, Kikatapula told Robinson 'that when LUG.GE.NE. MENE.NER first saw him she seemed much surprised and wanted to know what made him come to that part of the country: he quaintly replied, "to look after you"'.

The coastal smokes began rising again almost as soon as they waded ashore on Swan Island. This time Robinson sent Stansfield with Kikatapula, Pagerly, Wurati, Trukanini, and Ghoner, a Port Dalrymple/ Ben Lomond woman, back to the coast on 11 December. Ghoner was the oldest woman on Swan Island, one Robinson felt could be trusted. She was to locate those who had signalled; the others were to remain at Little Mussel Roe River until she took the newcomers there. Four days later they all returned to Swan Island with nothing but some kangaroo carcasses to show for their sortie. '[I]t appeared that the smoke I saw was occasioned by the embers of the fire I had left kindling and the wind had wafted it into a blaze', Robinson wrote. Perhaps it was.

Bored with island life, Kikatapula was beginning to cause problems for Robinson. 'Informed that Tom had been cohabiting with Jumbo [Pulara or Rramanaluna, a Little Swanport woman]', Robinson tut-tutted in his journal. 'He is a bad man. There is not a woman but he is endeavouring to cohabit with. I have taken measures to prevent it. These native men on the island are an abandoned set, and with such an example as Tom what may be hoped for?'[16] He rebuked the offender, who festered for four days before offending anew. Robinson:

Today the black men, headed by Black Tom, set the bird rookery on fire at the east end of the island. Sent two men and had it put out. Threatened Tom to put him in gaol, and reprimanded him about his conduct to PAGERLY and his cohabiting with the black women: he promised to conduct himself better in future.

Almost a year had passed since Robinson had last seen his family, and he decided to visit them. On 4 January 1831, taking Kikatapula, Pagerly, Wurati, Trukanini, a Little Swanport woman named Tikati, and Stansfield, he crossed to the mainland and struck out to walk some 300 kilometres to

Hobart. They reached the coast near the southern end of Bay of Fires next day and followed it southward. Robinson was soon suffering blistered feet and a bad cold, and by 8 January all his Palawa companions were snuffling and sneezing. But the air was opiate with summer scents, the light long lasting and golden, the countryside bountiful. Five swans and two ducks fell to their stones at Long Point that day. Kikatapula reminisced about previously having killed a boomer kangaroo there when passing through with a roving party. Approaching Swanport late next day, he told Robinson that two Palawa women were reportedly cohabiting there with Britons, but Robinson took no action. They called at Adam Amos's house 'but he did not come out nor did they enquire my business', Robinson wrote, 'but all the white men surrounded the people, gaping with astonishment'. Although several encounters with armed Britons during their hike reminded them that the Black War was not yet over, Palawa were now a rare sight. Robinson did not report seeing any during their two-week trek, but he would have been on the lookout, bounties in mind.

Two days afterwards they passed Lieutenant Hawkins's farm at Little Swanport. Later that day, as they walked through Silas Gatehouse's sheep run at Grindstone Bay, they saw the graves of Holyoake and Mammoa. Kikatapula told Robinson of the events there, and Robinson recorded them in his journal. Soon afterwards they were chillingly reminded that more than seven years after those killings, hostilities were still far from over. 'Saw two soldiers here', Robinson noted, '[who] said if they had not seen me they should have fired at the natives'.

By the time they reached Spring Bay on 14 January all the Palawa were drooping and feverish and dragging their feet. Robinson let them rest until late afternoon before rousing them to resume their journey. They forded Prosser River next day, crossed Prossers Plains in the direction of Pitt Water, and camped that night about 14 kilometres from Sorell.

The party reached Hobart at 6 pm on 17 January 1831, 10 days short of one year after boarding the *Swallow* to sail to Recherche Bay. Their historic first great trek was complete, but they were not yet done with footslogging. Even though the Black War was in its dying days, the few Palawa remaining at large were not to be allowed to live peacefully. Ethnic cleansing was unfinished; the sundering of Kikatapula's life was not quite complete.

18

'Tucker said he would shoot Black Tom'

The *Hobart Town Courier* of 22 January 1831 devoted considerable space to Robinson's return and the success of his mission, also providing some details of Palawa he had encountered and their culture, as well as descriptions of Swan Island and one or two notable guerrillas he had succeeded in incarcerating there. 'From every calculation that has been made (and even the names of most of them have been collected) there cannot exist at this time in the island more than 350 Blacks', the report concluded. Even that figure may have been optimistic.

While in Hobart Kikatapula and the other Palawa were accommodated in the Aboriginal asylum Robinson had established next to his home in Elizabeth Street. The only glimpses of them during their sojourn are two indirect ones, the first in the *Colonial Times* of 22 February 1831.

> It is quite amusing to see how civilized the blacks are becoming under the superintendence of Mr. Robinson. We see two or three of them are continually parading up and down the streets to show themselves, dressed in long superfine blue coats looking for all the world like gentlemen with no shoes on – the sight, in some persons' opinion, worth £250 per annum, besides odds and ends.

The last remark alluded acerbically to the rewards Robinson received for his efforts: a salary increase to £250 a year backdated to 1829, plus a land grant of 1036 hectares and a gratuity of £100. Some, like the *Colonial Times*, thought them excessive.

The same source also provided the second glimpse, a similar but no less derogatory one, of four Palawa who could only have been Kikatapula,

Wurati, Pagerly, and Trukanini, reporting them as 'two poor miserable blacks that are daily paraded up and down every street in the town, accompanied with their gins and their keeper'.

They too were rewarded for their efforts. Citing 'the unremitting exertions and uncommon fidelity displayed by the aborigines throughout the undertaking', Robinson recommended that Kikatapula and Pagerly be given a boat and clothing, Wurati and Trukanini the same, Piway clothing only. The two couples were jointly awarded one boat, which was let for hire on the Derwent and the income it produced put aside to buy luxuries for them.[1]

They were to spend a little over six weeks in Hobart, during which Kikatapula perhaps saw Hobart friends like Sarah. Although the Hodgsons still owned Lovely Banks, they had been living in town again since early 1827, when Edmund had started the Cascade Tannery on Birch farmland at South Hobart.[2]

In the meantime Robinson was conferring with the Lieutenant Governor, who wanted him to lead another expedition to capture the few Palawa remaining in the settled districts, particularly the troublesome Big River people. Robinson was unenthusiastic. He believed it was so soon after the Black Line that his Palawa guides would be in mortal danger from soldiers and gun-toting settlers, 'extirpationist to a man'. He also told Arthur a Palawa reserve anywhere in mainland Tasmania would be porous and probably unsafe for those confined there. A Bass Strait island, on the other hand, would be an ideal sanctuary and an inescapable place of confinement – a prison walled by the sea. Robinson proposed Gun Carriage (now Vansittart) Island, believing its supply of fresh water, abundance of mutton birds and shellfish, and good anchorage made it ideal for a permanent establishment where Palawa could be civilised. Existing sealers' huts would be available for their immediate occupation and it was close to *truwana* (Cape Barren Island) with its plentiful game. Equally important, it was about 30 kilometres from the Tasmanian mainland – far enough to make escape impossible but close enough to facilitate shipping supplies there. Arthur agreed and gave Robinson authority to eject all the sealers from the island and rescue their captive women, also appointing him Superintendent of Aborigines at the new establishment. Once it was operating satisfactorily Robinson would undertake Arthur's desired mission to the Big River people.

So on 3 March 1831 all the Palawa, including those from Robinson's Hobart asylum, with a few others and some Britons who were to staff the establishment, including a surgeon, a carpenter, and a small detachment of soldiers, boarded the government cutter *Charlotte*. The Palawa were Kikatapula, Pagerly, Wurati, and Trukanini; Tikati (who was unwell) and a woman named Lotabrah; a girl recorded only as Mary; Cowertenninner (Jack or Jack Woodburn); Wurati's sons Myyungge (David) and Droyyerloinne (Peter); Trometehennea and Pieyenkomeyenner, two women from the hospital; and five males released from jail including Ronekeennarener and Tremeboneener, the Black Line's only captives. A third released from jail was a Big River man named Weltepellemeener. Among the Britons to staff the new establishment was Henry Laing, a young convict architect who was to act as draftsman and secretary. But when the *Charlotte* sailed that afternoon it left behind a dumbstruck Robinson, who had not been informed of its departure. Irked, he crossed next day in his own boat to Kangaroo Point, struck out on foot, and caught up with the cutter at Spring Bay on 10 March.

The *Charlotte* then sailed for Maria Island, Robinson recording that the conduct of the Palawa aboard was 'highly praiseworthy'. Next day Tikati died. Already in a 'depressed state of mind and no inclination for food or nourishment', she deteriorated physically after the Palawa were forced to sleep unprotected on deck in bad weather.[3] Her body was taken ashore at Maria Island for burial.

> [A]t four pm, the corpse being enclosed in the coffin and placed on a bullock cart, the funeral proceeded on its way to the place of interment, accompanied by the commandant, the surgeon and the settlement guard, myself and son, Mr Clucas, and Black Tom and COWETINNER [Cowertenninner], two aborigines who knew this female and who requested to see the body interred, also many prisoners. A suitable grave was dug and the body interred (no remarks was offered on this occasion), after which the party retired.

He considered her death a severe loss to the mission, noting that she was 'tall and well made, about six feet [183 cm] in height' and 'remarkable good tempered'.

The *Charlotte* put to sea again the following day, and on 14 March anchored off Swan Island to disembark the Palawa. After two days they were re-embarked and removed to Preservation Island, where a temporary camp was set up for them near Horseshoe Bay. On the 18th they were moved again, this time to Gun Carriage Island, site of the proposed permanent establishment. Some, notably Kikatapula, were not impressed with it. 'The natives appeared to be contented with the change [of location] with the exception of Black Tom and two or three of the others who came from Hobarton who expressed their wish to return or go on the main land', Henry Laing noted in his journal. 'From these wishes I took much pain to dissuade them, assuring them that Mr. Robinson would do everything to make them comfortable. They generally employed themselves in wandering about the island and in gathering an immense quantity of birds.'[4] Despite Kikatapula's initial dissatisfaction, when Robinson showed him and Pagerly, Wurati and Trukanini, and Manalakina and Tanalipunya their huts and gardens they all appeared very pleased. But their contentment was short-lived.

Before long Robinson had 60 Palawa under his care on the tiny island, a bleak outpost only eight square kilometres in area. Both the water supply and the accommodation proved inadequate. Two Palawa, including Cowertenninner, soon died, 15 more were sickly, and other problems were mounting.[5] Some Britons attached to the establishment were disruptive and unresponsive to Robinson's authority, and Kikatapula, Wurati, Manalakina, and their wives refused to work their gardens or sleep in their huts, saying that 'if they slept outside the devil would cure them'. Robinson was much occupied coping with such problems, as well as investigating other islands and dealing with recalcitrant sealers. Moreover, Kikatapula and Wurati and their wives, who had not forgotten the reward due to them and were put off by neither Robinson's comings and goings nor his workload, frequently pestered him about their promised boat. In an effort to placate them Robinson wrote to Rev. William Bedford in Hobart on 1 June, asking him to ascertain how much rent the boat had produced on their behalf. (Its hire eventually earned £18 before it was lost a few days after Kikatapula's death.)[6]

Barely treading water in a rising sea of squabbles, administrative problems, and sick and dying Palawa, Robinson decided to leave it all to others while he set in train a mission to capture Umarrah, who was attacking settlers in Tamar Valley, after which he would find and bring in the hostile Oyster Bay–Big River people. On 20 June, at his base camp on mainland Tasmania opposite Swan Island, he wrote that he 'purposed taking my departure into the interior'. He would take Kikatapula and Pagerly, Wurati and Trukannini, Tanganuturra (Tibb), Robert, and Richard, as well as his son, Stansfield, Platt, Maclaine, and Mason, with two horses and a dog. Although he did not record it, he also took Malapuwinarana, known to whites as Tim or Timmy.

Led by Kikatapula, whom Robinson called his 'knowing friend', the party set off on 20 June 1831 for Boobyalla (now Ringarooma) River. They trekked for several windy and frequently rainy days through country usually much frequented by Palawa without encountering any or seeing any recent sign of them. On 24 June Robinson recorded a curious incident that had struck him forcefully. 'An aborigine who had been domesticated, asked me one night whilst gazing at the stormy firmament if I knew the planets Mars and Jupiter, and said that if the sky had not been so obscured he would point it [sic] out to me.' Whichever guide it was had obviously been educated to a degree beyond mere literacy, but Robinson regrettably did not name the man.

They trekked on through extreme cold, Robinson noting on 29 June that Mt Cameron East was covered in snow. As they were crossing Accession River two days later a dog's barking nearby suggested Palawa were tracking them, but the dog fled when Kikatapula and others went to investigate. They continued on through the bitter conditions, already short of rations. However, in yet another demonstration of his hunting skills Kikatapula was able to alleviate the dearth two days later by killing a boomer kangaroo.

On 6 July Robinson noted that the country they travelled through, north-east of Ben Lomond, 'was formerly occupied by the PY.EM.MAIR. RE.NER.PAIR.RE.NER [band of the North-East people], who were a fierce people ... They are now extinct. The country had formerly been burnt, and many trees were notched where the native women had ascended in quest of opossums. Tom related some exploits of his nation in their wars with these people'.

Crossing a plain the following day they discovered a Palawa *markenner* leading directly to the east bank of Tamar River. When they saw signs of recent use, Kikatapula's response was immediate and subversive. 'Tom on arriving at this spot set off without acquainting me with his intention with the two dogs to hunt, and whilst I was examining the country I heard the dogs yelping and saw them killing a boomer kangaroo, which were plentiful in this place', an angry Robinson noted in his journal.

> By this injudicious proceeding the whole country was thrown into alarm. Not content with this, he proceeded still further hunting; after waiting some considerable time I proceeded, when I met him and Tim returning with two kangaroos. As night was approaching I halted and though I was much displeased at his conduct, yet our scanty supply required recruiting and the dogs was in a starving state.

Next day Robinson was still riled. He grew even angrier when, soon after starting out, the guides discovered a new hut, proof Palawa had indeed been nearby. Even when Kikatapula further victualled the mission by catching a wombat, Robinson was not mollified. 'Here I would remark that the greatest forbearance is required with these natives when in the bush, for they feel more independent and shew a disposition to be very idle', he grumbled.[7] But what he saw as independence and idleness were in fact manifestations of their reluctance to cooperate with the mission – to passively subvert it instead. Having now experienced durance on a bleak island with little to occupy them, they were unwilling to betray others for a similar fate in perpetuity. Robinson never fully understood that, although his irritation with Kikatapula did not affect his faith in him as the mission's most dependable providore. 'Left Tom to hunt', he noted on 11 July, 'and proceeded with part of the natives'.

They pushed on through short days of crisp winter sunlight and chill rains and huddled close to their campfires through long frigid nights. Sometimes they saw Palawa signs – on 12 July 'in a particular spot many stones where the natives had had their fires and had been making spears' – but those who left such traces remained unseen. On 15 July the party climbed Mt Pedder, which took three hours.

> Descended into a deep ravine whose sides was so steep it required the utmost caution. The fern trees and rocks and immense forest around

us, the party winding down the steep and the light glimmering through rendered the object an interesting one for the painter. Ascending, we crawled over slippery logs which interrupted our road and whose mucid surfaces caused our feet to turn aside from us so that we was frequently thrown down.

As they warmed themselves at their fires on 15 July after completing another chill day's trekking, Wurati regaled them with stories of his martial exploits. When he went on to expound on Nununi creation beliefs, Kikatapula scoffed – perhaps as Christian convert, perhaps as quasi-Briton – saying 'he would not believe it, he only believed the white people's story'. That angered Trukanini, a Nununi. 'Where did you come from?' she spat back. 'White woman?'

Next morning they proceeded with frost cracking underfoot. The cold was so severe that Robinson complained of being unable to keep himself warm as they laboured over low hills dense with hop-pole and green forest and then more easily through less taxing light bushland. Provisions almost exhausted, they subsisted on wombat meat until they reached open grassland where kangaroos were plentiful. Freshly burnt country was frequently encountered, although those who had fired it were not, causing Robinson to observe that 'it is evident that only a small remnant of this once formidable race of aborigines remains'. Even his guides remarked the lack, if disingenuously. 'My sable companions frequently asked me what had become of the natives, as they had not discovered any trace of them. They supposed that they had been shot by the soldiers.'[8] Their reluctance to betray any more of their race can only have been strengthened by the silent spaces devoid of the ancient bands.

The mission's difficulties and frustrations continued.

20 July 1831: Crossed a large swamp up to our knees in water and continued my route along the north bank of this river [Forester River]; had purposed crossing to the south side, where I thought I should be most likely to succeed in meeting with the natives, but found after several attempts that it could not be effected as the river runs through a swampy tea-tree forest of several miles extent and some parts of it so close as could not be got through. The water was middle deep and full of old timber ...

Then Robinson's luck seemed to change. First the mission found empty swans' nests and newly broken eggshells, evidence that Palawa had recently been there. Later the same day Wurati found fresh tracks of six Palawa and their dogs, which they followed until dark and then eagerly took up again at first light, but stony ground stymied further progress. Kikatapula and the other guides could follow the trail no farther, they said.

Subsequent days brought similar results.

22 July 1831: Tom and WOORRADY out in quest of the native track, and the native women out hunting for opossum. The men returned unable to find the traces of the natives ...

23 July 1831: Sent Tom and WOORRADY to look out for traces of the natives.

24 July 1831: [T]he aborigines went in quest of opossums and to endeavour to discover traces of the natives ...

25 July 1831: WOORRADY having informed me that he had the previous evening discovered some tracks which he judged to be those of natives, I sent him and the other natives and Stansfield to endeavour to find them ... The natives returned unable to discover anything of the tracks of the aborigines.

Soon after noon on the 26th the mission trudged back to their coastal base camp opposite Swan Island. Thirty-six days of arduous travel and icy privation had taken them around a large area of north-eastern Tasmania from Piper River to Little Mussel Roe River without any sight of their quarry. Two days later a boatload of supplies from Swan Island reached them, and Robinson sent the guides to Big Mussel Roe to ascertain whether their elusive quarry had been there to gather swans' eggs. In the afternoon Kikatapula, Pagerly, Wurati, and Trukanini returned laden with fresh kangaroo meat, as well as swans' eggs gathered as a gift for Robinson, but the only tracks they reported were those of sealers' women who had also been there to collect eggs.

Hobart newspapers at this time made no mention of Robinson's renewed mission, but the *Launceston Advertiser* showed some interest because of recent Palawa attacks in Tamar Valley.

THE NATIVES – We learn this morning that Mr. Robinson's parties have been in close pursuit of the Natives in the vicinity of Piper's River, for the last ten days, but without being enabled to effect any intercourse with them. The George Town messenger, coming into town, was chased by the Natives on the road, but fortunately escaped unhurt. It appears that the Aborigines have been lurking about the farms down the Tamar, for the last several days.[9]

Robinson now resolved to abandon the Swan Island supply base and move it to George Town. He also sent to Gun Carriage Island for Manalakina, a respected local chief, and his wife Tanalipunya, expecting their knowledge of the north-east to provide crucial local expertise not being displayed by his guides who, instead of locating Palawa sign, passed their days hunting kangaroos. The familiar aroma of sizzling kangaroo meat on frosty night air helped mask the memory of captivity and despondency.

Manalakina arrived on 5 August without his wife but with Piway, and Robinson recorded his pleasure at seeing them both. A famous warrior, Manalakina now supplanted Kikatapula as Robinson's trusted aide, confidant, and lead guide. 'I proceeded on my journey', Robinson wrote,

led on by the chief [Manalakina] whom I had appointed as guide ... fully sensible that he was the only person amongst my sable adherents who knew where to find the natives. He had wandered over this extent of country for a long succession of years and his influence amongst his people was great. He was universally admired by all the native tribes who knew him ...[10]

Kikatapula, who also knew Manalakina and had sometimes been his ally fighting the Lairmairrener, deferred to him, partly because of his superior knowledge of the north-east, partly because Manalakina, who was about 55 at this time, was older and more senior. Ceding his place to Manalakina would also conveniently absolve Kikatapula of responsibility for further betrayals.[11] 'This morning I developed my plans to the chief MANNALARGENNA [Manalakina] and explained to him the benevolent views of the government toward himself and his people', Robinson wrote next day. 'He cordially acquiesced and expressed his entire approbation of the salutary measure, and promised his utmost aid and assistance.'

Manalakina briefly supplanted Kikatapula as Robinson's chief guide.
Portrait by Thomas Bock. (Courtesy British Museum)

Robinson then revealed not only his desperation but his willingness
to employ deceit. In Kikatapula's presence he told Manalakina he was
authorised to inform them they would be allowed to remain in their
own country and would be given flour, tea, sugar, and clothes if they
stopped attacking settlers – a heartless piece of duplicity (although in
June a letter from the Lieutenant Governor had suggested such a last-
ditch sweetener might be allowed for Palawa who jibbed at forced
offshore exile). In suggesting to Kikatapula and Manalakina that it was
a real possibility Robinson knew word of it would trickle down to other
Palawa, both captive and yet to be caught. Manalakina was said to be
delighted. To Kikatapula, having already endured the realities of island
incarceration, it perhaps seemed a beacon of hope, especially as he had
just learnt his life was in danger from sealers and from his own people.
Sealers visiting Gun Carriage Island were telling captive Palawa that their
internment was Kikatapula's fault because it was he who led Robinson to
those hiding in the bush. They themselves hated him because it was his
guiding Robinson to their camps that was costing them their sex slaves.

One, Thomas Tucker, was threatening to 'shoot Black Tom when he had an opportunity'.[12]

On 10 August Robinson left Swan Island for the mainland to resume his hunt for Umarrah's Stoney Creek band. He took his son George, Kikatapula, 10 other Palawa (including Tanalipunya, who had finally arrived from Gun Carriage Island), one white man, and the Tahitian Black Joe. Manalakina, who claimed to be in touch with spirits that would tell him which way to go, would be their guide. Robinson ordered the other Palawa to carry Manalakina's blanket and rug and noted that he 'seemed gratified at the attention paid him'. Kikatapula too deferred to him. 'Tonight [was] in conversation with Tom', Robinson wrote, 'who said the chief [Manalakina] knew where to find the natives; that [the spirits of] the two men who died at Gun Carriage was in him, and came away with him and walked about with him. Said that the chief can find the natives ... I did not ridicule what Tom said but listened with attention'.[13]

But this general kowtowing to Manalakina nettled Kikatapula, making him openly obstructive. Robinson's journal for the following day recorded a delaying tactic.

> Ere I set off my old friend KICKERTERPOLLER took the opportunity of telling me that the native tribe we were in quest of was a savage people and that they would kill LACKLAY [Prupilathina] the [Port Sorell] boy who accompanied us, that all the eastern natives had warred with his [Prupilathina's] people, that they had killed his [Prupilathina's] father and would kill him, that they would steal secretly toward him [Prupilathina] and then spear him.

Yet a day later Kikatapula the Christian was endorsing Robinson's Sunday proselytising to Manalakina, perhaps endeavouring to establish a quasi-British superiority over the man who had supplanted him. 'I ... told him [Manalakina] of man's creation', Robinson wrote, 'and that white man tell plenty and make books tell plenty, for all men to believe', to which Kikatapula added, 'if they believe not, they will go to the devil'. You sense again the sundering of his identity – black man's protector one day, white man's ally the next.

Trouble erupted that day while they were camped on Brougham River east of Mt Cameron. Most of the Palawa men were expecting the sealers' women freed from Gun Carriage Island to be given to them as wives. But when Stansfield appeared without the women, the men became angry. They had been promised wives. Where were they? Why had they not come? They must have been given back to the sealers. Manalakina agreed, fuelling their ire by saying it had been deceitful to promise them the sealers' women. Robinson sought to appease. He was not to blame, he said; the sealers were. They had deceived the Lieutenant Governor by telling him the women had begged to return to the sealers. That outraged Manalakina. 'No, no, no, they be bad men and by and by me tell the Governor,' he responded. To which Kikatapula added 'Yes, when we have done we will let the Governor know all about it'. Both had their wives with them, so neither was personally deprived. But they assured Robinson he would need the sealers' women if he expected to find the Big River people. Although they were originally from Oyster Bay bands, the women had most recently been with the Big River people and so would know where to look for them.

A day later Kikatapula's compass swung again. Despite their surroundings having been saturated by overnight rain, he managed to ignite some vegetation. The fire quickly spread, a widely visible signal of the mission's presence. 'The chief, Tom and two others had gone up the river to endeavour to effect a crossing', Robinson wrote, 'but this they found they were unable to do. As they had carried torches and in their way back had carelessly dropped some fire, in a short time the fire spread with rapidity. I felt angry with Tom, whom I blamed. Sent orders for them to go and put it out, which they with difficulty effected ...' Then, as if that were not enough, 'Tom again would not swim across and endeavoured to create a temporary disturbance by threatening to go to the Mistake [Little Mussel Roe River]; however, him and Richard afterwards swum over and everything was peaceable'.

Next day, 16 August, Robinson's interest in Palawa beliefs about the creation of man, which was often the subject of campfire talk, moved him to raise the subject again. Kikatapula took an active part in the discussion, although sounding a note of uncertainty that again points to a man uneasily straddling two cultures. 'He said he believed what the white people said', Robinson noted, but

When I spoke of heaven and how the good spirits live without food, Tom said how could they live without eating; and I explained. They said the devil live in the fire – some said on the big hill …Tom said the black people have a devil of their own, and the white people their own devil; and I told him there was only one devil. He said he did not know; he never saw him, he only heard him whistle, that was all.

Wet and windy weather was alternating with fine. The party tramped across winter plains and picked their way through open forest and forced arduous passage through dense bush. They found some Palawa sign, but none of it was fresh. With difficulty they crossed a tea-tree swamp and then Great Forester River on 20 August. To the north they could see Bass Strait and 'a large and stately vessel with her lofty canvas, gliding along the watery element', but 'No indications presented themselves to guide us to the long neglected and wandering aborigines'. They were preparing to camp for the night when Piway, reconnoitring from an adjacent hill, signalled that he could see smoke. After going up to see for themselves, Kikatapula and Manalakina assured Robinson that it was a considerable distance away, too far to travel in the fast-falling winter darkness. Next morning would have to do, Robinson decided, and continued with his camping preparations. Later Kikatapula presented him with four swan eggs.

Rain drenched the camp all that night and the following forenoon, when Robinson sent Kikatapula, Manalakina, and some others to search for the source of the smoke. They returned that afternoon without result. But there were unexpected developments later in the day when he allowed the guides to hunt. A short distance from their camp they found fresh tracks and a fire's traces, indicating that Palawa had been spying on them from nearby, although they had vanished at the guides' approach. While Kikatapula, Manalakina, and some others followed their trail, Piway ran back to inform Robinson, urging him to come quickly: 'The black fellow run away, the black fellow run away, make haste, gone this way.' Robinson was astounded, thinking Piway meant Manalakina. Incredulous, he asked if the old chief had really absconded. 'No, no, black fellow PANER,' Piway said. Now Robinson understood. He and Piway sprinted toward the spot, only to meet Kikatapula in full retreat because, he said, he was afraid the blacks would spear him. Perhaps it was another attempt at avoiding having to betray any more of his people, or perhaps he believed he was in danger from Palawa who resented his collaboration. 'I reprehended him', Robinson wrote, 'and said he ought to be ashamed of such conduct after what the government had done for him, and that I myself would go, that I was by no means afraid, but that I was sure my white face would alarm them. After this lecture he went reluctantly after them'. But when he returned that evening he was alone, once more incurring Robinson's wrath. Why had he not followed the strangers as Manalakina had? Kikatapula shrugged. He had been to their camp, their huts were huge, there were many tracks of men and women. A suggestion of superior numbers. Plainly a threat.

When Manalakina returned to camp after dark Robinson told him he wanted him, Kikatapula, and three of the women to follow the tracks next morning until they located the strange Palawa. They were not to come back until successful. 'Tom seemed dejected at this arrangement, fearful they should spear him', Robinson fumed.

> He is exceedingly timorous. I told him he should not act cowardly ... Little good can be expected from Tom. The chief ... told us that he had dreamed the previous night that the natives had come upon us and had speared us, at which Tom said, 'Ah, there, sir, there, a pretty set of black people you have got not to look out, we might have been speared' – and which might have been the case for all he did.

At daybreak on 22 August Robinson ordered the two men and the three women to follow the trail until they located those who made it. Again Kikatapula dragged his heels. To do that they would have to walk all the way to Launceston, he complained, for that was the direction their quarry had taken. Robinson, testy, pondered. Kikatapula was intent on being uncooperative. Very well. He ordered the five of them to stay out for one night and if by that time they had not located the fleeing Palawa, Kikatapula and two of the women could return while Manalakina and the other woman, Plorenernoopperner ('Jock'), kept searching. The recalcitrant yielded and the five departed.

Nobody came back that day. Nor, after the stipulated one night, did Kikatapula and the two women return, which caused great concern among the guides. Robinson too was worried. 'The general opinion of those aborigines with me,' he recorded on the 24th,

> is that Black Tom is speared by the native tribe ... and what appeared to confirm them in this opinion was the shadow of the earth on the face of the moon, that luminary not having yet arrived at the full. This they said was Black Tom: that the natives had killed him and that he had gone up into the moon ... It is strange certainly that Tom and two of the women have not returned. I told Tom he was to stop out only one night, and that the chief and Jock ... could come back after ... In the course of conversation with the woman remaining I found her of the same opinion as WOORRADDY, i.e. that Tom was killed.

The camp that night was subdued. Another sombre day followed, made even gloomier by the wind-whipped rain that flayed the countryside. 'The chief and Tom and the three women [have] not returned', a concerned Robinson wrote.[14]

By morning the weather had cleared but there was still no sign of the missing guides. Reluctant to move without them, Robinson was filling in time by writing in his journal when all five suddenly appeared out of the bush but without new captives. The rest of the mission gathered around to hear their story. They had followed their quarry for a long way toward Launceston, they explained, but had lost the trail and returned to tell Robinson of their failure. His relief at seeing them was greater than his disappointment that they had been unsuccessful. '[I]t is now five days since they left me', he wrote, 'and they could have absconded if they thought fit to do so, but the circumstance proves that they are faithful and can be trusted'. It does not seem to have occurred to Robinson that Kikatapula might have had another motive for remaining five days in the bush with three women, although he already knew of Kikatapula's unbridled concupiscence and would very soon be reminded of it again.

For the next 48 hours Kikatapula's only task was to hunt, at which he was successful on the second day. Later that afternoon Manalakina 'shook himself as usual', Robinson observed, 'which the natives said was the devil telling him where the natives was'. After this ritual 'heaving of the breast and trembling', he divined that the Palawa they were seeking had returned to the hills near where they had first been discovered. Robinson asked Kikatapula his opinion. Did he think Manalakina truly meant to lead them to their quarry or was he being deceitful? Kikatapula assured him that Manalakina really did want to find them and said his devil told him they were in that direction. So Manalakina led the mission westward to a point on the west side of Piper River, which caused Robinson some concern. He told Kikatapula he was surprised Manalakina had taken them there since it was 'dragging the people off their legs to no purpose'. Kikatapula replied that he did not know, but Manalakina's devil had told him to go there. As they stood on a sandy beach debating their next move, some of the guides noticed smoke wafting up from inland – Palawa smoke, Manalakina declared. A delighted Robinson decided to camp at some nearby lagoons while Kikatapula, Manalakina, and three women set out to locate the source of the smoke and bring in 'by every possible means' those whose fire it was.

As he awaited results next day Robinson's noontime writing was interrupted by the return to camp of two guides who had been out hunting. They brought four kangaroo carcasses and news that was even more welcome: 'the natives was coming'. Plenty of smoke was heading this way, they reported, which the natives were making to signal their approach. 'God grant it may be so!' Robinson wrote. With growing excitement he watched the progress of the smoke through the bush toward them.

> Shortly we heard voices and a cooee. I desired a native to answer. Another cooee was heard in answer. In a short time heard much talking; the natives was then crossing the river and coming through a tea-tree swamp. I saw them leaving the copse and coming on toward me. They were all loaded and walked in single file. They had fourteen dogs. I saw six men and one woman. It gladdened my heart; it was a blessed sight.

Kikatapula, Manalakina, and Plorenernoopperner were heading the procession. The newcomers were led by Umarrah, whose most recent of several flights from British service had been while a guide with the Black Line almost a year earlier. After Robinson gave them gifts of beads, buttons, and blankets, Umarrah's people consorted amiably with the Palawa guides. They spent the evening dancing and singing together. 'I took part in the hilarity', Robinson noted contentedly.

But the conviviality was ruptured next morning when armed sealers suddenly burst into the camp, intending to abduct Plorenernoopperner, who had been a sealer's woman. Tensions rose as they abused Robinson. A fight seemed inevitable; the Palawa prepared to flee. But although the sealers eventually departed without the woman, Palawa nerves were taut. Umarrah's men and the mission guides began to bicker. Kikatapula and Manalakina told Robinson that Umarrah's people were a savage lot who would kill both whites and blacks, Robinson wrote in his journal for 30 August. 'This tribe is called by the white people the Stoney Creek tribe, and are supposed to have perpetrated some of the most daring and cruel outrages that could be conceived.' He blamed them for recent killings along the Tamar and noted that Manalakina's past victories over them were the cause of the friction. Moreover, Manalakina had once speared Umarrah. When Robinson questioned Kikatapula about the rift, he asserted that the mission guides were not to blame; Umarrah's mob were at fault. He did not trust them and said 'it would be too late when we were killed'. Manalakina did not trust them either. Having armed himself with a spear since their advent, he told Kikatapula he wished Robinson would let him spear them. For further security he promised Robinson that he and Kikatapula would keep watch all night in case Umarrah's men tried to knock their brains out while they were sleeping. He was true to his word, but Kikatapula dozed off.

On 31 August the mission, with its added Palawa, set out for Forester River and Waterhouse Point. Travelling eased the tensions between the two groups, so the night of 1 September 'was spent in dancing and singing, and this hilarity was kept up to a late hour and much glee and satisfaction evinced'. Then a familiar problem arose. 'An instance of much depravity was evinced by Tom, who came to me and asked me to let him put away his wife PAGERLY and get another woman, and backed his proposition with a cash incentive, saying that when he got his money [from the hire of the boat] he would give it to me and that he only wanted a little tea and sugar.' Kikatapula had worked for wages and knew money's allure for white men. 'I was inwardly incensed at this conduct of Tom', Robinson continued,

> and although I could not give vent to my feelings, I gave him to know that I
> was exceeding angry at his conduct and that he should never more speak

to me on such a business. I had all along known the base conduct of this man and that one nor twenty women would suffice him ... The TYRE.LORE [sealer's woman] ... told me that Tom slept with several women and had not slept with PAGERLY for a long time, nor had given her anything to eat.

Some weeks later one of the women told Stansfield, who told Robinson, that Kikatapula had tried to persuade other Palawa to kill Wurati so he could have Trukanini.[15]

More friction followed next morning. Ningernooputener, one of Umarrah's men, parted from the mission with two dogs and a torch, saying he was going to his own country to meet his brother. An incredulous Kikatapula asked Robinson if he meant to let him go. 'Yes, certainly, if he can do better for himself', Robinson replied. He sent Kikatapula after him to tell him to come back and have breakfast, after which he could leave if he wanted to. Kikatapula soon returned with Ningernooputener, whom he had shamed into staying with the mission. Robinson's apparent indifference caused considerable talk among the guides because the threat of returning to island exile was unappealingly ever-present in their minds. Later in the day Umarrah presented Robinson with a kangaroo tail, the first of several such gifts over the next few days. 'Is this for Joe [Maclaine]?' Robinson asked, to which Kikatapula responded, 'No, for you ... we take care of you.' Robinson understood this and other offerings as bribes and knew why he was getting them. When both Umarrah and Manalakina endowed him with similar largesse a day later, he observed, 'These shew the gratitude of these people. The people don't want to go to the islands ...'

News of Umarrah's capitulation was soon announced in a Launceston newspaper.

Mr. G.A. ROBINSON, with LEMENA BINGNA [Manalakina] ... who has been for some time in pursuit of the natives on the eastern coast, and has been following in their track backwards and forwards from the bight of Ben Lomond for about 400 miles [640 km], at last ... had the good fortune to come up with and capture, between Forrester's River and the Little Piper, the fugitive Yumarrha, the Chief of the Stoney Creek tribe, with 5 other men, 1 woman, and 16 dogs ... It appears that there are now but three natives belonging to the Stoney Creek mob, in the bush, to whom Yumarrha promises to lead Mr. R.'s party.[16]

Umarrah's people were reluctant to go to either Launceston or George Town with Robinson because they feared the consequences of having attacked and killed settlers in Tamar Valley between March and May that year. After hearing the guides' tales of the unappealing Gun Carriage Island, the Stoney Creek people made plain to Robinson that they did not want to go there either. 'Nothing therefore remained but for me to go to Hobart Town', he sighed in his journal on 6 September. So they headed southward.

But the strife continued. Manalakina had a score to settle with his old enemy Umarrah and one of his warriors, so with Kikatapula's connivance he was stirring trouble among the Stoney Creek people as they crossed Tomahawk River and camped together by Montagu River. When Robinson was ready to set off on the day's walking on 8 September he found Umarrah's mob were not. Three of them headed in the opposite direction until Kikatapula and Manalakina went after them and brought them back. Why do you want to leave? Robinson asked them. Because Kikatapula and Manalakina were constantly antagonising them, they replied. Worse, the two guides had spread the word that Umarrah's people would be tied up when they reached Swan Island. A former sealer's woman with the party also blamed Kikatapula and Manalakina for persistently goading the Stoney Creek mob, adding that the two of them kept all the women for themselves. 'From what I subsequently learnt from another woman', Robinson wrote, 'I was fully convinced that Tom was at the bottom of all these proceedings … I made known to Tom the opinion I entertained of him and said he of all men ought to have been the last to have so conducted himself'. Unable to allay the newcomers' fears, Robinson again resorted to mendacity. They would not go near Swan Island, he told them, but turn inland toward Georges River – that is, southward rather than westward toward Launceston, so in the opposite direction from Swan Island. The lie seemed to mollify them; the party proceeded. But trouble travelled with them. 'Tom and the chief continually quarrelling with the people, are great impediments', Robinson fumed next day.

Kikatapula continued to be nettlesome. When Robinson camped that night (9 September) Umarrah's mob, with Kikatapula and some other guides, remained on the other side of the river, saying they could not cross and would rejoin the mission next morning, which they did. When the mission camped the following night on Tomahawk River, Robinson learnt that Kikatapula had helped himself to sugar, tea, and flour and distributed it to the others while they were isolated. Whether he thought he was acting *in loco princeps* for Robinson or was victualling them so they would be encouraged to abscond is unclear; in the light of later events the latter seems more likely. Although Kikatapula tried to excuse his behaviour by telling Robinson he and Tanalipunya had kept watch on the new arrivals all night, Robinson responded by saying, 'I told Tom and the chief not to hinder them if they wanted to go away, that we could easy find them again, and if they did not keep quiet I would get plenty of natives and go after them, and that I was going to their country. I was told that the natives was afraid of the chief and Tom ...'

When four of the newcomers, three men and a woman, took him at his word and absconded, a seething Robinson blamed Kikatapula.

> Notwithstanding they had been fourteen days with me, yet I was sure they would have remained yet longer if proper pains had been taken by Tom and my natives to render them contented; but Tom neither called them back nor told me they were going, but came and sat by the fire quite unconcerned. He is a bad man and a depraved disposition, and would sacrifice my interest to his base purposes and drive the people away so that he might cohabit with the women. I reprehended him severely.

Yet lust was hardly the sole cause of Kikatapula's behaviour. His casual attitude to retaining Umarrah's people reflected Robinson's own, evinced by his willingness on 3 September to let Ningernooputener depart. Moreover, the continuing tension between the newcomers and the guides was more serious than Robinson realised – so serious that it might eventually have proved lethal. When Robinson's coxswain later recaptured three of the four absconders, they told him they had left Robinson because Manalakina 'had killed three of their tribe, and that they had now come down to be revenged upon him as well as "Black Tom" and another youth named "Jemmy" [Prupilathina]'.[17] By then, however,

Kikatapula and the other two were far distant, somewhere in the vicinity of Lake Echo.

Nevertheless Robinson continued to blame Kikatapula, who was subtly encouraging them to escape.

> 11 September 1831: Am, the three men and one woman [of Umarrah's mob] who went away yesterday evening not [having] returned, I reprehended Tom for his gross neglect, whom had he gone after or stopped with until the ebb tide would have stayed with the other natives. Besides, Tom instead of encouraging the people, has all along done everything to make them uncomfortable.

That day Robinson proposed to Umarrah's remaining people that he take them to Waterhouse Island, about two kilometres offshore from Waterhouse Point, to forage for eggs while he went to George Town to free Palawa from the jail there. They were mistrustful but he was persuasive. He assuaged his conscience by rationalising that 'it was the most humane as being the only way to save their lives'. He then sent Kikatapula and the others to hunt kangaroos to feed them all while they were on the island. He also noted another reprimand of Kikatapula, whom he continued to blame for Umarrah's people's absconding.

> 12 September 1831: Proposed for Tom and MANNALARGENNA to go and look after the strangers [on Waterhouse Island]. They were satisfied with this arrangement ... Reprehended Tom for not looking after the [four] natives who went away.

Kikatapula's whereabouts for the next three weeks are not specified in Robinson's journal, but he and Manalakina probably did stay on Waterhouse Island while Stansfield, Maclaine, Robinson's son, and five unnamed Palawa scoured the bush for holdouts, and Robinson and two whites, with Piway and Prupilathina, left for George Town.[18] On 21 September Robinson sent a man to fetch those on Waterhouse Island and take them to Launceston, where he had been since the 19th. They arrived in the town on 1 October. Two days later, at Cook and Sherwin's store in Charles Street, Robinson bought clothing and other items for Kikatapula and Wurati.[19] The purchases included fustian jackets, drill trousers, waistcoats, and handkerchiefs, as well as tobacco, plums, pipes, sugar, tea, red ochre, fish hooks, marbles, and fishing line to the total value of £7.10.8, which was to be paid from funds due to the two guides from the hire of their boat on the Derwent.[20]

On 5 October the Lieutenant Governor arrived to speak to Robinson before he left to search for the remnants of the Oyster Bay and Big River people. They decided Gun Carriage Island was to be abandoned, as a local newspaper reported.

> The natives, when caught, are to be placed upon an island in the immediate vicinity of the one at present occupied as a depot for Aborigines, known as Great Island [now Flinders Island], being about 50 miles [80 km] in length – Gun-carriage island being too circumscribed to afford a livelihood for those placed thereon ... Mr. Robinson started this morning [8 October] in prosecution of his mission of conciliation to the aborigines. His expectation of success with the Oyster Bay and Big River tribes, which are said to have united, are most sanguine.[21]

With Umarrah conciliated it was time to round up all the remaining Oyster Bay and Big River people and end the war.

19

'This man Tom is a bad character'

Campbell Town, about 70 kilometres south of Launceston, was the immediate destination of the mission, which now included 15 Palawa: Kikatapula, Umarrah, Wurati, Manalakina, Prupilathina, Koleteher-largenner, Malapuwinarana, Piway, Robert, and the women Pagerly, Trukanini, Wulaytupinya, Plorenernoopperner, and Tanganuturra. They arrived there on 9 October 1831, making an interesting and unusual spectacle for residents of the little settlement, and remained until the 15th. During their stay Robinson bought four cakes of red ochre for his guides, again charging the cost against money due to Kikatapula and Wurati for the hire of their boat. He also visited George Simpson, two of whose employees, including John Guinea, had been Kikatapula's victims, but nothing of their meeting was recorded.

From Campbell Town the mission headed east, then south-east, occasionally finding fresh Palawa sign such as the remains of a large recent fire. On 20 October they stopped on the bank of Morriston River

> which Tom said was the Ross Bridge river and run into the Macquarie River and which I judged to be the case ... At 3 pm, on passing the acclivity of a hill, heard the barking of dogs. Tom stripped himself and went to ascertain the cause, and found that it was wild dogs. Tom caught one of the pups ...

After travelling through mountain passes next day they reached the place, west of Tooms Lake, where Kikatapula and Gilbert Robertson had captured Umarrah in 1828. The capture was the subject of much discussion among the guides. Around the campfire that night Kikatapula told Robinson that Manalakina's devil had told Manalakina where the Big River people were. Embers they had found at Macquarie River were the campsite of Parewareatar's brother Memerlannelargener who, with Umarrah's brother Kulipana, had now gone westward to meet other Palawa at Quamby Bluff. The Oyster Bay people, Kikatapula said, were now in their own country, where the Big River people would soon join them, and Robinson must not go around and around but should go straight to them at a place called *trungenyer* and another called *woreromemenner*. Neither has been identified.

They were already in Oyster Bay country, which Kikatapula knew intimately despite his frequent claims to the contrary, and on 22 October they 'Came to a place that Tom called the Big Rock; it was a steep rocky cliff. Tom said the natives hunted in those parts … The natives had often wandered over this country, many of them from childhood, and every part was familiar to them'. They moved on through pleasant scenery in good weather.

Next day Kikatapula and Umarrah told Robinson that Umarrah's wife Wulaytupinya, a Big River woman, knew where Palawa had cached weapons nearby. She showed him the place, from which he recovered a shotgun, a musket, 45 spears, five waddies, and ammunition.[1] Later that day Kikatapula took him to a hill to point out James Hobbs's farm, a frequent Palawa target, about 400 metres away. Later still, when smoke was seen, Robinson sent Kikatapula and Stansfield to investigate, but it proved to be a farmworker's fire.

Where they might find the Big River people was the topic of campfire talk that night, 25 October. Kikatapula said Manalakina would ask his devil. 'Accordingly, [Manalakina] went to work, Tom and his wife asking him occasionally where the natives rendezvoused', Robinson wrote.

> He said they was about the banks of the river. When he had finished he got up (it being dark) and said that a dead man's devil that had been put in a tree was walking about and would tell him about it. He set off in the woods; Tom and another native trembling followed him; the women lay as still as mice. They said I should know if he was there by his whistling. By and by heard a whistle and several whistles. They returned. I asked Tom if he had seen the devil; he said he had only heard him whistle. Said that when there

was a small fire he would come and look at us at night. I told them I would go and make a small fire in the woods and see if the devil would come, that if he made his appearance I would lay hold of his ears and pull him along and put him in the fire.

On the following day Kikatapula's intractability resurfaced (and was infectious) after Robinson reproached him for making too much noise and hunting instead of looking for Palawa sign. Wulaytupinya had told Robinson about a second cache of firearms, but she subsequently denied having done so. 'I judged therefore that Tom had persuaded her to this', Robinson wrote. 'I appeared angry about it'. By now, encouraged by Kikatapula, all the Palawa guides were subversive whenever possible. One woman lit a large fire while Robinson was busy writing his journal. He did not notice it at first, but when he finally did he was furious. 'Of course this smoke could have been seen by the hostile tribes and would necessarily prevent their approaching me', he fumed.[2]

By the following day it was clear to Robinson that the guides were deliberately wasting his time in Oyster Bay country. Once populous, it was now devoid of Palawa. He told them that if they did not immediately lead him to the Big River people he would waste no more time there, and he again blamed Kikatapula for the mission's lack of success. 'I reprehended Tom for not exerting himself, seeing it was his own country and he had the strange woman [Wulaytupinya] to assist him', he wrote, still failing to understand Kikatapula's attitude. Nearly two years had passed since he had last been in his country – it was now October 1831 – and the even greater Palawa void must have been obvious. He had been aware for at least a decade of the destruction of the Aboriginal landscape and the disappearance of his people, but now the dearth of them in country they had inhabited immemorially cannot fail to have troubled him. The hopelessness of his own situation and his complicity in their disappearance were daily being driven home to him, feeding his despondency and hardening his resolve against cooperation.

So next day Robinson decided to change direction and head westward toward Big River country, but his guides were dilatory. Big River country was very cold and would surely kill them, they said. Robinson countered that it was nearly summer and warm weather was ahead, but Kikatapula, who had often hunted and raided in Big River country and knew it well, gave another reason not to go there. He told Robinson that Wulaytupinya 'said that there was plenty of devils in that country and that they would kill strange black people, especially if they saw them carrying knapsacks. I told Tom I had no opinion of his country, that it was no good country'. Kikatapula knew that traversing parts of Big River country would be laborious and uncomfortable, and he undoubtedly knew it was where the Big River people would be found. But Robinson prevailed, and the mission turned west.

Kikatapula soon led them astray again. In heavy rain on 3 November, 'I set out on my journey', Robinson recorded,

> taking a NE course, Tom taking the lead as he had ofttimes wandered over this country with his tribe and I was anxious to travel the native track ... [A]bout 5 pm on arriving at the summit of the hills on the east side of the township of Oatlands, Tom was arrested in his progress on discovering the big lagoon [Lake Dulverton] there.

Kikatapula's feigned surprise at finding himself there peeved Robinson.

> I had in the whole course of my route observed to Tom that my course lay west and that he was keeping too much to the north. Previous to reaching Oatlands Tom was keeping still further to the northward, and UMARRAH had [also] kept to the northward. I expressed my astonishment to Tom that he should so far mistake as to bring me into the township of Oatlands when our road was through Jericho [13 km farther south] and I wished to keep the native road.

Around the campfire that night Kikatapula tried to appease Robinson by promising that when they located the Big River people he and Wulaytupinya, both of whom the Big River people knew well, 'would go first to them, lest they might suppose it was a strange tribe ... come to fight with them'.

Keeping well clear of white habitations the mission crossed the Hobart–Launceston road on 4 November, Manalakina viewing 'with much surprise the fragments of stones which had been broken to metal the road'. The country they passed through was well settled; they could hear roosters crowing and wood being chopped. 'Though great danger was to be apprehended from the hostile natives', Robinson wrote, 'still in passing through the settled districts more danger was to be apprehended from white people ...' A settler Robinson approached for supplies reported killing seven Palawa nearby and then following the fleeing survivors and killing 10 more. Entering the Central Highlands to the north of Captain Wood's farm the mission encountered a detachment of the 63rd Regiment en route to Bothwell, a town the mission could see as they crossed a high tier. 'Farms and cultivated land was to be seen in different directions', Robinson noted.

On 6 November they traversed Weasel Plains, about 14 kilometres north of Bothwell, arriving mid-afternoon at Shannon River. This was country Kikatapula had once terrorised. The mission briefly halted at Dr Ross's farm – a stockkeepers' refuge in 1826 and 1827 when Kikatapula attacked Thomson's neighbouring run – and later passed close to Thomson's itself, but Robinson did not record any discussion of the attacks. Travelling in unseasonal heat they reached Ouse River which Robinson observed 'meanders in its course between lofty tiers of hills covered with herbage and thinly timbered. Large patches were quite free from copse, along which was seen the kangaroo bounding, others feeding in abundance'. When they camped for the night Kikatapula told Robinson 'he knew where there was several dead men [interred] in trees [nearby]' and offered to show him.

A day later Robinson and his guides decided their quarry would most likely be found in the country beyond Lake Echo. They would search that first and, if unsuccessful, would head for Great Lake. So they crossed the Ouse and camped for the night at Bashan Plains, where Kikatapula attempted blatant sabotage. After sighting Palawa smoke in the direction of Lake Echo he tried to alert their quarry by starting several grass fires, which a furious Robinson berated him for.

Next day they set out for Lake Echo. On the way 'Tom pointed out a small marsh where him and MANNALARGENNA had fought with the LAIRMAIRRENER. Tom said they was obliged to retreat as the LAIRMAIRRENER was too strong for them'. They soon saw smoke, which Robinson urged the mission toward. But the guides stalled, saying they first needed to arm themselves by making spears, otherwise the Big River people would spear them. They also wanted to roast a kangaroo. 'I said if we made a fire [the Big River people] would see our smoke', a vexed Robinson recorded,

> and [I] appeared angry with them for their dilatoriness and particularly addressed myself to Tom whom I said ought to have been the first to have set the example and that if we did not get to them now it was uncertain when we should again find them. But all the argument I could adduce could not divert them from their purpose of hunting ...

Returning to camp on 9 November Kikatapula and the other scouts reported seeing smoke from Palawa fires rising from camps near the river. Robinson was eager to proceed but the guides were in no hurry; they again wanted to roast kangaroos. Robinson protested, angry at the delay and fearing their quarry would be alerted by the smoke, but grudgingly consented. To fill time he climbed to the top of a high cliff that gave him a sweeping view of the country around them – good open country and snow-topped mountains, he noted. Moving on once their meal was finished, they found Palawa sign, so he sent Kikatapula, Umarrah, Malapuwinarana, and two women ahead to scout, but their effort was half-hearted. They 'returned and said they had been to where they [the Big River people] had had their fire, and [the guides] had warmed themselves at their fire, but had seen nothing of the natives', Robinson crossly chronicled that night.

> I appeared exceedingly angry with them and told them that it was their own neglect or I might have been with those natives long ago, that instead of hunting for kangaroo they ought to have gone and looked after the natives, that I was incensed at their conduct and that unless they adopted a better line of conduct I must of necessity have recourse to some other measure.

Next morning he further harangued Kikatapula before questioning him again about cached firearms; the previous day he had pointed out a hill where Palawa had such a hoard. After recovering the weapons the guides shouldered them 'and these with their spears and waddies and dogs and the horse and knapsacks had a pleasing and singular effect' on Robinson. At noon they came to a plain that Palawa had set ablaze; the trees were still burning and the nearby sound of dogs suggested the Big River people were close. After going out to look for them Kikatapula and the others returned, claiming the dogs were just wild dogs. But they had found Palawa tracks heading south-south-east, they said. Robinson immediately sent guides off in various directions to look for more sign, and when Wurati returned to say he had seen smoke not far away Robinson urged the others to go immediately to its source. But they were laggard, causing Robinson to remonstrate furiously with them. 'At last I prevailed on Tom, who went away first', he wrote, 'and then I said if no other person would go I should go myself ... and set off accordingly. This had the desired effect, and three other men and two of the women accompanied me'. They soon found a group of five unoccupied bark huts and they could see smoke rising from behind a distant hill, but it was too far away for them to reach before nightfall.

On 11 November, Robinson sent Kikatapula, Manalakina, Umarrah, Wurati, and the five women ahead with their blankets and dogs. He accompanied them on horseback for about five kilometres, then turned back at a marsh where wild cattle grazed. 'This open marsh is skirted by an open forest of stringy bark, gum and peppermint trees, and was of considerable extent', he wrote.

> As we passed along the skirt of this marsh [we] met with numerous native huts and remains of native villages. Some of these habitations had been very recently erected. At one of these huts they had been eating emu ... This is the country where the blacks have constantly domiciled and had remained undisturbed by their white enemies. Kangaroo was in abundance ... and this country must be a fine resort for natives, there being thousands of acres of clear land and excellent pasture.

In drizzling rain next day he rode back to the marsh to meet Wurati and Trukanini, who returned with Tanganuturra, whom Kikatapula had ordered back after quarrelling with her. Wurati told Robinson they had gone to the fires, that the bush there was still burning despite all the rain, and that they had seen plenty of Palawa footprints. When they found the route their quarry had taken, Kikatapula had declared they were close, so he and Pagerly would continue on their trail. All next day, a wet Sunday, Robinson waited eagerly for the couple to return with news of the Big River people and intelligence about the country ahead, but it was not until the following afternoon that they came back. They had not been successful. After tracking the Big River mob as far as River Dee they had made a fire on a peaked hill, they said, and stayed all night before returning to tell Robinson that 'the country through which the natives had gone was so densely wooded that they had to break their way through, that it was covered with fallen timber'.

Robinson was sceptical. 'I did not expect they would succeed', he wrote, 'as there appeared a great want of perseverance among them'. When the guides told Robinson that the Big River people had seen them and run away, he disbelieved them. 'I cannot effect anything without these people and yet I am harassed and perplexed by them', he fumed.[3] Their efforts seemed to him increasingly feeble. Haranguing them, urging them to greater exertion, was now almost a daily necessity. A few days later he noted:

> The natives appear to be less diligent, less assiduous, less obedient than on former occasions. Seldom conversed on the plans to be adopted relative to meeting the natives. Seldom expressed a wish to meet with them … They appeared more intent at hunting opossum than in that of looking out for the smoke of native fires or in their endeavouring to communicate with their countrymen.[4]

Having looped around the northern end of Lake Echo in early November, the mission headed in a generally southerly direction, backtracking to Bradys Sugarloaf in the middle of the month before turning south-east and then south-west. Around 20 November, near Thistle Hill, they changed direction again, this time travelling back the way they had come, although by a varied route. Passing through good country and bad, they avoided settlements and white habitations except when supplies were needed. Rarely were they short of meat, for kangaroos and possums were plentiful, in addition to which Umarrah and Wulaytupinya ate three thylacine cubs Prupilathina had killed and at another time a native cat was eaten. But they complained whenever flour, tea, sugar, and tobacco were exhausted, necessitating a visit to a farm or stock hut to resupply. Occasionally there were other reasons to visit. On 22 November, when a strong current made the Ouse difficult to cross near James Triffett's farm, Kikatapula told Robinson that when he had been there with Robertson's roving party they had always crossed in Triffett's boat, so they diverted to Triffett's. But his vessel had drifted away during the night, forcing them to go farther along the river to use John Young's.

In places they encountered physical evidence of fierce Palawa hostility. A day after boating across the river they 'Saw the remains of an old hut which had frequently been burnt down by the natives. Many people had lived here, but were driven away by the natives'. When Manalakina announced that day that his devil had told him the Big River natives had gone to Swanport, far away on the east coast, Robinson derided the notion. He told the guides they would head for Ouse River, which Kikatapula objected to because, he said, they did not like travelling backwards and forwards – another indication that boredom and fatigue were adding to their recalcitrance. No matter how fresh the Palawa sign they encountered, the Big River people always seemed to be a step ahead in a cat-and-mouse game that was to continue for many wearisome weeks on top of the five months the mission had already spent scouring the bush. Kikatapula knew this country well, but although he generally appeared to be cooperative he continued to mislead whenever possible, and the other guides, mindful of his reputation and unwilling to betray any more of their race, followed his example. Breaking the monotony were occasional false alarms, often caused by barking dogs, and sometimes they saw smoke from Palawa fires, but the Big River people effortlessly eluded them.

On 25 November, in 'heavy rain with boisterous wind', Robinson began the day by castigating his guides for their contumacy before starting out in a new direction that 'led to the unexplored and unsettled parts of the territory'. During the day they encountered recently constructed Palawa huts but saw nothing of those who built them. While the mission was making camp that evening Robinson and Kikatapula pushed a further two kilometres northward to reconnoitre, finding the country ahead to be thick forest. They returned to camp where the guides, still smarting from that morning's scolding, refused to help Robinson build himself a shelter.

They reached the southern extremity of Lake Echo on the 27th and left it behind a day or two later to travel northward as far as Skittleball Plains, where they turned east and skirted the southern shore of Great Lake. Changeable weather hampered their progress and worsened their mood. 'The climate ... is subject to great vicissitudes: yesterday it was exceeding hot; today it is very cold with snow, rain, wind and sleet', Robinson wrote on 28 November. Three days later he noted:

> A continuation of rain, snow, sleet and boisterous winds, accompanied by thunder and lightning and dense cloud. The weather has been exceedingly cold ... very changeable and uncertain ... and frost and snow are here frequently met with in the midst of summer. The altitude of this part of the country must be great ...

Rain-swollen rivers made crossings dangerous, and relations between guides were deteriorating. Umarrah and his wife were in fear of Kikatapula, Malapuwinarana, and Manalakina because the three had declared they would kill Umarrah and Koleteherlargenner, a Tayarinutipana man now with the mission. The reason, Manalakina told Robinson on 4 December, was that the two of them had killed his son Plairnrooner at some past time. It led Robinson to fear that Umarrah and his wife were intending to abscond for their own safety. Late that day, when the mission camped at the source of River Shannon at Great Lake, he sent his guides out to look for tracks. Although they discovered recent signs, including a fire and a fresh kangaroo carcass minus its hind legs, they made no attempt to follow up, so Robinson 'again reprehended very severely the natives' for another indifferent effort.

His hopes rose on 6 December when they found fresh Palawa tracks. Manalakina claimed the credit by pointing to his chest, signifying his personal devil was responsible. When Robinson asked Kikatapula why *he* could not tell which way their quarry had gone, Kikatapula tartly replied that he had no devils. Subsequently, as they were crossing the Shannon, he 'fell and got a ducking which amused the rest of the people', although not the prideful and dripping duckee. From Great Lake they travelled east, reaching Arthurs Lakes next day. When he discovered Umarrah and his wife had disappeared, the 'exceedingly excited' Robinson sent Kikatapula and Wurati to look for them, fearing they had indeed absconded, which a triumphant Manalakina said was right. But they eventually returned.

A despatch dated 6 December from a correspondent in Bothwell apprised the *Courier*'s Hobart readers of Robinson's recent activities.

Perceiving by last week's *Courier*, that some apprehension has been felt on account of Mr. Robinson and his party, it will no doubt be gratifying to learn that a few days ago he was near the Lakes (15 miles [24 km] west of Lake Echo) endeavouring to procure an interview with the Big river natives. The black female who was present at the murders of poor Captain Thomas and Mr. Parker [Wulaytupinya], and who is now with Mr. Robinson, succeeded in leading him three several times upon this tribe; but the blacks invariably fled at his approach. On the last occasion (ten days ago, fifteen miles from Lake Echo,) such was their hurry to escape that they left behind them a considerable quantity of arms, &c, consisting of *eight stand of fire arms* ... together with a bag of bullets and shot, and a large looking glass, &c. The party fell in with traces of several considerable villages or encampments of the natives; from the number of the huts it is supposed they take up their winter quarters in that neighbourhood. The guns were all in good order ...[5]

Boredom and indifference were now rife among the guides, their reluctance to betray exacerbated by the testing terrain, the torturous lake-country weather, and a landscape constantly fraught with natural obstacles: dense scrub, near-impenetrable forest, tarns, marshes, fallen timber, and extensive open tracts thickly coated with uneven rocky rubble. Their willingness to continue was fast evaporating. Mid-morning on 7 December, about 10 kilometres east-south-east of Arthurs Lakes, they paused at a marsh where Kikatapula said he and his people had once battled with the Tayarinutipana. After some refreshment – Umarrah and Wulaytupinya ate a platypus they had dug out of its burrow – the guides were loath to move at all, so Robinson 'rather too freely gave vent to that just indignation ... such disgraceful conduct is sure to call forth and which is so justly deserved, and reprehended them in severe terms'. Grudgingly they resumed their trek.

Late next afternoon they came to a rare British toehold in that remote region: a group of three huts where Kikatapula said 'he had been ... with his tribe and had taken away flour'. Robinson wanted to avoid them but the guides ignored him. They pressed on, frightening into flight two Britons who were repairing a bridge over Lake River.

In lashing wind-borne rain, hail, and snow five days later a frozen and weary Robinson realised with exasperation that the route his guides were taking was not going to lead to the Big River mob. When he demanded to know why, they said they wanted to go to a place a long way off where they could get red ochre. Suppressing his anger, he persuaded them that a detour would be counter-productive, and they reluctantly agreed to a postponement, although Kikatapula made a sardonic comment: 'You missed a very fine thing to go for red ochre; what would the Governor think of it? If the Governor asked Mr R where was the blacks, Mr R must shew him the red ochre and say, there, Governor, there is the natives'. After all, he seemed to say, might not the Big River people also be there grubbing for ochre?

An elongated anticlockwise loop around Western Tiers brought them back to Arthurs Lakes on 14 December. Several times during their circuit Kikatapula's obstreperous behaviour further infuriated Robinson.

13 December 1831: I had wished the woman [Wulaytupinya] to proceed by the north end of the Great Lake, but she said there was no road, that her way was the way the natives went. It was a roundabout way, but I had no alternative but to yield to the woman who had in conjunction with the old chief [Manalakina] the ascendancy. I could scarcely suppress my indignation and blamed Tom and assured him although I apparently [acquiesced] it was contrary to my view.

18 December 1831: The natives went in the evening to hunt kangaroo. Tom and the chief had quarrelled. Tonight UMARRAH told my servant to tell me that Tom and the chief said they would spear him [Umarrah]. This man Tom is a bad character; I am compelled to reprimand this ruffian.

19 December 1831: [The guides] said they wanted to go ... south-east ... Neither Black Tom nor any of the other people informed [me] of their intention and their object for going in the direction referred to ... I was exceedingly indignant at their proceedings and could not refrain from severely reprehending them. It has always been with considerable reluctance that I have at any time ventured to reprove, but when necessity has required it I have been necessarily compelled thereto from a sense of duty, and it is a matter of astonishment that all the counselling and reproof that I have from time to time had occasion to bestow on some of them,

particularly on Black Tom, that still this individual remains obdurate and callous to all my advice and reproof.

From Arthurs Lakes they tramped south to Lagoon of Islands and then in an easterly loop as far as Lake Crescent and Lake Sorell and back to Lagoon of Islands. On 22 December the mission followed a zigzag route north-west from west of Lake Crescent. 'Passed through a succession of exceedingly wet marshes', Robinson recorded,

> and anon over stony hills and through some fine open forest of stringy bark trees of large growth ... Gum and peppermint trees were also to be met with. Kangaroo was very plentiful. Saw some old native huts and trees that had been barked by the natives were to be seen in every direction ... Halted for the night about two miles [3 km] south-east of the Lagoon of Islands.

He was worn out. Frustration and hardship had ground him down and were adding to his growing fear of failure. 'Self unwell; have been much indisposed for this week past, debilitated. My mind has been much perturbed, which has added to my indisposition.'

He was still much indisposed when they reached St Patricks Plains late in the afternoon of the 24th. Two days later, while the mission was camped on the east side of the Ouse about 13 kilometres north of Shannon Point, his malaise was aggravated by a reproachful letter from the Colonial Secretary, delivered by two of his men bringing supplies.

> His Excellency is exceedingly anxious that you should fall in with the [Big River] tribe, and it appears to him very extraordinary that the aborigines who accompany you experience so great a difficulty leading you to their haunt ...[6]

The letter salted his wound by noting the success another Palawa-hunter – a convict, moreover – was having. 'I am also to transmit to you the copy of a letter from Mr Curr detailing the success of Alexander McKay in the capture of four of the natives ...'[7]

That stung. His mind still much perturbed, Robinson recorded next day that he was 'Greatly at a loss how to proceed'. His guides, in mortal fear of the Big River mob, remained unhelpful, deeming their quarry to be 'the most savage of all the aboriginal tribes ... by whom they said they would be surely murdered (a feeling which had induced them on several occasions to lead me considerably astray)', he wrote.[8] He was aware by now that they were sabotaging his mission. In desperation he explained to them the Colonial Secretary's letter, at which 'they all evinced a strong desire to communicate with the people. They say they have taken me to all their haunts but that [the Big River people] are now away, as they had before informed me'.

The following day, 28 December, he sent two of his men, Tyrell and Platt, ahead to Bashan Plains while he halted the mission at a small lagoon so he could write despatches.

> Had just commenced when the report of a gun was heard in the direction of the River Ouse. I at once concluded it was some of my people and immediately despatched Black Tom and two other people to see what it was, when in a short time after[,] Tom was seen running toward us. I run to meet him, when at once he informed me that the natives was at Bashan Plains, that Platt ... had returned with the news. Not a moment was now to be lost ... in a few moments we were all on a jog trot on our way back to the river ... I urged them on and told them the Governor only wanted me to get to the Big River tribe and then our troubles would be over ...

But at Bashan Plains they found it was Platt who had fired the shot, giving some excuse that Robinson disbelieved. No Palawa were there. Platt had lied to Kikatapula, apparently as a joke.

Heading north-east next day they searched around the usual Palawa crossing place over Ouse River but found no footprints. Robinson then sent Kikatapula and Wurati to the top of a high hill, possibly Fishers Sugarloaf, on the opposite side of the river to look for smoke. 'In a short time after they had ascended the hill they were seen coming hastily down', Robinson wrote,

> and in a short time I was informed that they had seen a large smoke of the natives in a south-westerly direction. Set off with all promptness in the direction mentioned. Proceeded by the usual track of the natives to Lake Echo and from thence to the Three Mile Marsh [just north of Lake Echo].

They spent the night camped on the east side of the marsh about a kilometre from the Ouse, and next morning headed north-west toward where they had seen the smoke. After crossing a high rocky tier about eight kilometres in extent they reached Skittleball Plains, where Kikatapula told Robinson the remains of three Lairmairrenener, his and Manalakina's victims at some past time, were to be found. It was a tract of open country stretching as far as the western side of Great Lake. When they saw smoke rising not far away to the west Robinson dispatched Kikatapula, Wurati, Umarrah, Malapuwinarana, Prupilathina, and Wulaytupinya to investigate.

Watching the smoke as he waited for their return, Robinson was overcome by impatience and set out toward it. After walking about five kilometres he saw Umarrah and Wulaytupinya coming back, and soon Kikatapula and the others joined them. They brought welcome news. Having gone up Platform Bluff (now Skittleball Hill), about five kilometres east of Lake Fergus, to get a good view of the surrounding countryside, 'They informed me they had crossed the Derwent River [*sic*, Little Pine River] and been to the fires, that it was the Big River tribe', Robinson wrote. The news should have exhilarated him, but he remained subdued and pessimistic despite having himself seen the smoke. He felt 'somewhat disappointed, still hoping for the best and heartily tired of this sort of life'. Two years' bitter experience had taught him that Palawa could be as elusive as smoke itself, and he feared this sighting would be no more than another wild-goose chase leading only to another abandoned campsite, another failure. His enthusiasm waning with the daylight, he decided to return to camp and wait until dawn before going to the fires. Sensing Robinson's despondency, Kikatapula assured him of his and Wurati's support.

We can surmise that sound sleep was not general that night. The mission was finally about to confront the combined Oyster Bay–Big River peoples – the fierce fighters who, initially under Kikatapula's leadership, had spearheaded resistance to the British. Now they were fugitives living in a remote region where they thought they were safe from pursuit and harassment. They would certainly be furious when they discovered they had been tracked into this haven and betrayed by some of their own. They would surely respond with vengeful spears and waddies. As the campfires burned low, some in the mission, weary though they were, awaited dawn with apprehension.

In the first light of a fine mild morning the subdued party moved out, heading south-west through bad country toward the Big River camp some distance away in a thickly wooded sanctuary a few kilometres north of Lake Echo. Their hushed voices fell silent as they neared their objective. Robinson signalled a halt about 100 metres from the Big River fires. In whispers and gestures he ordered forward as envoys seven adult guides (including Wulaytupinya) and the boy Prupilathina. All the whites and Manalakina and the remaining guides concealed themselves to wait as the eight emissaries made their cautious way forward. Their quarry had not posted sentries, thinking themselves secure in this wild and unpeopled place where they had sought sanctuary after eluding a posse of 84 armed Britons on Freycinet Peninsula in mid-October.[9] Now, relaxed and unsuspecting around their fires, they were astounded to see eight strangers walking into their camp. They seized their weapons and jumped up ready to fight.

In their hiding place down the hill Robinson and the others were enduring an edgy wait. Suddenly the Big River people appeared and surged toward them, their wild whoops and the menacing rattling of their spears shattering the tense silence. Manalakina immediately fled, crying that the natives were coming to spear them. As other guides prepared to follow and the women began to whimper, Robinson managed to stay them. But they all feared the Big River people were hostile, and their fear swelled to panic as the spear-rattling warriors loomed larger and their warlike shouts grew louder. For a heart-stopping few seconds all in the mission thought their envoys had been killed, for they could not see any of them among the advancing horde. But as the Big River people closed on their hiding place Robinson saw that Wulaytupinya and the others were indeed with them, and his fears were further assuaged when the Big River women following the men 'lifted up their hands three times, the signal of peace, which is inviolable with the Aborigines'.[10]

Much relieved, Robinson realised that his guides' unthreatening approach had been successful. They had called out assurances once they were sighted and then grasped the Big River warriors' arms in a gesture of amity. After explaining why they were there, the emissaries pointed to where Robinson and the others were concealed, and they all charged toward him with the Big River warriors shouting their war cries. Robinson stepped out to greet them, surprising them by explaining in their own language the purpose of his mission. They said they had heard of him. He offered them food and a few trinkets, which they accepted, and a little later they agreed to place themselves under his protection. Afterwards he went with them back to their camp, where 'the evening was spent in mutual good humour, each party dancing alternately'.[11]

After more than six months' arduous trekking Robinson's mission had located and pacified the last of the once-mighty Oyster Bay and Big River peoples – 'the most sanguinary in the island' – including the one-armed Oyster Bay chief Tukalunginta and the Big River chief Muntipiliyata. Shockingly few were left. Although their combined population had once been many hundreds, now they numbered just 16 men, nine women, and a newborn infant.[12] Many of them bore the scars of gunshot wounds inflicted by Britons trying to exterminate them, Robinson noted, adding 'there was scarcely one among them – man, woman, or child, but had been wounded by the whites'.[13]

Kikatapula was assuredly one of the eight emissaries who risked their lives that morning to go forward and end the Black War. Only the previous month he had promised Robinson that he and Wulaytupinya would lead the approach to them in case the Big River people thought the mission had come to fight them, and no other guides were better qualified than they to confront their quarry, for Kikatapula had been one of them, a leader and a hero, and Wulaytupinya was one of their own.[14] Yet neither Robinson's official report nor an account of the event he gave years later to the Aborigines' Protection Society mentioned by name any of the eight guides who were sent forward on the last day of 1831 and succeeded in conciliating a potentially hostile numerically superior mob. The glory would go to only one man.[15]

This climactic day, this abject end for his own Oyster Bay people, for their Big River allies, and for Palawa resistance must have deeply affected Kikatapula. The pitiable composition of the bullet-scarred little band surely shocked him – a mere 26 people. During his boyhood only a generation before, they had been the two largest Palawa affiliations, their combined population perhaps more than 1000 people. Their posterity had seemed assured by the three and four generations in whose midst he had grown up. Now only a handful were left. Worse, there was only one child: a direful sign. Kikatapula had been instrumental in starting the war that brought them to this; now he was instrumental in his people's final defeat. Whether recognition of that duality shocked him with the force of a spear thrust or was simply the painful climax of intensifying despair and despondency as he trekked with Robinson across a landscape now desolate of his people can never be known. But his own paramountcy in causing this double disaster ate at him. And metastasised.

20

'I greatly deplored the loss of this aborigine'

Next morning, 1 January 1832, as the newly enlarged mission broke camp, Big River women were sent to fetch four large bundles of spears secreted nearby. The whole party then set off for Lake Echo with the surrendered weapons, their ultimate destination Hobart. Before they had gone far Muntipiliyata took Robinson to the top of a thickly wooded hill where there was 'a newly erected native hut, the interior of which was decorated with an assemblage of rude sketches representing birds, beasts, human forms, &c, and were for the most part tolerably well executed'. Adjoining the hut was a huge hollow tree whose cavity served as a hiding place for three shotguns and three muskets, all primed and loaded and in good condition. Muntipiliyata tried to surrender them to Robinson but he refused to accept them, instead asking the Palawa to carry them to Hobart for surrender to the Lieutenant Governor.[1]

They resumed their journey. At Robert Espie's hut at Bashan Plains the Big River warriors had to be restrained from killing an employee who had shot dead one of their number during a raid the previous August.[2] Concerned at this still-simmering vengefulness, Robinson sought reinforcement. Farther on, near the junction of the Shannon and the Ouse, was George Thomson's farm, which Kikatapula had so devastatingly struck in 1826 and 1827. There Robinson was able to enlist a stockkeeper named Henry Smith to help herd the Palawa into Bothwell, the nearest town.[3] They then resumed their march.

They reached Bothwell on the afternoon of 4 January. The Palawa entered the town boldly and made camp opposite the military barracks while Robinson availed himself of the comforts of the Castle Hotel.[4] Asked if he needed assistance to keep the Palawa secure and quiet, he demurred, and they remained orderly throughout their stay.[5]

Toward evening, curiosity took into the town a young man named George Russell, a Scot who had been in Tasmania and working near Bothwell for 10 months without ever seeing a Palawa. He recorded his impressions years later.

> There were about sixty or seventy of the Tasmanian natives, including men, women, and children, the largest number being grown-up men. Some of the men were stout and active-looking; but the women were poor miserable-looking creatures. They were clad in rags made of the skins of the opossum and some of them had blankets around their bodies ...[6]

That night, outside the inn where Robinson was recuperating, they sang and danced around their fires as of old. It was the last corroboree ever performed in Oyster Bay/Big River country. None were left now to perform another.

Next morning, while the Palawa went to hunt between Den Hill and Kempton, Robinson sent the Colonial Secretary a preliminary report of his success, noting:

> No restraint in any way has been placed upon them since they have been with me.[7] They hunt &c. Complain loudly of the injuries done to them and their progenitors by the whites ... I have promised them a conference with the Lieut Govr and that the Governor will be sure to redress all their grievances.

In a despatch to Robinson the Colonial Secretary ordered that while the Palawa were to be treated humanely, all possible precautions were to be taken to prevent their escape.[8]

Robinson's party left Bothwell later that day, and two days afterwards made a grand entrance to Hobart. The *Hobart Town Courier* had publicised their imminent arrival.

> It is with no small pleasure we announce the gratifying news that the whole of the Oyster bay and Big river tribes ... have surrendered themselves to Mr. Robinson, by whose conciliatory intervention the desirable event has been mainly brought about. They ... may be expected in town to day ...[9]

The news sparked great interest among Hobartians. From an early hour that Saturday morning they positioned themselves wherever they thought they would have a good view, but it was not until 10 am that Robinson and his Palawa cavalcade appeared, eliciting 'the most lively curiosity and delight' from the spectators. Except that the Big River people had all been fitted with trousers before being allowed into town, their appearance was more or less as Russell had noted at Bothwell. As a newspaper reported:

> The hair of the women was shaved closely, and their covering a blanket: the hair of the men, on the contrary, was clotted with a sort of red ochre and grease, resembling very much little strings of bugles; the upper part of their bodies was also well greased, and reddened with a portion of the same earth.[10]

Accompanied by their large pack of dogs they strode down Elizabeth Street to Government House (now the site of Franklin Square and Hobart Town Hall) where onlookers gathered to gawk. Though the Palawa had agreed to cease fighting, they were not cowed. Each warrior carried three long spears in his left hand and one in his right, and they were singing what a spectator described as their war song. At Government House they were met by the Lieutenant Governor, whom they had threatened to spear if he did not offer them redress for wrongs done to them. He listened to their grievances, talking for some time with Kikatapula and others who could speak English, explaining to them that they would all be shipped to Flinders Island where they would have peace and plenty. They were agreeable, or perhaps resigned. He gave each of them a loaf of bread before they repaired to the Government House lawn to listen with interest to a concert by a military band specially ordered for the occasion. Then, 'in the greatest good humour and with an evident desire to make themselves agreeable', they put on a show of their own. A shutter was placed against a tree and a mark chalked on it that the warriors were asked to use as a target for their spears. 'The immense force with which these instruments of destruction were darted through the shutter was truly astonishing', a newspaper observed, 'but the men did not perform well, the crowd pressing too closely upon them, and the wind being very strong at the time'.[11] Finally, they were persuaded to board the ketch *Swan River Packet*, which was to accommodate them until the *Tamar* was ready to transport them to Flinders Island.

Launceston's *Independent* newspaper, after acknowledging the huzzas in Hobart, shrugged off a *Colonial Times* suggestion that chicanery had been used to get the Big River people to capitulate.

> They were cozened into Hobart Town under the idea of laying a statement of their grievances before the Governor ... We [consider] the small deceit that has been played off against the Aborigines as the merest possible bagatelle ...[12]

The conciliation of the last of the Big River and Oyster Bay peoples was a climactic event in Tasmanian history. The submission of that pathetic remnant signalled the end of the Black War on whites in the settled districts, although occasional attacks in the north-west would continue for some years.

The white war on blacks, however, would last much longer.

Kikatapula (bottom row, sixth from left) in Hobart, 1832, waiting with other Palawa for removal to Flinders Island when they were sketched by John Glover.
(Courtesy of the State Library of NSW)

They stayed in Hobart for 10 days. On 15 January Lieutenant Governor Arthur inspected the *Tamar* and the *Charlotte*, both of which were being readied to take the Palawa to Flinders Island, and ordered the work expedited so they could sail on the 17th. The *Tamar* did, leaving that day with all 40 Palawa aboard, carrying Kikatapula and the others to Preservation Island for transfer to the *Charlotte*, which took them first to George Town (on 3 February) and then to Launceston the following day to await Robinson.

At that time he was still in Hobart. He left little record of his 5½ weeks there at the beginning of 1832, although he spent some of the time reporting to and negotiating with the Aborigines Committee, which rewarded with a gratuity of £100 his roundup of the Oyster Bay–Big River remnants. After some hard bargaining the committee agreed to pay him a further £1000 if he captured all the Palawa from the uncolonised west, a quite unnecessary exercise because they had taken no part in the war. As further reward he was then to be appointed superintendent of the Aboriginal establishment in Bass Strait. The committee also approved his recommendation that the mission guides' services be recognised with the award of a flock of sheep 'by which means they may be induced to a more settled mode of life'. A flock of 50 were duly shipped on the *Tamar* for them and landed at the Bass Strait establishment on 1 March 1832.[13]

While in Hobart in late January Robinson received a letter from Anthony Cottrell, a special constable at Evandale, near Launceston, who had been in John Batman's roving party. 'Since I wrote you last I have brought in another [Palawa] woman', it said, 'who says she is the woman you took from Launceston jail and states she left you on account of Eummarah and Black Tom beating her – this of course is only *her statement*'.[14] Four months later Cottrell was to arrange construction of a simple marker that would be Kikatapula's sole physical memorial. One, like his name, not destined to last.

On 13 February Robinson departed Hobart for Launceston, travelling overland. He reached the northern settlement late on the 16th and was accommodated at his friend George Whitcomb's house. Waiting for him in Launceston were nine mission Palawa: Kikatapula, Pagerly, Wurati, Trukanini, Umarrah, Wulaytupinya, Manalakina (who had rejoined the mission after the apparent danger of 31 December had passed), Tanalipunya, and Piway. Among those in Launceston jail were Umarrah's brother Kulipana and Piway's brother Pintawtawa.

Two days after arriving, Robinson left for George Town, taking with him the nine mission Palawa, his son, and another man. They arrived the following day to join the *Charlotte*, which had sailed from Launceston with five Palawa from the jail but without Robinson and his cohort. Contrary winds prevented the cutter from leaving George Town until 25 February, when it sailed for Green Island, landing the Palawa there the same day. Green Island was the nearest safe anchorage to The Lagoons on Flinders Island, which the Aboriginal establishment had been moved to since Robinson's last visit the previous year.

Kikatapula had some news for Robinson the day after their arrival: two sealers based on Green Island still had Palawa women who needed to be rescued. 'Black Tom also informed me that a male aborigine had been shot on Great Island by one of those sealers named Mansell.' Robinson, who was ill, kept busy for the next few days making inquiries about the shooting.

On 4 March Kikatapula's linguistic and pastoral skills came to the fore when Robinson conducted the first church service on Flinders Island. 'Today the whole of the aborigines on the establishment (near a hundred in number) attended divine service under a large awning', he wrote. 'Tom explained to the natives the nature of the service.' It was Kikatapula's last recorded diaconal duty.

It is not known precisely when he learnt that ethnic cleansing was not yet finished and that he was now required to help Robinson round up for island incarceration all the Palawa in the mainly uncolonised (and therefore generally peaceful) west and north-west. But it is fair to surmise that it was another bitter blow to a man already desponding at the catastrophe that had befallen his people and the corroding awareness of how much he had contributed to it.

Robinson wasted no time before leaving Flinders Island to pursue those Palawa remaining and the promised £1000 reward, a very attractive sum in 1832: four times his already generous annual salary. He and his son embarked in the *Tamar* on 9 March with 15 Palawa including Kikatapula and the other eight guides he had brought with him from Launceston. The vessel berthed in Launceston on the 13th. During the three weeks they stayed there he noted that sickness had begun to manifest itself among his guides.

> 22 March 1832: UMARRAH and Robert have been ill and confined to the hospital.

> 23 March 1832: Robert died this morning at six o'clock ... of an inflammation of the chest.

> 24 March 1832: EUMARRAH died this morning of dysentery at ½7 am. The aborigine Robert ... was buried at 4 pm ... The fourteen [mission] aborigines followed the corpse.

> 26 March 1832: Eurmarrah was buried at 5 pm. Myself and natives attended.

Robert, who had been baptised as a child, was buried with Christian rites; Umarrah was not. Kikatapula attended both burials. At Umarrah's interment, Robinson noted, 'One of the natives, on being asked why he painted himself [for the occasion], riposted by asking the enquiring individual, "what do you wear fine clothes [to a funeral] for?"'. Such a tart (and grammatical) retort can have come from only one man: Kikatapula.

After being delayed because five other Palawa guides were still unwell, Robinson and the mission finally proceeded on 4 April on their expedition to the western natives, with a cart and two packhorses to carry their supplies. 'My son and four of the men accompanied the cart', he wrote, 'and also fourteen natives, three of whom were invalids and two dangerously ill'. He did not name the ailing Palawa, but subsequent events suggest Kikatapula and Wulaytupinya, Umarrah's widow, were the two who were dangerously ill. A day later he noted the 'two invalid Aborigines in a very dangerous state'. Perhaps exacerbating Kikatapula's malaise was the knowledge that he was now to help exile peaceful Palawa who had taken no part in the war.

The mission reached Westbury township on 6 April but continued on, crossing Meander River at *wyyareroeby*, where the town of Deloraine would soon be founded. On the 7th Anthony Cottrell and some mainland

Aborigines wearing European clothes joined the party. As they progressed, Robinson expressed little concern about his ailing guides, making only such occasional notes as, on 9 April, 'Proceeded on with the expedition; as I had two invalids I conceived I should not be justified in leaving them'. He ordered the cart unloaded so they could be carried in it.

On 10 April they reached Mersey River. When they saw smoke on the eastern side of the river two days later – the only Palawa sign they had encountered in six days' travel – the guides traced it to the fire of a lone woman named Prarenaner. They pressed on through several wet days that were followed by pleasant weather: Epping Forest on the 14th, Middlesex Plains on the 15th, Vale of Belvoir on the 16th, River Leven on the 17th, Burnieside the next day, and on the 19th Hampshire Hills, where they stayed until 27 April. On the day they arrived, Robinson noted 'Several of the natives taken ill with dysentery'.

He performed divine service on 22 April with all the Aborigines attending. On the 26th, after dispatching to Emu Bay several members of the mission including his son, Cottrell, and the mainland Aborigines, he noted 'The greater part of the natives [are] afflicted with dysentery'. Despite the misery so many ailing people must have felt at being forced to keep moving, Robinson drove the mission on. 'The country through which I passed consisted chiefly of a succession of high rocky wooded hills intersected by rivers and ravines', he wrote.

> Occasionally met with some small sword grass plains ... About four miles distance from Hampshire Hills [we] passed through a myrtle or green forest overgrown with espalier shrub and other small trees, the stinkwood, sasafras [sic] &c, through which we forced our way with some difficulty, sometimes crawling for yards upon the entwined branches and sometimes on our hands and knees on the ground beneath them ... Sometimes [we] would have to bend and twist the body round the branches and through the interstices.

That day, 27 April, they came to a place the Palawa were eager to visit because red ochre was found there. Robinson wrote, 'when they arrived at the spot the first mineral they met with they patted with their hands and kissed it ... They maintained the greatest good humour ...'. He noted too:

The whole country has an exceedingly wild and romantic appearance: it may be called a riot of wildness, immense wooded hills intersected by ravines. The cragged tops of the hills quite bare are seen above the forest trees. The appearance of the country was rendered still more wild by its having been burnt at different periods by the natives.

Rain fell all day on the chill and windy 28th, and the bitter cold persisted. In his journal on 30 April Robinson mentioned Kikatapula by name for the first time since joining him in Launceston on 13 February, 11 weeks earlier, noting that he, Pagerly, Richard, Karnebutcher, and Wulaytupinya were still sick. Kikatapula was clearly no longer in the forefront of Robinson's thoughts, not attracting attention in any way as his brief candle guttered. Despair and hopelessness had helped render this fit and hardy 30-year-old passive and susceptible to illness. For eight years he had criss-crossed Tasmania as guerrilla and guide, everywhere experiencing the vast silent emptinesses whose nights only a generation earlier had blazed with the fires of his people and rung with their songs and laughter. Now they and that life were gone. Now there was no escape, no future for what was left of his people, only involuntary exile and a living death on a windswept island prison. Robinson's silence about him shows that Kikatapula was now only a passive appendage to the mission, a man losing the will to live.

On 2 May, Robinson ordered Cottrell, who had rejoined the mission the previous day, to take the invalids to Emu Bay. Too sick and weak to walk, they were put on packhorses and carried there. Robinson himself intended going straight to Emu Bay but constant heavy rain kept him and the rest of the mission at Hampshire Hills for two more days. Only on 6 May did they join the ailing Palawa at the embryonic settlement, a tiny outpost of the Van Diemen's Land Company that comprised just a store, a small jetty, a handful of cottages, a paddock and garden, and a blacksmith's shop and sawpit. Heavy rain was again falling, a downpour that continued through the following day, when Robinson noted

KICKERTERPOLLER extremely unwell and two females also indisposed. At Emu Bay there was neither accommodation nor sufficient supplies for the natives. Gave orders for the invalids to be forwarded to Circular Head by the sloop *Fanny* ... The ... great unpleasantness of having sick attached to this service induced me to send them back.

But nothing happened. The sick Palawa remained behind at Emu Bay when Robinson and his mission moved out on 8 May, bound for Cam River.

Three days later Cottrell wrote to Robinson, who was then at Detention River, to tell him that although the others were improving, Kikatapula's condition had worsened. He wrote again on 14 May, this time with the news that Kikatapula had died and been buried at Emu Bay on the point near the company's store.[15]

Robinson received the letter two days later while camped on East Inlet at Circular Head. 'Informed of the death of the aborigine KICKERTERPOLLER alias Black Tom', he wrote in his journal.

> I greatly deplored the loss of this aborigine. He had been a faithful servant and had laboured hard in the service of the aboriginal mission. I regretted that I had had the invalids removed from Hampshire Hills. Emu Bay was a miserable place for invalids to be stationed at. The removal was with the concurrence of the natives, but God's will be done.

He answered Cottrell's letter next day. 'Requested that some mark might be put up to point out the spot where the ashes of this faithful servant was laid.' Cottrell complied and notified Robinson of what he had done. 'Mr Cottrell said he made a coffin for Tom and interred him at the back of the store and all the people attended. He read the burial service over the corpse; and also as I directed put a log fence round the grave.'[16]

Kikatapula's was a wretched dying and lonely death far from his country. Because Emu Bay had no cemetery his grave was solitary. Even when a cemetery was consecrated there some years later it was distant from his, the fledgling city's first Christian burial, so the site remained solitary. Its log fence, Kikatapula's only substantive memorial, ensured that his memory did not immediately die. But, like him, like his great tragic tale, like his people, their songs, their stories, their customs, their ancient culture, it gradually disappeared, effaced by the omnivorous advance of time and tyrant civilisation.

Epilogue

History, as we have seen, has largely ignored Kikatapula or at best has touched on only part of his epic story, and even that was not done accurately or well. Yet he was very important to history: a major force who two centuries ago helped shape, more than any other Palawa, the future of Tasmania and the fate of its Indigenous people. The difficulty for a biographer is to see whole a man who, although literate, left no written record of his life or thought and whose character and motivations have to be inferred from reports written by others, not all of whom were friendly.

This much is obvious: he was a complex man and a charismatic one. Plainly he was intelligent, intellectually adventurous, a natural leader. He was able to demonstrate fidelity and did whenever doing so was not against the grain. He obviously cared deeply about what was happening to his country and his people and he suffered the agony of divided loyalties because, all too soon, he could see their fate writ plain. He had a lively sense of humour that was offset by a volatile temper – or a culturally inculcated urge – that moved him to seek revenge for perceived wrongs. His career as a guerrilla was sustained by rage. He had a healthy self-regard, except in the final months of his life, by which time his anger had turned inwards and become despair.

His charisma cannot be doubted. His own people were willing to follow him to hopeless war, and many Britons, from the Lieutenant Governor down, liked him and were prepared to trust him, then to forgive even his most serious transgressions and trust him again.

Some may see him as a traitor to his people – a man who, after defecting to the enemy, assisted in rounding up and permanently exiling the remnants of his race; perhaps, as a resistance leader, he should have fought to the bitter end and the last man. But Kikatapula was a realist. He fought for as long as he was able; then, realising the hopelessness of his cause, he took the line of least resistance, however bitter or unpalatable it may have been, in the hope of saving some of his people and something of their culture. But neither he nor anybody else could have understood then that it would all end so disastrously.

To some it might seem reprehensible that a man professing Christianity should prosecute a savage war against other Christians, personally participate in their destruction, and be celebrated for it. But what little evidence exists suggests that despite his baptism and his church attendance when he was part of the Birch household, Kikatapula's embrace of Christianity was no more than nominal until George Augustus Robinson began evangelising to him in Hobart jail in 1828. Regardless, Christianity is pliable. Its tenets and strictures have always been donnable or doffable to rationalise or excuse or ignore injustice and torture and killing if deemed necessary. History abounds in bloody examples. A Christian attempting by violence to free his country of invaders, Christian or otherwise, is far from unusual and certainly undeserving of special focus here. As Lyndall Ryan observes in her Foreword, Kikatapula was 'a true patriot whose paramount purpose was to save his people from extermination'.

He was unquestionably the most important Palawa in history, one of the most important people of any race in the annals of colonial Tasmania, and one of the most significant men in all the violently racist history of post-invasion Australia. His life was paradigmatic of how Palawa life evolved after 1803: shock, fear, uncertainty, curiosity, familiarity, resentment, resistance, submission, and finally despair unto death.

Kikatapula died in the service of his people. With the best intentions he led resistance against the British invasion, which hastened the ultimate catastrophe, and with the best intentions he subsequently aided, if half-heartedly at best, the British war against Palawa via the roving parties and the Friendly Mission and the final soul-corroding Flinders Island incarceration. So it must truthfully be said that, however good his intentions, he was responsible for aiding in two opposing ways the Tasmanian apocalypse.

Epilogue

Because of that, he must be seen as one of the most tragic figures in all Australian history.

Kikatapula's death was not reported in any of the newspapers he had once so frequently and fearsomely featured in. His part in helping the invaders in their push to ethnically cleanse Tasmania of its Indigenous inhabitants was not noted or commemorated in print or in any other way. Even his major claim to a place in history – leading resistance to the invasion – was nearly forgotten, as was his service to the invaders. As one historian has observed, 'Kickerterpoller and Mungo-Jack [another roving-party guide] largely faded from memory, their significance deliberately underplayed and then quickly and genuinely forgotten'.[1] Only once, four years after his death and 8½ years after he had broken his spear, was Kikatapula's struggle referred to in a newspaper, when *Bent's News and Tasmanian Three-penny Register* briefly resurrected him, although only to pound a final nail into the coffin of Palawa rights and liberty. Commenting on the undesirability of ever again allowing Palawa the freedom of their own country, the paper recapped with fear, resentment, and unconcern for accuracy the four bloody years of Kikatapula's fight against invasion and dispossession.

> [W]e need only refer to the murderous conduct of Black Tom, who was civilized, by living for ten long years in the family of the late Mr. Thos. Birch, and who, notwithstanding, afterwards took to the woods, joining the most hostile tribes of his countrymen, and taking the most leading part of such tribes – himself spearing to death numerous white men, women, and children.[2]

And that was all. That was his only obituary, his only epitaph.

Kikatapula is as uncommemorated today in his native Tasmania as he is little known. One-hundred-and-forty years ago a man named William Brodribb had a parcel of land called Black Tom's Run at Native Corners, an area Kikatapula sometimes frequented, but any connection with him is only conjecture, and the name may not have survived.[3] In the early 20th century, on the York Plains farm Handroyd, there was some wooded country known locally as Black Tom's Scrub, and although it is geographically and historically likely to have been so named because of Kikatapula's activities in that region – colonial Tasmania briefly also boasted a bushranger named Black Tom – Handroyd's present owner says the name is no longer used.[4] Only Kikatapula's time at Duck-Hole Farm, near Richmond, and no doubt his subsequent notoriety, has been commemorated by applying the name Black Tom's to the waterhole below the dam in Coal River.[5] And that is all. For a man who led the fight to resist invasion and later helped the invaders to clear Tasmania of its traditional owners, it is nothing like an adequate memorial. Although Kikatapula served both parties in the conflict, it is depressingly ironic that he is today remembered by neither.

Yet throughout the decades that indelible but not-quite-perceptible imprint of his name on Tasmania's collective subconscious has surfaced faintly (and quaintly) now and again. Alexander Laing, as we have seen, made several references to Kikatapula in his 1867 unpublished (and unreliable) memoir. In 1910 a descendant of another Pitt Water pioneer mentioned Black Tom in an interview with the English field naturalist Ernest Westlake, but it was a misidentification.[6] The Birches' grandson Thomas Sutcliffe wrote briefly about Kikatapula in his quoted *Critic* article on Macquarie House, published in 1915, although it sparked no further public interest in the man. Seven years later, nine decades after Kikatapula's death, an Oyster Bay Palawa named Tom Birch appeared as a character in a novel about life on the Tasmanian frontier (also starring, *inter alia*, Musquito). This fictional Tom Birch's natal name is 'Malanagena', presumably a mangling or misremembering of Mannalargenner (Manalakina), and he is a man of such small stature that the author describes him as a 'pigmy'. The novel, *The Luck of 1825* by Horace B. Pithouse, was published in 1922 and serialised in the *Circular Head Chronicle*.[7] As nothing more than a faintly history-flavoured highly fanciful tale of frontier derring-do that expropriated Kikatapula's English name for a fabricated character, it is ineligible for anything more than a passing nod.

Once disturbed, however, Kikatapula's dust did not immediately resettle. Newspaper features about pioneering days in Burnie briefly brought him to life again in 1928 and 1931 by recalling his death and burial there. The first described him as 'an intelligent aboriginal' and 'Mr.

Robinson's trusted assistant', the second as an 'intelligent native boy'.[8] Nothing more.

Two years later, in an article titled 'Burnie's Old Cemetery', the same newspaper reprised the same melancholy details, this time calling him 'a "tame" aboriginal'.[9] Since British expansion into the north-west had barely begun during the years of Kikatapula's spear-and-waddy war on Britons, knowledge in that region of this remarkable man was limited to his unremarkable end.

And then even that was forgotten.

After Kikatapula's death **George Augustus Robinson** trekked on, resolved to reap the rewards of capturing and exiling every one of the few Palawa remaining in the bush. In June 1832 he incarcerated 23 of them on Hunter Island (and then Flinders Island) before heading southward along the coast to Arthur River, where he was attacked by Palawa who intended to kill him. Robinson, who could not swim, escaped only because Trukanini, who could, propelled him on a makeshift raft across the river to safety. By 1834 his mission was finished; only about a dozen Palawa were thought to remain at large in all Tasmania. But although the theft of *lutruwita* was complete, ethnic cleansing was not. The following year Robinson took charge of Wybalenna and its unwilling internees. But

> Flinders Island was an unhealthy place. The rations were inadequate, the Aborigines' huts damp and badly ventilated and their drinking water impure, and they died of disease and despair at an alarming rate – 59 of them in the 3½ years after Robinson arrived as superintendent. An independent inspector, Major Thomas Ryan ... sent by Lieutenant Governor Arthur to the island in March 1836, reported that it was difficult 'not to draw the conclusion that the Aborigines were being deliberately exterminated in a manner that involved considerable pain and suffering'.[10]

In March 1839 Robinson was appointed Chief Protector of Aborigines at Port Phillip (Melbourne). He took with him 15 of the handful of surviving Palawa, partly to preserve their lives by removing them from Flinders Island, partly because he thought they could help him conciliate Port Phillip Aborigines. Those taken included Tanaminawayt (Piway) and his wife Planobeenna (Fanny), Malapuwinarana (Timmy), Wurati, and

Trukanini. Only six of them ever saw Tasmania again. Robinson returned to England in 1852 and died at Bath in 1866, aged about 75.

Gilbert Robertson, Robinson's rival and Kikatapula's friend, was dismissed from the police in 1832 for giving wine to convict servants at a festival. For a short time afterwards he edited the *Colonist,* then started his own newspaper, the *True Colonist,* but in 1835 he was jailed for libelling Lieutenant Governor Arthur. Later he was briefly Superintendent of Agriculture on Norfolk Island before returning to Hobart in 1847. Broke and landless, he was appointed overseer of a farm in Colac, Victoria. For a time he seems to have thrived, becoming editor of the *Victoria Colonist* and secretary of the Constitutional Committee. He also stood (unsuccessfully) for Geelong Town Council. Robertson died at Geelong in 1851 after suffering a massive heart attack and falling from his horse.

Edmund Hodgson, his fellow immigrant, died in Hobart in 1884, aged 92, surviving Sarah and three of his six children and leaving an estate of £1305. His obituaries noted only his interest in politics and his vociferous advocacy of railways.[11] His connection with Kikatapula was as long forgotten by then as Kikatapula himself.

Sarah Birch Hodgson survived Kikatapula by 36 years. Since she was not a worldly woman, especially (and unsurprisingly, given contemporary women's rights) concerning monetary matters, her marriage to Edmund Hodgson was unhappy, as two of her children testified in *Hodgson vs Hodgson*, and soured by his cavalier attitude to debt. In 1860, when he declared insolvency, he was living with his stepson Samuel Birch while Sarah resided at their marital home, Glen House in Macquarie Street, South Hobart. Her genuine and lasting affection for Kikatapula is beyond doubt, as is her courage in fighting for him. Probably she saw in him qualities possessed by neither her eccentric first husband nor her feckless second. She certainly understood his uniqueness and never ceased to mourn him. Interviewed about him in old age by James Bonwick, 'She repeatedly spoke of "Poor Tom"'.[12] Sarah died of pneumonia, aged about 75, at Glen House on 31 March 1868.

By then most of Kikatapula's Palawa companions in the Friendly Mission were long dead. Umarrah's widow **Wulaytupinya** died at Emu Bay in May 1832, just a few days after Kikatapula. Manalakina's wife **Tanalipunya** died on Flinders Island on 1 May 1835, followed on 4

December that year by **Manalakina** himself. **Parewareatar**, who once escaped death at the point of Kikatapula's spear, also died about that time, precise date and circumstances unrecorded. Kikatapula's widow **Pagerly** survived the illness that killed her husband and in early 1834 absconded from Robinson's mission with Karnebutcher, although both were later recaptured and, like Robinson's other faithful servants, rewarded for their service with forced island incarceration. Robinson's journal for 2 July 1834 reported that Pagerly was anxious to leave Flinders Island, but she never did. History's final sight of her is in an 1837 list of Palawa buried at Wybalenna.[13]

Kikatapula's acolytes **Tanaminawayt** and **Malapuwinarana** (Piway and Timmy) died violently in embryonic Melbourne. Having absorbed Kikatapula's campfire tales of his and Musquito's martial exploits, they absconded from a Port Phillip Aboriginal reserve in September 1841 with Planobeenna, Trukanini, and a Paytirami woman named Mathabelianna (Matilda) and terrorised settlers in the area until captured two months later. During their breakout they stole firearms, slew two men and wounded others, and in December all five were tried for murder. Although Trukanini was probably guilty, she and the other women were exonerated, but Malapuwinarana and Tanaminawayt were not. They were hanged on 20 January 1842 in Melbourne's first public execution, a festive event witnessed by most of the population of Port Phillip – nearly 5000 men, women, and children. Trukanini, with the other two women, was shipped back to Flinders Island later that year, but her husband Wurati died at sea and was buried on Green Island.

Once the object of Kikatapula's desire, **Trukanini** outlived them all. Fourteen years after returning to Flinders Island she and the 13 other surviving Palawa were removed to *putalina* (Oyster Cove) on D'Entrecasteaux Channel opposite Bruny Island, her birthplace. There she married the last Palawa man, William Lanne, who died in 1869. After the last of the other women died at Oyster Cove in 1873, Trukanini was taken to Hobart to live out her final years among the alien race that had dispossessed and destroyed her people. Perhaps, like Kikatapula, she was haunted by the knowledge of her own part in their displacement and destruction, for her all-consuming anguish is devastatingly apparent in photographs of her in her final years. A man who took her fishing on D'Entrecasteaux Channel late in her life recalled that her profound despair prevented her fishing that day. '[W]ith tears rolling down her black cheeks … for some time she never spoke a word … Then she broke down and sobbed afresh. She told me they were all dead now, excepting herself …'[14] Trukanini died a lonely death in Hobart on 8 May 1876, 72 years and eight months after the first invaders splashed ashore at Risdon Cove. Her service as Robinson's companion and saviour was lost in her melancholy celebrity as the 'last of the Tasmanians'. The desolation pervading every day of her final years cannot begin to be imagined. Only Kikatapula's in his final weeks might have been as profound.

In 1899, 23 years after Trukanini's death, and again in 1903, a woman named Fanny Cochrane Smith (1834–1905), who was believed to be the last native speaker of a Palawa language, made some wax-cylinder recordings of Palawa songs. Born on Flinders Island two years after Kikatapula died, she later lived at Oyster Cove with her mother Tanganuturra (the 'Tibb' who had travelled with Kikatapula and Robinson) and Trukanini. One song she recorded, called 'Corroboree Song', is said to have been composed and sung in honour of a great Palawa leader.

> *Lo! With might runs the man:*
> *My heel is swift like the fire.*
> *My heel is truly swift like the fire.*
> *Come thou and run like a man;*
> *A very great man, a great man,*
> *A man who is a hero!*
> *Hurrah!*[15]

The great leader is not identified by name, yet whom he was can hardly be doubted. In all the short and terrible story of the British theft of *lutruwita*, only one Palawa leader truly stood out, only one is known to have been truly worthy of being called a very great man, a hero.

Appendix 1

What remains of the warrior

Few sites associated with Kikatapula are visible today. Macquarie House, his first urban home, is extant, although it is nearly impossible to see from the street because of beleaguering 20th-century buildings. It is private property.

The St David's church Kikatapula saw being built in 1819–1823 a few metres north of Macquarie House on Macquarie Street (and attended services in) has long gone, replaced on the same site in the 1870s by the present St David's cathedral. (However, the original church's organ, whose music so enchanted Kikatapula and the other Palawa when Robinson took them to services there, can still be seen and heard at St Matthew's church, Rokeby. And the clock from its tower is at St Luke's church, Richmond.) Diagonally opposite the cathedral, the old jail where Kikatapula was a prisoner and then a clerk for almost a year 1827–1828 (and where Musquito and Black Jack were hanged) has also long gone, replaced by beautifully preserved Victorian buildings. But the old Supreme Court, in which Kikatapula faced justice in 1828, survives. It is the two-storey stone building, built 1824–1826 (and now part of the Treasury Complex) on the opposite corner of Murray and Macquarie streets. Behind that, heading north, are Franklin Square and Hobart Town Hall, where Government House once stood and where Lieutenant Governor Arthur greeted the returning Friendly Mission, including Kikatapula, on their entry into Hobart in 1832.

Farther down Macquarie Street, on the opposite side, City Hall now occupies the block that was the site of the Market Place in November 1824 when 64 visiting Palawa led by Kikatapula were sheltered there. The precise site of the Aboriginal establishment at Kangaroo Bay they were subsequently moved to is uncertain but was probably close to Kangaroo Bay Rivulet, which flows between Eastlands shopping centre and the public golf course and, after becoming a stormwater culvert, empties into Kangaroo Bay.

George Augustus Robinson's Hobart home – believed to have been where 112 Elizabeth Street is now, about three doors down from Warwick Street – and the Aboriginal asylum adjoining it that sometimes housed Kikatapula have gone. But to stand in the small park on the corner of Elizabeth and Warwick streets is to stand in the northernmost corner of Robinson's land, which extended south-west along Warwick Street almost to Murray Street and a shorter way south-east down Elizabeth Street toward Hobart CBD.

The Sorell jail, site of Kikatapula's first incarceration, disappeared in 1910 from the corner of Gordon and Fitzroy streets in that town, replaced by a newer building. But the Richmond jail, where he was sometimes housed and was once briefly incarcerated, has been preserved and is now a much-visited tourist attraction. Because of its public accessibility it has the most tangible Kikatapula associations.

There is one other: Kikatapula's burial place. The only contemporary record of its location is the entry in Robinson's journal for 22 May 1832 reporting that Kikatapula was interred at the back of the Van Diemen's Land Company's store, meaning on or close to Blackman Point at the western end of Emu Bay in the city of Burnie. Robinson asked 'that some mark might be put up to point out the spot where the ashes of this faithful servant was laid'.[1] Anthony Cottrell reported back to him that a log fence had been built around the grave.[2]

For 96 years after the burial there was no mention of the grave in any record. Then, in September 1928, probably prompted by an item that appeared the previous month in the same newspaper, Burnie historian Richard Hilder published an article stating that 'Tom Birch ... succumbed to an acute attack of dysentery and was decently buried under the boobyalla bushes at the extreme north end of Wilson Street [Burnie]'.[3] Wilson Street did not exist at the time of Kikatapula's death but the grave was recognisable as such for at least two or three decades after the burial (see below) and from 1843 was locatable by its proximity to the northern end of the then-newly named Wilson Street. (At the time it was called Ladbrooke Street. The Wilson Street of 1843 is today's Mount Street.)

Hilder repeated his statement in a subsequent article. Kikatapula, he wrote in 1931,was buried at Blackman Point 'in a sandy grave at the extreme north end of Wilson Street, Burnie'.[4] This time he did not mention boobyalla bushes but did usefully note that the soil there was sandy. He added that Blackman Point had been so named because it was reportedly the site of an ancient Palawa midden and possibly also because of Kikatapula's burial. Hilder was born in Burnie in 1856, so the grave must still have been fenced and recognisable when he was a young man in the 1870s, or a little later.

Two years after Hilder's second article was published, H. Stuart Dove, a Hilder correspondent, enlarged upon those two claims by confirming that 'As a youth, Mr. Hilder saw the fenced-in resting-place of poor Tom Birch' who 'when dying besought those about him not to bury him in "The Swamp" (the ancient cemetery), but to put him in the dry, clean beach-sand and within sight of the deserted midden on Black man's Point'.[5] His story of Kikatapula's supposed dying request not to be buried in the 'ancient cemetery', which is not known to have existed at the time Kikatapula died and was never consecrated, can safely be dismissed as filigree or folklore, but the detail about his being buried in beach sand echoes Hilder's 1931 piece and is important. Dove's article further pinpointed the grave's exact location as 'just where the hand-gate opens on to the [railway] line as one goes to the sea-beach'.[6]

Burnie researcher Brian Rollins, a surveyor by profession, has clearly identified the gate on a plan of survey made for the Railway Department on 2 October 1930. The gate was indeed at the extreme northern end of today's Wilson Street and was there so pedestrians could cross the railway line, which was opened in 1913, to get to the beach. He has determined that the grave was therefore about 230 metres from the south-western rear corner of the VDL Company's store, whose location is well established because it is clearly shown in other old plans. The store's front faced in the opposite direction, toward the waters of Emu Bay, so Kikatapula was indeed buried at the back of it.

In agreement with Hilder's comment that the grave was sandy, Rollins points out:

Blackman Point itself was notoriously thinly covered with soil and was underlain by basalt columns. The grave site obviously needed to be some distance westward of the store in order to find soil or sand of sufficient depth to accommodate the burial.[7]

The store was demolished in 1886 to allow extended shipping infrastructure at Blackman Point. Although the entire area to the immediate west of the store and the site of the store itself were excavated for their rock, Kikatapula's grave, having been dug in sandy, rock-free soil, was far enough away to have escaped that. The site is also unlikely to have been disturbed by the laying of the railway line, which would have required no excavation work, only the application of a layer of ballast to form a solid base for line-laying atop that sandy soil.

So the site is still identifiable although unmarked – the log fence has of course long gone – and the grave is almost certainly undisturbed. Its location is within a paved and landscaped waterfront parkland called The Boardwalk (aka Hilder Parade) that hugs the coastline between North Terrace and West Beach. An imagined extension of Wilson Street in the direction of the beach would cross the railway line (which laterally bisects The Boardwalk) at a place Rollins confirms was 'just where the hand-gate opens on to the [railway] line as one goes to the sea-beach', as Dove noted. The line is bordered by steel-mesh fencing, one panel of which replaces the gate that was there in the 1930s. A scrappy unmarked strip just inside the first fence, between it and the railway line where that imaginary extension of Wilson Street's western side would cross the line, is where Kikatapula lies – anonymous, unremarked, uncommemorated.

A heroic defender of his country deserves better.

Kikatapula's remains are believed to be under the twiggy debris
in the foreground between fence and train line.
(Photograph by author)

Appendix 2

Justice perverted: The trials of Musquito and Black Jack

Farce is a word that has sometimes been used, and used very accurately, to describe the trials that sent Musquito to the gallows, but *travesty* and the modern term *show trial* fit too, especially the latter. Musquito was convicted solely on the basis of John Radford's testimony about the Grindstone Bay killings, but that testimony, as has been shown, was perjured and the colonial government knew it was.[1] Moreover, there were other anomalies that have never been examined.

It must be remembered that Black Jack was executed for killing Patrick McCarthy at Sorell Plains in early 1824, not for anything to do with the Grindstone Bay killings the previous year (despite his part in them), so his trial and his culpability or otherwise in the McCarthy case are not discussed here. The perverted justice referred to was in his and Musquito's trials for aiding and abetting the murders of William Holyoake and Mammoa at Grindstone Bay.

In the first place, by the time the two stood in the dock in December 1824, more than a year after the killings, the colonial authorities were well aware of a crucially relevant matter never mentioned in court: the part Kikatapula had played in inciting the attack on the victims, which *prima facie* means he was as culpable as Musquito. The authorities were aware of it because, without trial, they had already punished Kikatapula by sentencing him to a term of imprisonment at Macquarie Harbour months before Musquito and Jack were even in custody. So when the two did stand trial for their part in the Grindstone Bay killings, the authorities already knew what had caused the attack and of Kikatapula's incitement, which might have been mitigating circumstances in Musquito's favour.

Moreover, it seems undeniable that the same colonial authorities ordered Radford not to mention Holyoake's shooting the Nununi woman because it would have weakened their case, and they may even have coached him about what to say in his testimony, for an assured outcome is essential to a show trial. That Radford was granted his certificate of freedom – fully pardoned – a few months after giving damning evidence at Musquito's trial looks anything but coincidental.[2]

Musquito and Black Jack faced Chief Justice Pedder and a jury of six military officers in Hobart on 1 December 1824. Neither of the accused was represented by legal counsel and, because they had not been baptised and therefore could not swear an oath on the Bible, neither man was allowed to give evidence in his own defence. Both pleaded not guilty. With the administration's deliberate silence about Kikatapula's complicity and with Radford's perjured testimony omitting Holyoake's shooting of the Nununi, the stage was set for a farcical trial whose outcome was never in doubt.

First, both men were tried for aiding and abetting the murder of William Holyoake. Musquito was found guilty, but Black Jack was surprisingly exonerated. Both were then tried for aiding and abetting the murder of Mammoa, and this time both were exonerated. (Black Jack was subsequently remanded to a later date and convicted on 21 January 1825 of killing McCarthy, then hanged the following month with Musquito. No record of his trial survives.) Yet the testimony of Radford, the only Caucasian witness, did not mention Musquito's playing any part in either killing beyond enticing Mammoa across the creek, away from Radford and Holyoake, then leading the Palawa back across it to the hut, where he took possession of the stockkeepers' dogs. No evidence was presented that he personally attacked or was among those who pursued Holyoake and Radford, and his 'guilt' in Holyoake's case seems to have been based solely on the fact that he was the leader of the tame mob at the time.

Black Jack's exoneration on both Grindstone Bay charges is also strange, since Radford's testimony indicates that it was likely he who stole the firearms from the hut before the attack, thereby aiding and abetting both deaths. Moreover, Radford later told George Meredith that it was Black Jack who speared him in the side, yet he did not mention that in his testimony, although it would have led to Black Jack's being charged with attempted murder.

In the wake of the 1824 attacks on settlers, the colonial authorities seem to have been determined to make an example of some Aboriginal people, especially Musquito, who was the best known, since he had been identified as present at Grindstone Bay and subsequent attacks, by making him or them pay with their lives. As revealed in *Baptised in Blood*, there exists a privately held legal document, an indictment dated 29 November 1824 and signed by Attorney-General Joseph Tice Gellibrand, charging Musquito with the attempted murder of Joseph Gerram at Pitt Water on 25 July 1824.[3] The indictment was never used and may have been intended to be lodged with the court as a fallback charge if Musquito was exonerated of the two Grindstone Bay counts. So it is clear that the authorities were determined to hang Musquito, and it is obvious that, if necessary, they were willing to bend the law to do so.

Calder noted as much in 1875, writing that 'as it may have been thought necessary to make a few examples [Musquito] may have been sacrificed to intimidate his surviving brethren into submission to the superior race'. He further observed:

> it is not easy to understand on what it was he was convicted; for whatever may have been his guilt, there was no legal proof of any, beyond presence at the hut with fifty or sixty more, and some slightly suspicious circumstances … [F]rom what I remember of the Governor of the time, of the judge who tried them, and of military juries generally, I don't believe that justice, or anything like it, was always done here fifty years ago.[4]

Appendix 3

Alexander Laing:
Cover-up and downfall

Alexander Laing's life was unusually parabolic. Born in Scotland about 1791, he was a soldier who, convicted in 1813 of theft, was sentenced to seven years' transportation. After landing in Tasmania in 1815 he seems to have ingratiated himself with influential people and at the beginning of 1820, while still a prisoner, he was appointed a District Constable at Sorell. (Most of Tasmania's earliest police were convicts or former convicts.) In the ensuing years his star waxed as he was given additional government appointments – pound-keeper, jailer, postmaster, and commissariat storekeeper – and additional salaries, culminating in his appointment in April 1824 as Sorell's Chief District Constable, the apex of his parabola. He also received several substantial grants of land (including much of the present-day Hobart dormitory suburb of Midway Point and the three acreages between Orielton and Runnymede he called Bank Head Farm), so he was successful, apparently respected, and well off.

But Laing began to fall from grace soon after attaining that apex. His plunge began early in November 1825 when he failed to capture the Pitt Water serial killer Charles Routley, complicit in the robbery and sadistic murder of the merchant Alexander Simpson.[1] Routley, an ex-convict turned farmer, had previously murdered three other men, all convicts, but had not yet come under suspicion. However, when he was suspected of being a party to slaying Simpson, a respectable free settler, he fled to the bush and was harboured by criminal sympathisers around Pitt Water. Laing knew that but failed to find him, although he may not have tried very hard, for the two of them were old acquaintances.

That apparently minor blemish to Laing's character was exacerbated later the same month when the bushranger Matthew Brady and his gang captured the Sorell jail and a military garrison billeted in it. They shot at Laing in his own home and seriously wounded the garrison's commander, Lieutenant William Gunn. What Laing actually did with himself after he fled from the scene is uncertain because of a falsified newspaper report and, much later, purloined official records.[2] But, whether by accident or design, he disappeared from sight about the time Gunn was shot and he remained invisible until long after the bushrangers had gone and a civilian had freed the military garrison. Whatever did happen to Laing that night, that incident and several others were falsified in his 1867 memoir to make him appear in a heroic light.

So Laing was already under a cloud by the time he left Sorell shortly before midnight on 8 December the following year to go to Robert Grimes's rescue at Bank Head Farm. He probably knew he was in disfavour and was determined to try to rescue his reputation by teaching Kikatapula's mob a severe lesson. Possibly he was drunk that Saturday night as he marched out, for he was a confessed alcoholic.

What is very significant, and *prima facie* inexplicable, is that Laing earned no public praise after apprehending Kikatapula (as Gilbert Robertson did in 1828 for capturing Umarrah). On the contrary, his career trajectory turned steeply downward instead of ascending, as might have been expected after such an important arrest. In the wake of the Brady raid and Bank Head Farm he had clearly come to be seen as a dangerous liability – a weak link on the one hand and a ruthless killer on the other, so not to be trusted. As a drunk who seems to have been garrulous, he would also have to be carefully handled to ensure he kept his mouth shut. He would need to have his activities watched and he would need to be answerable to a trustworthy superior.

The first evidence that he was in bad odour came within weeks of Bank Head Farm. In early 1827 the Executive Council had recommended Tasmania be divided into six police districts, one of them Sorell. Yet when the districts were promulgated in March that year there were only five, none of them Sorell. Instead of becoming a discrete police district as recommended, with Laing as Chief District Constable, Sorell was inexplicably lumped in with neighbouring Richmond. Even when the new system was finally implemented in early 1828 with nine districts instead of five, Sorell was not one; it remained subsumed in Richmond. Laing was consequently demoted from Chief District Constable, an office he had been promoted to only 19 months before the Brady raid, to constable. The combination of Brady and Bank Head Farm with a need to cover up the latter seems to have made his name execrable to the government, resulting in Sorell's downgrading and Laing's position as Chief District Constable becoming untenable. That obviated the need to dismiss him outright. Perhaps one intention was to get him out from under the aegis of local magistrate James Gordon, but even he could not prevent Laing's demotion through the Sorell police district's downgrading.

Some of the official correspondence that might have revealed more has not survived, but what is left permits reasonable inference of its content. It suggests that although the government wanted to get rid of Laing, someone in it was willing to protect him. His immediate protector was obviously Gordon; their collusion in the Bank Head Farm cover-up meant it was in his interest to protect Laing in order to protect himself. For the same reason Arthur must have protected Gordon, and through him Laing, even as he was a party, via the Executive Council, to downgrading Laing to a minor player in Pitt Water affairs so he could do no more harm. It seems to have been done in a way that would make it appear he was not being punished.

The first such letter, dated 4 May 1827, five months after Bank Head Farm, was from Dudley Fereday, the Sheriff of Van Diemen's Land, to Laing.

> In reply to your letter of the 27th April last relative to an order sent to you by Dr Garrett requiring you to confine a Prisoner. I consider that [illegible] applies to you as Chief Constable and not as Gaoler therefore I could not interfere – but I think it would be better were you to resign the Chief Constableship as I conceive it must interfere very considerably with your Duty as Gaoler.[3]

That seems to have been the second intimation that Laing was in official disfavour, the first being Sorell's omission from the promulgation in March of the new police districts, from which Laing probably sensed what was happening. He undoubtedly understood Fereday's advice was meant as a fairly painless way for him to fall on his sword, for if mere incompatibility of duties were truly a problem, it had taken the administration a full three years to realise it, Laing having been jailer since 1822 and Chief District Constable since April 1824. Moreover, if the positions were genuinely incompatible he could just as easily have quit being jailer and kept the more prestigious and better-paying job of Chief District Constable, as in fact the Lieutenant Governor was to suggest to him, probably two-facedly, in a letter dated 18 May. So Fereday's letter was voicing the government's opinion. Quit the job you've demonstrated your unsuitability for, it was saying, and we'll let you keep the lowlier position so you won't be destitute.

Whether Laing's response to Fereday showed him prepared to go quietly or was actually an implied appeal for protection is uncertain – in it he made sure Lieutenant Governor Arthur knew he was being pushed, so it sounds like the latter – but he duly offered his resignation to the Colonial Secretary on 7 May 1827, five months after Bank Head Farm.

> I beg leave to enclose a communication I received from D. Fereday Esqr., Sheriff of Van Diemen's Land which I beg you will be placed before His Excellency the Lieut Governor relative to my Situations of Chief District Constable and Gaoler wherein it is the Sheriff's opinion that I would better resign the Constableship.
>
> I therefore humbly beg that His Excellency in his most gracious consideration may be pleased to allow me to resign the Office of Chief District Constable which I have filled in the District of Gloucester upwards of seven years.[4]

Further communication between the government and James Gordon ensued, and perhaps certain unrecorded compromises were reached. On 2 June 1827 Laing again offered to resign.

> I beg leave to acknowledge your letter of 18th May last wherein His Excellency the Lieutenant Governor is pleased to express his approbation of my conduct as Chief District Constable and that His Excellency has been graciously pleased to allow me to reconsider the matter[,] it being possible that [it] may be most advantageous for me to continue in the Office of Chief District Constable and assign that of Gaoler –

I beg to state that I am perfectly satisfied with the Salary and the Indulgences His Excellency is pleased to allow me and [indecipherable] if His Excellency will be pleased to accept my resignation as Chief District Constable and permit me to hold that of Gaoler as my health is considerably impaired since November 1825 when I had a severe illness which I have not quite recovered [from] and the duties of Chief District Constable in this populous District are sometimes hard for me to perform requiring me to be frequently in the Bush at night on purpose to secure those delinquents required and search for property stolen.[5]

The letter is curious, difficult to interpret. Perhaps Laing, knowing his neck was on the block, offered his resignation as a face-saving gesture. Yet there is a little evidence that he may have been angry at being forced to do so. Laing had been a convict in Tasmania since 1815, yet no blemish was noted on his conduct record until 2 June 1827 – the precise date he wrote that letter of resignation. On that date, for reasons unknown, he was charged with neglect of duty. (Whether charge or resignation came first is unknown.) A bench of three local magistrates – Gordon, Butcher, and Glover – acquitted him.

Nevertheless, the government was willing to accept his resignation, and on 13 June asked Gordon to nominate a successor. But Gordon preferred Laing to remain in office. On 21 June he told the Colonial Secretary that Laing was the only man for the job and then turned the blame for Laing's malfeasance back onto the administration for failing to appoint enough constables at Pitt Water.

In reply to your letter of the 13th of June in which you request me to name a proper Person to succeed Mr. Alexr. Laing in the Office of Chief District Constable he holding at the same Time the Office of Gaoler, which are considered incompatible in the same Person[,] I beg leave to say that I have attentively considered the subject but at present I am unable to name any Person for His Excellency's Consideration[.] I take the Opportunity further to observe that the Situation[s] of Gaoler [and Chief District Constable] are incompatible[.] [W]hen a very constant Attention to the Duty of Gaoler is required it would be out of the Power of one Man to perform both, but in this instance the Duties of Gaoler are light, and when the Case is otherwise, as having two or three Prisoners held for further Examination, his Position as Constable might be dispensed with for the Moment, if there were a sufficient number of Petty Constables, which I must say is not the Case at present as there are only two in the District of Gloucester and in the adjoining District of Sussex where there used to be four we have at present only one. Also in his Situation as Gaoler he is in some Measure relieved by the Sheriff having placed two Javelin Men in Attendance at the Gaol – I have stated this much in Hope that His Excellency will not at present accede to Mr. Laing's Request to resign his Situation of Constable as I certainly do not know any Person, (who would take the Situation) so competent to take Charge of the Sunday Muster and make proper and correct Returns, where there is a Prisoner Population of near 250 scattered over a Space of fourteen Miles by four [22.5 km by 6.4 km, or 144 km²].[6]

The matter remained in stalemate, although five months later, in November 1827, a Laing-led posse failed to catch the bushranger Thomas Pearson and an accomplice near Sorell despite having been given accurate information about where they were camped. As G.T. Lloyd wrote, 'The escape of two runaway prisoners on foot from six vigorous and efficiently armed men, did not add to the chief constable's fame as a general'.[7] (Laing did lead a later party that apprehended Pearson, although he falsely claimed in his memoir to have personally captured the bushranger.)[8] However, the impasse was resolved bloodlessly in 1828 when the Sorell police district disappeared and Laing's office of Chief District Constable disappeared with it. On 8 November that year the *Hobart Town Courier* reported Gilbert Robertson had been gazetted a Chief District Constable and Laing a constable and pound-keeper.

Laing's subsequent career was chequered for he had a knack for rubbing people up the wrong way. In 1836 the local parson, Rev. James Norman, and a Sorell businessman named Robert Doctor were said to be conspiring to have him sacked, but their attempts failed.[9] He resigned from the constabulary in December 1838, but what he did for the next few years is uncertain. In the 1842 census he was shown still at Sorell and seemingly prosperous, for he was recorded as owning and occupying one Sorell property, owning property at Midway Point, another house and other property in Sorell, and Bank Head Farm at Orielton. Yet by the time of his death 26 years later he had lost it all.

For a while he seems to have remained at Pitt Water, presumably farming and still battling alcoholism. In 1845, while working as overseer for James Gordon's widow at Forcett House, a few kilometres from Sorell, he drunkenly attacked another employee, costing him a £5 fine. Early the following year he moved on. In the ensuing years he was recorded as a constable at Norfolk Bay (Taranna) – while there he signed a pledge of abstinence – a jailer at Richmond, and acting commissariat storekeeper at Norfolk Bay, under-jailer at Norfolk Bay, and a petty constable at Point Puer at a penny an hour, which he was bitter about. Later he was under-jailer at Hobart, jailer at Richmond, and jailer at New Norfolk. In 1856 he was appointed a wardsman at Royal Derwent Hospital, New Norfolk's lunatic asylum. The year after his appointment he sought and was given a testimonial from the hospital's medical superintendent that read, in part, 'Mr. A. Laing has been employed as wardsman at this institution for the last twelve months ... [D]uring that time his habits have been perfectly steady and sober ...'.[10]

But on 10 July 1862, after about 12 years at the asylum, he was sacked for being drunk on duty, whereupon he returned to Pitt Water. He and his remaining family moved in with his daughter Susanna and her husband Bartholomew Reardon III at Green Hills, Forcett, where he spent the rest of his life. In the same year, G.T. Lloyd, who had lived at Pitt Water for some years from 1820 but was now resident in London, published a book, *Thirty Three Years in Victoria and Tasmania*, that disparaged Laing. Laing was indignant about it. 'George T. Lloyd', he wrote,

> has published a work entitled 'Twenty Three Years a Resident in Tasmania' [*sic*] ... In his book Mr. Lloyd makes mention of Brady's gang, Charles Routley and Pearson the bushranger, and gives me credit for jumping through one of my windows to escape from Brady's gang, and also of being too fat and broken winded to catch Pearson the bushranger, matters that he knew nothing about, only from hearsay.[11]

In 1867, in attempted repudiation, he wrote a 40,000-word memoir – never published but often unquestioningly quoted from – in which he falsified history to show his own actions in the best possible light, hid his misdeeds, falsely inflated the peripheral parts he played in some events, and mendaciously put himself at the heroic centre of other actions that he had taken no part in.

Although mentioning his involvement in Kikatapula's 1826 capture, the memoir omitted almost every relevant detail – 'we fell in with ... them' was its only description of Laing's capturing Kikatapula at Bank Head Farm. He also lied about the place and the date of the incident, and he obscured other details in a narrative rife with obfuscations, falsehoods, and omissions.

> After bushranging nearly ceased, the Aborigines became troublesome and commenced murdering the white population indiscriminately. They murdered a settler and his wife and a shepherd within a few miles of Sorell, and severely wounded others in the neighbourhood, especially a female at the Carlton, named Judith Pearce ... I was ordered out by the Police Magistrate [Gordon] to head a party in pursuit of them. I marched off with three soldiers and two constables. After four days travelling, we fell in with ten of them, five males, three females and two boys. Amongst them were Mosquito [*sic*] ... and Black Tom, generally called Birch's Tom. He was reared from his infancy and educated by Mr. Birch, a merchant at Hobartown, and when he grew up to between sixteen and seventeen years of age, he absconded and joined his country people the rest of the Aborigines. Those two Mosquito and Tom could talk English fluently. They were the first gang of Aborigines that had been captured. I was well acquainted with Black Tom Birch, as I had often seen him when he was nursing Mr. Birch's children at Hobartown. I lodged them all safe in the Gaol on the 4th January 1829. Colonel Arthur the Governor, came to Sorell to see them, and held a long consultation with Mosquito and Tom. They acknowledged the murder of Thomas Coffin and his wife at Clapson's Point ... [but] denied murdering Mr. Stacey's shepherd at the Cherry Tree Opening [Pawleena]. His Excellency ordered them to be removed to the Richmond Gaol, where they would be turned out for exercise under the care of the constables and javelin men. They remained at Richmond for upwards of two months and Colonel Arthur sent instructions to the Police Magistrate to furnish them with an ample supply of blankets and provisions and turn them out at large in the bush. They were not heard

of several months. At length they commenced in the Oatlands district, murdering and wounding every European that came their way, and burning down stock keepers, shepherds and sawyer's huts.

That is mostly arrant nonsense. Musquito and Kikatapula were never captured together. Emma Coffin was slain on 18 September 1829, more than eight months after the date Laing gives for their fictitious tandem capture and two years and nine months after Kikatapula's actual capture at Bank Head Farm. Her husband was wounded the following year. The attack on Judith Pearce was on 15 March 1830, 14 months after Laing's invented double capture of Musquito and Kikatapula and three years and three months after Bank Head Farm. John Stacey's shepherd was killed in October 1830, 21 months after Laing's fabricated dual capture date and nearly four years after Kikatapula's actual capture.[12] Moreover, none of those incidents involved Kikatapula or the long-dead Musquito – as Laing would have known, since in 1829 he and Kikatapula were both working for Gilbert Robertson. So why did he lie? The ostensibly bloodless capture of Kikatapula and his band was, on the face of it, one of Laing's few real achievements as a lawman and one he might have wanted posterity to know about in detail, for he was not averse to bragging.

Late in his life, as he composed his memoir, Laing's memory, even for dates, was generally good and his recall demonstrably quite accurate – as long as he had nothing to lose by telling the truth. But his account of Kikatapula's capture is so convoluted and confusing that it amounts to nothing more than an obvious and deliberate falsification. His connecting Musquito and Kikatapula is absurd, for although the two were comrades-in-arms in 1823–1824, Musquito was hanged in February 1825, as Laing well knew. Moreover, Laing played no part in capturing and jailing Musquito, who was never incarcerated in Sorell jail with or without Kikatapula; Laing, Sorell's only jailer until years after Kikatapula's death, would have known that too. The date he gives for incarcerating the Bank Head Farm survivors, 4 January 1829, is also misleading nonsense. Musquito had been dead for nearly four years by then, and Kikatapula, captured twice after Musquito's execution, including once by Laing, had changed sides by that time and was working as a guide for Gilbert Robertson, Laing's immediate superior, as Laing would have known.

Most significantly, his memoir does not even mention that Kikatapula was captured on his own farm, something he would hardly have forgotten, but he took care in writing about it to place the event well away from there. He knew very well that his farm was not four days' travel from Sorell, as he claimed; according to a newspaper report it took his party about four or five *hours* (on foot) to get there from Sorell. And the memoir's juxtaposition of the 1830 attack on Judith Pearce at Carlton, which is south-east of Sorell, with Laing's 'subsequent' 1826 capture of Kikatapula at Orielton, which is in the opposite direction, north-west of Sorell and a long way – about 35 kilometres – from Carlton, is part of that deliberate falsification.

Yet there is no doubt the memoir was referring to his capture of Kikatapula; he gave enough factual details to evince that. If, as seems unquestionable, local people knew there had been Palawa slaughtered at Bank Head Farm, Laing would have wanted it remembered that it was he who captured Kikatapula but would not have wanted it known that the capture was associated with something shameful like killings (possibly of women and children as well as men) in a surprise attack. So he claimed the capture, and therefore his own action, happened well away from Bank Head Farm and was peaceable. That would imply not one but two separate events: the commonly known and talked-about bloodshed at Bank Head Farm involving unnamed persons on both sides, and Laing's purportedly bloodless capture of Kikatapula supposedly four days' travel from Sorell, so a long way from Bank Head Farm and the bloodshed there.

There can be little doubt that Alexander Laing was a man with something so shameful on his conscience that he attempted to falsify history in order to cover it up.

Acknowledgements

As always, people readily responded to requests for information or assistance, and I thank all of them: Alison Alexander, the Burnie Historical Society, the British Museum, Nick Brodie, Peter and Judy Cocker, Barbara Cox, Kathy Duncombe, Mike and Renata Jakupec, Douglas Lockhart, Tony Marshall, Ian McFarlane, Mary and the late Andy McKinlay, Liz and Gerard McShane, Hamish Maxwell-Stewart, Robyn Mosley, John Olding, Christopher Pearce, Michael Powell, Mary Ramsay (Bothwell Historical Society), Tony Rayner, the late Irene Schaffer, Rebe Taylor, Ian Terry, Jaydeyn Thomas (Burnie Regional Museum), and David Thompson. Thanks too to those staff at the Tasmanian Archive and Heritage Office who cheerfully shared their expertise, particularly Fiona Macfarlane and Kim Pearce.

I am also fortunate to have had invaluable contributions from Birch family members Nancy Birch and Jenny Yates. Their knowledge of the family's history and willingness to share it made possible my piecing together hitherto unknown details of Kikatapula's life in the difficult period 1819–1824. I am profoundly grateful for their cooperation.

The contemporary Palawa community was equally forthcoming in responding to requests for assistance, and I acknowledge with thanks the help of Tony Brown (Tasmanian Museum and Art Gallery), puralia meenamatta/Jim Everett, Julie Gough, Greg Lehman, Zoe Rimmer (Tasmanian Museum and Art Gallery), Annie Reynolds (palawa kani Language Program, Tasmanian Aboriginal Corporation), Theresa Sainty (Tasmanian Aboriginal Corporation), and Gaye Sculthorpe (British Museum).

Nick Clements kindly offered trenchant comments on the manuscript and generously shared invaluable material from his own research. I am much in his debt.

To Lyndall Ryan, a source of encouragement and assistance for more than a decade, I register my sincere appreciation, not least for her generous Foreword. And I am beholden to Henry Reynolds, who read and unhesitatingly endorsed the manuscript.

Appendix 1, which reveals the location of Kikatapula's gravesite in the city of Burnie, was greatly facilitated by Brian Rollins, whose professional skill as a surveyor and knowledge of the records of the Van Diemen's Land Company were crucial. His selflessness in sharing his expertise is very much appreciated.

Working with the team at Wakefield Press has been a personal and professional pleasure. Thank you Julia Beaven, Michael Deves, Stacey Zass, Poppy Nwosu and Maddy Sexton.

Immeasurable gratitude is owed to my grandfather, William Parsons, who first lit my word-fire, and my remarkable mother, Phyllis Cox, who fuelled it with books. I also gratefully acknowledge opportunities and encouragement given long ago to a fledgling writer by Richard Slatter and the late Susan Yorke.

My greatest gratitude, as always and with everything, is owed to my dear wife Lou, who demonstrates daily that love is absolute and never self-serving. Her contributions to this book, directly and indirectly, are innumerable.

Bibliography

BOOKS

– *Historical Records of Australia* Series 3 Volumes 1–6

– *Van Diemen's Land: Copies of All Correspondence Between Lieutenant Governor Arthur and His Majesty's Secretary of State for the Colonies, on the Subject of the Military Operations Lately Carried on Against the Aboriginal Inhabitants of Van Diemen's Land*, Hobart, Tasmanian Historical Research Association, 1971

Bonwick, James, *The Last of the Tasmanians*, London, Sampson Low, Son, & Marston, 1870 (facsimile edition, Adelaide, Libraries Board of South Australia, 1969)

Bonwick, James, *The Lost Tasmanian Race*, London, Sampson Low, Marston, Searle, and Rivington, 1884

Bowden, K.M., *Captain James Kelly of Hobart Town*, Melbourne, Melbourne University Press, 1964

Boyce, James, *God's Own Country: The Anglican Church and Tasmanian Aborigines*, Hobart, The Social Action and Research Centre Anglicare Tasmania, 2001

Boyce, James, *Van Diemen's Land*, Melbourne, Black Inc., 2008

Breen, Shayne, and Dyan Summers, *Aboriginal Connections with Launceston Places*, Launceston City Council, 2006

Breen, Shayne, *Contested Places: Tasmania's Northern Districts from ancient times to 1900*, Hobart, Centre for Tasmanian Historical Studies, 2001

Brodie, Nick, *The Vandemonian War: The Secret History of Britain's Tasmanian Invasion*, Richmond, Hardie Books, 2017

Calder, Graeme, *Levée, Line and Martial Law: A History of the Dispossession of the* Mairremmener *People of Van Diemen's Land 1803–1832*, Launceston, Fullers Bookshop, 2010

Calder, James (ed. 'Eustace Fitzsymonds'), *Brady, McCabe, Dunne, Bryan, Crawford, Murphy, Bird, McKenney, Goodwin, Pawley, Bryant, Cody, Hodgetts, Gregory, Tilley, Ryan, Williams and their associates, bushrangers in Van Diemen's Land*, Adelaide, Sullivan's Cove, 1979

Calder, J.E., *Some Account of the Wars, Extirpation, Habits, &c., of the Native Tribes of Tasmania*, facsimile edition, Hobart, Fullers Bookshop Publishing Division, 1972 (orig. pub. 1875)

Cameron, Patsy, *Grease and Ochre: The blending of two cultures at the colonial sea frontier*, Launceston, Fullers Bookshop, 2011

Clements, Nicholas, *The Black War: Fear, Sex and Resistance in Tasmania*, St Lucia, University of Queensland Press, 2014

Cotton, William Jackson, *Land of the Sleeping Giants: Untold History and Mythology of the Tasmanian Aborigines*, Hobart, Wellington Bridge Press, 2013

Cox, Robert, *A Compulsion to Kill: The Surprising Story of Australia's Earliest Serial Killers*, Brisbane, Glass House Books, 2014

Cox, Robert, *Baptised in Blood: The shocking secret history of Sorell*, Hobart, Wellington Bridge Press, 2010

Cox, Robert, *Steps to the Scaffold: The untold story of Tasmania's black bushrangers*, Pawleena, Cornhill Publishing, 2004

Duyker, Edward (ed.), *The Discovery of Tasmania: Journal extracts from the expeditions of Abel Janszoon Tasman and Marc-Joseph Dufresne 1642 and 1772*, Hobart, St David's Park Publishing, 1992

Dyer, Colin, *The French Explorers and the Aboriginal Australians 1772–1839*, St Lucia, University of Queensland Press, 2005

Ellis, Vivienne Rae, *Trucanini: Queen or Traitor?*, Canberra, Institute of Aboriginal Studies, 1981

Evans, G.W., *A Geographical Historical and Topographical Description of Van Diemen's Land*, Melbourne, William Heinemann Ltd, 1967 (facsimile of 1822 original)

Fornasiero, Jean, Peter Monteath, and John West-Sooby, *Encountering Terra Australis: The Australian Voyages of Nicholas Baudin and Matthew Flinders*, Kent Town, Wakefield Press, 2004

Harman, Kristyn, *Aboriginal Convicts: Australian, Khoisan and Maori Exiles*, Sydney, Newsouth Publishing, 2012

Johnson, Murray, and Ian McFarlane, *Van Diemen's Land: An Aboriginal History*, Sydney, Newsouth Publishing, 2015

Lawson, Tom, *The Last Man: A British Genocide in Tasmania*, London, I.B. Tauris & Co. Ltd, 2014

Bibliography

Lennox, Geoff, *Richmond Gaol and Richmond Police District*, Rosetta, Dormaslen Publications, 1993

Levy, M.C.L., *Governor George Arthur: A Colonial Benevolent Despot*, Melbourne, Georgian House Pty Ltd, 1953

Manne, Robert (ed.), *Whitewash: On Keith Windschuttle's Fabrication of Aboriginal History*, Melbourne, Black Inc. Agenda, 2003

Mason-Cox, Margaret, *Lifeblood of a Colony: A History of Irrigation in Tasmania*, Hobart, Rivers and Water Supply Commission, 1994

McFarlane, Ian, *Beyond Awakening: The Aboriginal Tribes of North West Tasmania: A History*, Launceston, Fullers Bookshop, 2008

McKay, Anne (ed.), *Journals of the Land Commissioners for Van Diemen's Land 1826–28*, Hobart, University of Tasmania/Tasmanian Historical Research Association, 1962

McKenna, Mark, *From the Edge: Australia's Lost Histories*, Carlton, The Miegunyah Press, 2016

McKinlay, Mary, *Forgotten Tasmanians*, Richmond, Mary McKinlay, 2010

Melville, Henry, *The History of Van Diemen's Land from the Year 1824 to 1835, inclusive*, Sydney, Horwitz-Grahame, 1995 (facsimile of 1835 edition)

Meredith, Louisa Anne, *My Home in Tasmania*, London, John Murray, 1852

Morgan, Sharon, *Land Settlement in Early Tasmania: Creating an Antipodean England*, Cambridge, Cambridge University Press, 1992

Mortimer, George, *Observations and Remarks Made During a Voyage to the Islands of Teneriffe, Amsterdam, Maria's Islands near Van Diemen's Land; Otaheite, Sandwich Islands; Owhyhee, The Fox Islands on the North West Coast of America, Tinian, and from thence to Canton*, London, George Mortimer, 1791 (facsimile edition published in Amsterdam by N. Israel and New York by Da Capo Press, 1975)

Nash, Michael, *The Bay Whalers: Tasmania's Shore-Based Whaling Industry*, Woden, Navarine Publishing, 2003

Nicholls, Mary (ed.), *The Diary of the Reverend Robert Knopwood 1803–1838, First Chaplain of Van Diemen's Land*, [Hobart], Tasmanian Historical Research Association, 1977

Nyman, Lois, *The East Coasters: The Early Pioneering History of the East Coast of Tasmania*, Launceston, Regal Publications, 1990

Parramore, W.T., (ed. Shelton, D.C.), *The Parramore Letters, Written from Van Diemen's Land 1823–1825*, Epping, n.p., 1993

Plomley, Brian, and Kristen Anne Henley, *The Sealers of Bass Strait and the Cape Barren Island Community*, Hobart, Blubber Head Press, 1990

Plomley, N.J.B., *A Word-List of the Tasmanian Aboriginal Languages*, Launceston, n.p., 1976

Plomley, N.J.B., *The Aboriginal/Settler Clash in Van Diemen's Land 1803–1831*, [Launceston], Queen Victoria Museum & Art Gallery, 1992

Plomley, N.J.B. (ed.), *Friendly Mission: The Tasmanian Journals and Papers of George Augustus Robinson 1829–1834*, [Hobart], Tasmanian Historical Research Association, 1966

Plomley, N.J.B. (ed.), *Friendly Mission: The Tasmanian Journals and Papers of George Augustus Robinson 1829–1834*, Queen Victoria Museum and Art Gallery and Quintus Publishing, 2008

Plomley, N.J.B. (ed.), *Jorgen Jorgenson and the Aborigines of Van Diemen's Land*, Hobart, Blubber Head Press, 1991

Plomley, N.J.B., *Tasmanian Aboriginal Place Names*, Launceston, Queen Victoria Museum & Art Gallery, n.d.

Plomley, N.J.B., *The Tasmanian Tribes* and *Cicatrices as Tribal Indicators among the Tasmanian Aborigines*, Launceston, Queen Victoria Museum & Art Gallery, n.d.

Plomley, N.J.B. (ed.), *Weep in Silence: A History of the Flinders Island Aboriginal Settlement*, Hobart, Blubber Head Press, 1987

Powell, Michael, *Musquito: Brutality and Exile*, Hobart, Fullers Bookshop, 2016

Rae-Ellis, Vivienne, *Black Robinson, Protector of Aborigines*, Carlton South, Melbourne University Press, 1996

Reynolds, Henry, *Fate of a Free People*, Penguin Books Australia, 1995

Roth, H. Ling, *The Aborigines of Tasmania*, Hobart, Fullers Bookshop, n.d. (facsimile of 1899 second edition)

Ryan, Lyndall, *The Aboriginal Tasmanians*, St Lucia, University of Queensland Press, 1981

Ryan, Lyndall, *Tasmanian Aborigines: A History Since 1803*, Sydney, Allen & Unwin, 2012

Stephens, Geoffrey, *Knopwood: A Biography*, Hobart, n.p., 1990

Tardif, Phillip, *John Bowen's Hobart: The Beginning of European Settlement in Tasmania*, Hobart, Tasmanian Historical Research Association, 2003

Taylor, Rebe, *Unearthed: The Aboriginal Tasmanians of Kangaroo Island*, Kent Town, Wakefield Press, 2002

Taylor, Rebe, *Into the Heart of Tasmania: A Search for Human Antiquity*, Melbourne, Melbourne University Press, 2017

Turnbull, Clive, *Black War: The extermination of the Tasmanian Aborigines*, Melbourne, Cheshire-Lansdowne, 1965

Weatherburn, A.K., *George William Evans, explorer*, Sydney, Angus & Robertson, 1966

Weatherburn, A.K., *Australia's Interior Unveiled: A Biography of George William Evans ((1780–1852), Surveyor, Explorer and Artist*, Sydney, self-published, 1987

Weeding, J.S., *A History of the Lower Midlands*, Launceston, Mary Fisher Bookshop, 1980

West, John (ed. Shaw, A.G.L.), *The History of Tasmania*, Sydney, Angus & Robertson, 1973. First published 1852.

Windschuttle, Keith, *The Fabrication of Aboriginal History: Volume One, Van Diemen's Land 1803–1847*, Sydney, Macleay Press, 2002

PAPERS, JOURNALS, MANUSCRIPTS, etc.

Amos, Adam, Diary of Adam Amos, TAHO NS 323/1

Anon, Untitled folder of miscellaneous papers re Aborigines, TAHO

Anon, 'Hand-written account of livestock and sundry farming operations by Edmund and Sarah Hodgson and Mrs. Edmund Birch [*sic*] in Van Diemen's Land in the years 1826 and 1827', TAHO CRO 630.9946 HOD

Brodie, Nicholas Dean, 'He had been a faithful servant': Henry Melville's lost manuscripts, Black Tom, and Aboriginal negotiations in Van Diemen's land [online]. *Journal of Australian Colonial History*, Vol. 17, 2015: [45]–64

Burbury, Stephanie, 'Lovely Banks[,] Stoney Hut Valley and Serpentine Valley: Notes in preparation for a walk May 1996', TAHO TLQ 994.626 BUR

Cox, Robert, 'Black Tom Birch: Fact and Fiction', Tasmanian Historical Research Association *Papers and Proceedings*, Vol. 60 No. 1, April 2013

Fels, Marie, 'Culture Contact in the County of Buckinghamshire Van Diemen's Land 1803–1811', THRA *Papers and Proceedings*, Vol. 29 No. 2, June 1982

Gatehouse, George, folder, TAHO

Hobler, George, Journal, 1825–1871, Mitchell Library, Sydney

Horton, Rev. William, Wesleyan Missionary Papers, BT 52 Vol. 4, Mitchell Library, Sydney

Laing, Alexander, *The Memoir of Alexander Laing*, 1867, unpublished manuscript, typed transcription, TAHO NS1116/1

Longman, Murray J., 'Songs of the Tasmanian Aborigines as Recorded by Mrs. Fanny Cochrane Smith', *Papers and Proceedings of the Royal Society of Tasmania*, Vol. 94, pp. 79–85

Powell, Michael, 'Assessing magnitude: Tasmanian Aboriginal Demography and the significance of Musquito in the Black War', *History Compass* 13/8 (2015): 375–384, 10.1111/hic3.12248

Rayner, Tony, 'Mannalargenna: Plomley's incorrect identification of Mannalargenna as a chief of the Oyster Bay Tribe', unpublished paper TAC 1996: 2–3. Copy in author's possession.

Robertson, Gilbert, Journal of the Proceedings of a Party, TAHO CSO
1/332/7578
Robertson, Gilbert, Memorandum for a Journal, TAHO CSO 1/331/7578
Sutherland, James C., Diary, TAHO NS61

WEBSITES

http://macquariepoint.com/wp-content/uploads/2013/04/Macquarie-
Point-Historical-Summary.pdf http://connectingthefamily.blogspot.com.
au/2014/04/52-ancestors-in-52-weeks-15-sarah-birch.html
http://connectingthefamily.blogspot.com.au/2012/05/notes-from-mc2-george-
guest-mary.html
http://www.law.mq.edu.au/research/colonial_case_law/tas/cases/
case_index/1824/r_v_musquito_and_black_jack/
http://www.law.mq.edu.au/research/colonial_case_law/nsw/other_features/
correspondence/robinson_speech_1838/ (report of George Augustus
Robinson's speech to the Australian Aborigines Protection Society, 19
October 1838)

NEWSPAPERS

Tasmanian newspapers and periodicals from 1810 and Sydney newspapers
from 1808. Specific items therefrom quoted in the text are cited as endnotes.

Notes

TAHO is the Tasmanian Archive and Heritage Office, formerly called the
Archives Office of Tasmania (AOT). CSO is the prefix of numbered records of
the Colonial Secretary's Office, CON the prefix of convict records, and NS the
prefix of non-state (unofficial) records held at TAHO.

Notes

Preface

1 Clements, *Black War*, p. 4.
2 *ibid.*, p. 208.
3 *ibid.*, pp. 3–4.
4 Respectively, *Hobart Town Courier*, 17 November 1827; *Hobart Town Gazette*, 2 December 1826; *ibid.*, 8 May 1827; *Colonial Times*, 11 May 1827; the *Tasmanian*, 16 November 1827; *Colonial Advocate*, 1 October 1828.
5 George Thomas Lloyd, *Thirty Three Years in Tasmania and Victoria*, London, Houlston and Wright, 1862, p. 211.
6 http://www.utas.edu.au/telling-places-in-country/historical-context/historical-biographies/kickerterpoller
7 Greg Lehman, 'Regarding the Savages' in Lehman and Tim Bonyhady, *The National Picture: The art of Tasmania's Black War, Canberra*, National Gallery of Australia, n.d., quoting Shayne Breen, 'Extermination, extinction, genocide: British colonialism and Tasmanian Aborigines' in Rene Lemarchand (ed.), *Forgotten genocides: oblivion, denial, and memory*, University of Pennsylvania Press, Philadelphia, 2011.
8 Clements, *Black War*, p. 79.
9 Ryan, *Aboriginal Tasmanians*, p. 83.
10 Plomley, *Friendly Mission*, p. 571.
11 Cox, 'Black Tom Birch: Fact and Fiction', THRA *Papers and Proceedings*, Vol. 60 No. 1, April 2013.
12 *Mercury* (Hobart), 2 June 2019.
13 H. Maxwell-Stewart, 'Competition and Conflict on the Forgotten Frontier, Western Van Diemen's Land 1822–33', *History Australia*, 6, 3 (2009): 1–19.
14 Rhys Jones, 'Tasmanian Tribes' (seminar paper, Department of Prehistory, RSPS, ANU, 1971), p. 20.
15 Plomley, *Friendly Mission*, 1st edn, p. 978.
16 Greg Lehman at http://www.utas.edu.au/library/ companion_to_tasmanian_history/P/Palawa%20Voice.htm

Chapter 1 ~ 'A timorous, harmless race of people'

1 Recent research on Clark Island in Bass Strait indicates it had been inhabited it for at least 41,000–45,000 years. (ABC Radio news, 11 September 2017, at http://www.abc.net.au/news/2017-09-11/

scientists-tracing-ancient-aboriginal-fire-practice-on-tasmania/8891626). And artefacts excavated at *kutalayna*, in Jordan River valley not far from Hobart, in 2009–2010 were similarly dated. See Taylor, *Into the Heart*, p. 2.

2   Anthony Trollope, *Victoria and Tasmania*, London, Chapman and Hall, 1875, p. 128.

3   Quoted in Dyer, *French Explorers*, p. 85.

4   *Mercury*, 10 August 1936.

5   Mortimer, *Observations and Remarks*, p. 19.

6   Matthew Flinders, *A Voyage*, vol. 1, p. clxxxvii, quoted in Miriam Estensen, *The Life of Matthew Flinders*, Crows Nest, Allen & Unwin, 2002, p. 79.

Chapter 2 ~ 'They rushed them at their fires'

1   Plomley, *Friendly Mission*, 20 November 1831.

2   *ibid.*, 25 October 1830. The palawa kani preferred spelling of his band's name is Paytirami.

3   http://sydney.edu.au/arts/research/baudin/voyage/timeline.shtml

4   Captain E. Bunker to Governor King, 5 October 1803, *HRNSW*, Vol. V, p. 231.

5   Some experts believe the average age of first memories is three years and six months, but 'with the vast majority of subjects dating their first recollection somewhere between ages two and five years'. See for instance Barrett, D (1980). 'The first memory as a predictor of personality traits'. *Journal of Individual Psychology* 36 (2): 136–149.http://psycnet.apa.org/?fa=main. doiLanding&uid=1982–01271–001 and Barrett, D (1983). 'Early Recollections as Predictors of Self Disclosure and Interpersonal Style'. *Journal of Individual Psychology* 39: 92–98. Quoted at the website http://en.wikipedia.org/wiki/ Childhood_amnesia#cite_note-7. So it is likely that Kikatapula, aged between two and five, did see and remember seeing a ship of the Baudin–Péron expedition and that his birthdate therefore was somewhere between 1797 and 1800, probably nearer the latter.

6   Ryan, *Aboriginal Tasmanians*, p. 17.

7   *ibid.*, and Horton, Wesley Missionary Papers, pp. 1268–1274.

8   *Waddy* is a Dharug (New South Wales Aboriginal) word probably introduced to Tasmania by either colonists who had spent time in Sydney or transplanted NSW Aborigines such as Musquito, although it does not seem to have been recorded in Tasmania before 1823. After that it was in general use by colonists and apparently by some Palawa. Oyster Bay people had at least three of their own words for waddy: *hillar, lergah*, and *lughrana*. Each possibly represented a different type of hunting stick or club.

9   Boyce, *Van Diemen's Land*, p. 16.

10 Plomley, *Friendly Mission*, 6 January 1831.

11 *ibid.*, 11 January 1831.

12 *ibid.*, 15 October 1830.

13 *ibid.*, 20 October 1830.

14 Adolphe Schayer, 'La Terre Van-Diemen', in *Novelles Annales Des Voyages et Des Sciences Geographiques*, Librairie de Gide, Paris, 1839, p. 15.

15 *HRA* Series III Vol. III p. 355.

16 Nash, *Bay Whalers*, p. 39.

17 George Augustus Robinson quoted in the *Colonist* (Sydney), 31 October 1838. However, Robinson did not arrive in Tasmania until two decades after the slaughter and was reporting hearsay.

18 *Sydney Gazette*, 5 June 1808; the *Colonist* (Sydney), 31 October 1838.

19 Robinson, Speech to the Australian Aborigines Protection Society, 1838.

20 Quoted in Fels, 'Culture Contact', p. 59.

21   K.R. von Stieglitz, *The History of Bothwell and its Early Settlers at the Clyde in Van Dieman's Land*, n.p., n.d. [1958], p. 79; William J. Lines, *Taming the Great South Land: A History of the Conquest of Nature in Australia*, Berkley and Los Angeles, University of California Press, 1991, p. 44.

22   Knopwood's diary, 14 February 1807.

23   *Derwent Star*, 29 January 1810, quoted in West, *History of Tasmania* Vol. II, p. 9.

24   *Derwent Star*, 29 January 1810. Quoted in Morgan, *Land Settlement*, p. 155.

25   Quoted in Turnbull, *Black War*, p. 47.

26   Robinson to Colonial Secretary, 23 September 1829, in Plomley, *Friendly Mission*, 1st edn, pp. 76–77.

27   Plomley, *Friendly Mission*, 15 December 1831.

28   Boyce, *Van Diemen's Land*, p. 63.

29   *Review of Reviews*, Vol. II, 9 September 1890, p. 235; Roth, *Aborigines of Tasmania*, p. 172.

30   *Hobart Town Gazette*, 24 May 1817.

31   *ibid.*, 31 August 1816 and 19 October 1816.

32   Plomley, *Friendly Mission*, 11 July 1831.

33   Knopwood's diary, 7 July 1814.

34   *Van Diemen's Land Gazette and General Advertiser*, 20 August 1814.

35   Knopwood's diary, 15–17 November 1815.

36   *ibid.*, 22 May 1816.

37   Rowland Hassall, 1891, *Hassall Papers* Vol. 2, part 1, MLA860, Mitchell Library, 17 March 1817.

38   *Hobart Town Gazette*, 24 May 1817.

39   *ibid.*, 13 February 1819.

40   *ibid.*, 25 April 1818.

41   *ibid.*, 26 September 1818.

42   Presumably the same four girls mentioned in Knopwood's diary on 24 and 26 March 1818.

43   'Monitor', in *Hobart Town Gazette*, 26 December 1818.

44   *Hobart Town Gazette*, 28 November 1818.

45   Plomley, *Friendly Mission*, 25 October 1830.

Chapter 3 ~ 'Nursing Mr. Birch's children at Hobartown'

1   Register of Baptisms, TAHO NS282/8/8.

2   Thomas Sutcliffe, 'Notes by the Way', the *Critic* (Hobart), 5 February 1915.

3   Bonwick, *Last of the Tasmanians*, p. 95; Plomley, *Jorgen Jorgenson*, p. 75.

4   Executive Council Minutes, 10 April 1828. TAHO EC4/1/1, p. 303.

5   *Hobart Town Gazette*, 2 December 1826; Roth, *Aborigines of Tasmania*, p. 126. Also *ibid.*, p. 115, quoting Davies, R.H., 'On the Aborigines of V.D. Land', *Tasm. Journ. Science* II, pp. 409–420. Launceston and London, 1846.

6   Calder, *Levée, Line and Martial Law*, p. 221.

7   See for instance Plomley, *Friendly Mission*, 26 December 1829.

8   In 1818–1819, while the Colonial Hospital was being built, Hobart's General Hospital was in rented houses. At the time of Kikatapula's baptism it was in a house belonging to R.W. Fryett, who owned a building in Bathurst Street and another on the corner of Liverpool and Harrington streets (now the site of the Shamrock Hotel). Also in 1819, surgeon Edward Luttrell had a temporary hospital for Palawa at Fisk's Mill (later called Waterloo Mill) 'contiguous to Wellington Bridge' – roughly next door, on the Elizabeth Mall side, to today's Myer department store in Liverpool Street – that was ordered closed in November 1819. Whether it was

operative as early as February that year is unknown, but in 1820 Arnold Fisk was paid £11.17.2 for the quarter ending 31 December 1819 for 'Rent of House used by Sick Natives 23 weeks & 5 days' (*Hobart Town Gazette,* 1 April 1820).

9   *HRA* Series III Vol. 3, p. 364. Regardless, the rite could not have been performed in church because Hobart's first real church, old St David's, was still under construction and was not consecrated until 1823, although the first recorded service was held there on Christmas Day 1819, possibly with Kikatapula in the congregation.

10   *Hobart Town Gazette*, 5 May 1827.

11   *ibid.*, 18 November 1826.

12   Plomley, *Friendly Mission*, 11 January 1830.

13   The website http://stravaganzastravaganza.blogspot.com.au/2011/05/ all–time– richest–australians.html names Thomas Birch as the 11th-richest person in Australian history.

14   *HRA* Series III Vol. III, p. 354.

15   Nash, *Bay Whalers*, p. 40.

16   *Colonial Times*, 20 March 1838.

17   *ibid.*

18   *ibid.*

19   In the biographical notes to Henry Savery's *The Hermit in Van Diemen's Land* (St Lucia, University of Queensland Press, 1964, pp. 51–52) the annotator wrongly identified Edmund and Sarah Hodgson as the proprietors in 1829 of the Macquarie Hotel, Hobart, when in fact John Edward Cox was the licensee (*Colonial Times*, 13 November 1829). Although Savery did not name either the proprietor or his wife, the annotator's mistake has led at least one source to claim Savery's favourable remark about the wife applied to Sarah Hodgson, but Savery was clearly writing about Mrs Cox.

20   Thomas Sutcliffe, 'Notes by the Way', the *Critic* (Hobart), 5 February 1915.

21   *Memoir of Alexander Laing.*

22   See Appendix 3, above. Also Cox, *Baptised in Blood.*

23   Bonwick, *Last of the Tasmanians*, pp. 95–96.

24   Brodie, *Vandemonian War*, pp. 355–356.

25   West, *History of Tasmania* Vol. 1, p. 68.

26   Rush to Simpson, 22 June 1828, TAHO CSO1/316, p. 141.

27   TAHO CON31/1/15, p. 42.

28   *Hobart Town Gazette*, 23 June 1827.

29   *Colonial Times*, 29 June 1827.

30   *Hobart Town Gazette*, 1 December 1821.

31   *ibid.*, 2 March 1822.

32   Bonwick, *Last of the Tasmanians*, p. 202.

33   The *Courier*, 6 December 1848.

34   *Colonial Times*, 23 May 1848.

35   Letter to the *Colonial Times* reproduced as an advertisement in the *Courier*, 3 June 1848, p. 1.

36   *Colonial Times*, 20 March 1838.

37   *ibid.*, 12 April 1842.

38   Cassandra Pybus, 'Robinson and Robertson' in *Whitewash*, p. 270.

39   Cassandra Pybus, 'The Colourful Life of Gilbert Robertson', at http:// launcestonhistory.org.au/wp–content/uploads/2012/03/ CassandraPybus20112.pdf.

40   *Van Diemen's Land: Copies of All Correspondence*, p. 48.

41 Bonwick, *Last of the Tasmanians*, p. 96. The *Hobart Town Gazette* also suggested alcohol was a factor. In an item published after Kikatapula had achieved notoriety, it confirmed Musquito's luring him from the Birch family's service 'but not before he had become addicted to rum and tobacco, for the procuration of which it cannot be doubted his subsequent offences have been perpetrated' (*Hobart Town Gazette*, 16 July 1824).

42 Plomley, *Friendly Mission*, 1st edn, p. 104 n. 45. Robinson was not in Tasmania in 1822 when Kikatapula abandoned Hodgson to join Musquito, so he was not writing of something he knew about first-hand. The problem of sexual frustration would always have existed for Kikatapula when he lived on white farms or at Macquarie House.

43 Batman to Aborigines Committee, 1 April 1834, TAHO CSO1/327, p. 129.

44 Bonwick, *Lost Tasmanian Race*, p. 79

45 Plomley, *Aboriginal/Settler Clash*, p. 58.

46 *Hobart Town Gazette*, 30 November 1822.

47 Calder, *Some Account of the Wars*, p. 92.

48 See for instance Evans, *Description of Van Diemen's Land*, p. 14; Government notice in *Hobart Town Gazette*, 13 March 1819.

Chapter 4 ~ 'They are very dangerous and troublesome'

1 TAHO CSO 1/323/7578, p. 288.

2 Meredith, *My Life in Tasmania*, p. 198.

3 West, *History of Tasmania* Vol. 2 p. 12.

4 TAHO CSO 1/323/7578, p. 197.

5 *Van Diemen's Land: Copies of All Correspondence*, p. 55.

6 *Hobart Town Courier*, 25 September 1830.

7 Amos, Diary, 3 May 1823.

8 Quoted in Cox, *Baptised in Blood*, p. 23.

9 'Recollections of a Short Excursion to Lake Echo in March 1823', *Hobart Town Almanac & VDL Annual*, 1830, p. 180, in Jetson, T. (1987) 'The Roof of Tasmania – The History of the Central Plateau', University of Tasmania, History, MA, p. 33.

10 Horton, Wesley Missionary Papers, pp. 1268–1274.

11 K.R. von Stieglitz, *The History of Bothwell and its Early Settlers on the Clyde in Van Dieman's Land*, n.p., n.d. pp. 65–66.

12 This surprisingly common misidentification appears to date from James Hobbs's testimony to the Aborigines Committee in 1830. West repeated it in *The History of Tasmania* Vol. 2, p. 14 (1852) and it was perpetuated in numerous newspaper historical features and books during the 19th century and later.

13 Arthur to Viscount Goderich, 10 January 1828. *HRA* Series III Vol. VII, pp. 26–27.

14 Bonwick, *Last of the Tasmanians*, p. 93.

15 *Van Diemen's Land: Copies of All Correspondence*, p. 48.

16 *ibid.*

17 The number of Big River women among Musquito's female associates probably indicates the paucity of Oyster Bay women by this time.

18 Thomas Dove, quoted in Roth, *Aborigines of Tasmania*, p. 57.

19 Gilbert Robertson opined that 'Musquito must have committed murders within 18 months after he went into the bush' (quoted in *Van Diemen's Land: Copies of All Correspondence*, p. 48), but since Robertson did not arrive in Tasmania until 1822, three years after that, his opinion can have been based only on hearsay.

20 Musquito's culpability seems unlikely. In mid-September 1818 he led a reward-seeking ticket-of-leave man named John McGill to the bushranger Michael Howe's hideout near the Clyde, although Howe escaped after a struggle. Musquito then

returned either to Hobart or to Edward Lord's service to await his promised repatriation, which did not eventuate. As far as is known, in mid-November when Kemp was slain Musquito was still in the south awaiting repatriation and did not join the tame mob until the following year. (See R.F. Minchin, *The First; The Worst? Michael Howe and Associated Bushrangers in Van Diemen's Land*, Sandy Bay, R.F. Minchin, 2001, pp. 88, 112–113.) Moreover, the attack on Kemp's camp was not a raid to steal supplies. Because of the destruction of the whites' catch, it was clearly punishment for their transgression against Palawa country and resources. Musquito, not being an Oyster Bay man, had no need to be part of such punishment.

21 'Old Talbot', quoted in Bonwick, *Last of the Tasmanians*, p. 95.
22 Quoted in Plomley, *Jorgen Jorgenson*, p. 95
23 Ryan, *Aboriginal Tasmanians*, p. 83.
24 Plomley, *Tasmanian Aboriginal Place Names*, p. 62.

Chapter 5 ~ 'Oh my God, the black-fellows have got me'

1 Amos, Diary, quoted in Nyman, *East Coasters*, p. 35.
2 Calder, *Native Tribes of Tasmania*, p. 54.
3 Trial transcript published in *Hobart Town Gazette*, 3 December 1824.
4 TAHO CON 1/31/1/18, p. 97.
5 Distances according to George Meredith as related to Louisa Anne Meredith, *My Home in Tasmania*, Vol. I, pp. 193–194, and converted.
6 Trial transcript published in *Hobart Town Gazette*, 3 December 1824; Meredith, *My Life in Tasmania* Vol. I, pp. 193–197.
7 Parramore, *Letters*, p. 31.
8 Plomley, *Friendly Mission*, 13 January 1831. In a footnote to Robinson's entry, Plomley, who edited the journals for publication, identified the graves as those of William Holyoake and Thomas Colley. But Colley, slain at John de Courcy Harte's property Bellbrook, on the Wye River near Great Oyster Bay, in April 1826, would have been buried at Bellbrook, not next to Holyyoake on Gatehouse's farm at Grindstone Bay about 50 kilometres south along what Calder referred to, even half a century later, as 'one of the worst bush roads in Tasmania'. Although Harte did have property at Grindstone Bay, the *Colonial Times* of 2 June 1826 reported Colley's killing as being at Oyster Bay and the *Hobart Town Gazette* of 23 and 30 September 1826 reported its having occurred at Great Swan Port – that is, Oyster Bay. The grave Plomley identified as Colley's was clearly Mammoa's, as Kikatapula's words indicated. The other, as Robinson noted, was Holyoake's, for he was 'Meredith's man'. Slain a week or more before their bodies were found, the two would necessarily have been buried on the spot without delay.
9 Letter dated 11 December 1827, TAHO CSO 1/323/7578, pp. 70–71. Although he used the words 'Oyster Bay', O'Connor was unquestionably referring to the Grindstone Bay killings because the body of the letter refers to Kikatapula on the point of being exiled to Macquarie Harbour for this incitement and, as discussed at pp. 55–59, that happened within a month (and as a consequence of) the Grindstone Bay killings. The Grindstone Bay location is also confirmed by what Kikatapula told George Augustus Robinson when they visited Gatehouse's property in 1831 and saw the graves of Holyoake and Mammoa; see p. 48. At that time 'Oyster Bay' was often used generically to mean any part of the east coast between Spring Bay and Oyster Bay.
10 Quoted in Melville, *History of Van Diemen's Land* p. 40n, but emphasis added. However, Melville does not name the European Musquito related this to, only that it was a 'person, who fell into [Musquito's] power in a defenceless condition, in a remote place, [but] was recognized by him as a former benefactor, and

treated with great kindness by him and his tribe'. While that is obviously not perfect provenance, the chronological and basic accuracy of the details lends considerable weight to the quote's veracity, especially the part that I contend pertains to the conflict at Grindstone Bay. That part also offers further evidence, if such be needed, that the upper echelon of Hobart society – Melville was a newspaper editor – knew who and what had really set off the conflict and that Radford's subsequent testimony was perjured.

11 Thomas McMinn quoted in Plomley, *Jorgen Jorgenson*, p. 95.
12 Nelson is believed to have been a sister of Pagerly, who later became Kikatapula's wife. She is usually recorded as having been one-armed, although how she lost the arm is unknown, possibly as a result of Holyoake's shotgun wound – if she were whom he shot, which is not certain.
13 *Hobart Town Gazette*, 27 August 1825.
14 Meredith, *My Home in Tasmania* Vol. I, p. 197.
15 *ibid.*, p. 198.
16 Amos, Diary, 20 November 1823.
17 *Hobart Town Gazette*, 3 December 1824.
18 Trial transcript published in *Hobart Town Gazette*, 3 December 1824.
19 Meredith, *My Home in Tasmania* Vol. I, pp. 208–210. However, some details therein, such as the date, are erroneous, and Buxton's elder son was three in 1823, not 15. The attack, though not the fatality, is also reported in Nyman, *East Coasters*, p. 36. The name of the dead man is unknown, and neither the attack nor the death is recorded in Plomley's *Aboriginal/Settler Clash*.
20 Quoted in Nyman, *East Coasters*, p. 36.

Chapter 6 ~ 'Poor Tom Birch was soon captured'

1 *Hobart Town Gazette*, 3 December 1824. Its report of Musquito's and Black Jack's trials, more than a year after the killings, was the only time it ever mentioned the Grindstone Bay attack.
2 *ibid.*, 29 November 1823.
3 Bonwick, *Last of the Tasmanians*, p. 94.
4 *ibid.*, p. 95–96.
5 Tasmania's Supreme Court was legally set up in October 1823 but heard its first criminal trial only on 24 May 1824.
6 Bonwick, *Last of the Tasmanians*, p. 96.
7 Plomley, *Jorgen Jorgenson*, p. 75; Roderic O'Connor letter to W.T. Parramore, TAHO CSO1/323/7578, pp. 70–71.
8 *Hobart Town Gazette* of 7 October 1826 and *Van Diemen's Land: Copies of All Correspondence*, p. 39.
9 Bonwick, *Last of the Tasmanians*, p. 96.
10 Plomley, *Jorgen Jorgenson*, p. 75.
11 Hamish Maxwell-Stewart, pers. comm.
12 See Dan Sprod, *Alexander Pearce*, pp. 146–150.
13 Roderic O'Connor to W.T. Parramore, TAHO CSO1/323/7578, pp. 70–71.

Chapter 7 ~ 'The notorious companion of Musquito'

1 West, *History of Tasmania* Vol. 2, p. 13.
2 *Hobart Town Gazette*, 23 January 1824.
3 A family history website, http://justoneaustralian.blogspot.com.au /2011/07/story-of-patrick-mccarthy-part-3.htm, offers the following: 'Patrick was speared by a Palawa named Black Jack (who had also been given the name Jack Roberts [*sic* and incorrect]). It's unclear exactly what the course of events were, but a

contemporary source [not cited] suggests that while returning home through the bush, Patrick, his wife Mary and a child in her arms ... were attacked by several natives. Patrick urged Mary to flee while he bravely held the natives at bay. This act cost him his life, but saved that of Mary and her child.'

4   Amos, Diary, 15 March 1824.

5   TAHO CON22/1/3, p. 45.

6   TAHO CSO1/323/7578, p. 289.

7   Plomley, *Aboriginal/Settler Clash*, p. 25.

8   *ibid.*

9   *ibid.*

10 Ryan, *Tasmanian Aborigines*, p. 115.

11 However, see H. Maxwell-Stewart, 'Competition and Conflict on the Forgotten Frontier, Western Van Diemen's Land 1822–33', *History Australia*, 6, 3 (2009): 1–19.

12 Plomley, *Friendly Mission*, 4 November 1831.

13 *ibid.*

14 Amos, Diary, entries for dates in the text.

15 *Hobart Town Gazette*, 9 April 1824.

16 Ryan, *Aboriginal Tasmanians*, p. 97; Weeding, *History of the Lower Midlands*, p. 32.

17 *Hobart Town Gazette*, 2 April 1824.

18 Boyce, *Van Diemen's Land*, p. 189, citing Adam Amos's diary.

19 *Hobart Town Gazette*, 18 June 1824.

20 The settler was Eli Beagent or Begent, a former *Indefatigable* convict and one-time accomplice of bushranger Michael Howe. He farmed at Tea Tree.

21 Extracted from *Hobart Town Gazette*, 16 July 1824. Two later versions of the attack also exist, both based on what Mary Osborne told others. They are different from each other and shorter than and different in some relatively unimportant details from the *Gazette*'s. Robert Jones, a neighbour of the Osbornes, related his in testimony to Thomas Anstey in 1830 (quoted in Plomley, *Jorgen Jorgenson*, p. 94). The other version is testimony Dr Hudspeth gave to the Aborigines Committee the same year (TAHO CSO1/323, pp. 327–331). However, it is probable that the *Gazette*'s account, furnished 'by the afflicted widow' only a month after the attack, is the most accurate, not having been transmuted by time and other people's memories. Hudspeth's account confirmed Mary Osborne's that Kikatapula led the attack, but Jones did 'not recall what tribe it was. I think it was what is called a tame mob, a mob of half civilized Blacks, such as have much intercourse with white men'.

22 Deposition of Robert Jones, 15 March 1830, quoted in Plomley, *Jorgen Jorgenson*, p. 94.

23 *Hobart Town Gazette*, 16 July 1824.

24 *ibid.*, 30 July 1824.

25 Thomas Sutcliffe, 'Notes by the Way', the *Critic* (Hobart), 5 February 1915.

26 *Hobart Town Gazette*, 19 March 1824.

27 However, Lovely Banks was robbed, soon after Musquito moved on, by a party of prisoners, including Matthew Brady, who had escaped from Macquarie Harbour. No other details have survived. *Hobart Town Gazette*, 2 July 1824.

28 'Hand-written account of livestock and sundry farming operations by Edmund and Sarah Hodgson and Mrs. Edmund Birch [sic] in Van Diemen's Land in the years 1826 and 1827', TAHO CRO 630.9946 HOD. Unnumbered page. Despite the title, it also includes some entries for 1824.

29 Samuel Johnson's *Dictionary of the English Language* 1756 online edition at http://www.whichenglish.com/Johnsons-Dictionary/1755-Letter-C.html; *Johnson's*

Dictionary, Improved by Todd, Abridged for the Use of Schools, Boston, Charles J. Hendee, 1836, p. 64.

30 Murderers Plains is now York Plains, east of Oatlands, so not in the Abyssinia region.

31 TAHO CSO1/316/7578, pp. 8–9.

32 Meredith, *My Home in Tasmania* Vol. I, pp. 202–204.

33 See Cox, *Baptised in Blood*, pp. 237–238.

34 *Hobart Town Gazette*, 6 August 1824.

35 *ibid.*, 29 October 1824.

36 Quoted in Plomley, *Friendly Mission*, 1st edn, p. 100, n. 3.

37 Plomley, *Friendly Mission*, 1st edn, p. 100, n. 3.

38 *Hobart Town Gazette*, 5 November 1824.

39 Letter in the *Tasmanian*, 10 December 1830, signed 'William Penn', pseudonym of Dr G.F. Story. I am indebted to Michael Powell for drawing my attention to this item. See also Bonwick, *Last of the Tasmanians*, pp. 83–84.

40 G.W. Rusden, *History of Australia*, London, Chapman and Hall, 1883, Vol. I, p. 625.

41 See also Ryan, *Tasmanian Aborigines*, p. 79.

42 Parramore, *Letters*, pp. 60–61.

43 Usually said to be on Bellerive Bluff but more likely to have been nearer present-day Rosny Park where Kangaroo Bay Rivulet empties into Kangaroo Bay. The rivulet would have provided a necessary supply of fresh water. Nowadays a stormwater culvert, the rivulet runs parallel to Rosny Park Public Golf Course down to Kangaroo Bay through the parklands and sports ground adjacent to Rosny College. A likely spot for the Palawa camp would have been slightly farther inland from there, perhaps near the site of today's Clarence City Council offices.

44 Arthur to Goderich, 10 January 1828, *Van Diemen's Land: Copies of All Correspondence*, p. 3.

45 Diary of John Hudspeth, Royal Society of Tasmania Archives, University of Tasmania, 8/RS/1901/034. I am indebted to Lyndall Ryan for drawing my attention to this killing.

46 *Hobart Town Gazette*, 24 December 1824. See also West, *History of Tasmania*, p. 269.

47 The *Tasmanian*, Wednesday 12 January 1825.

48 See for instance Plomley, *Friendly Mission*, 25 October 1830, 29 November 1831, and 8 December 1831.

49 The *Tasmanian*, Wednesday 12 January 1825.

50 *ibid.*, 19 January 1825.

51 George Augustus Robinson Journal, 25 Feb 1825, A7022 vol. 1, part 4.

Chapter 8 ~ 'Fire, you white cowards'

1 *Van Diemen's Land: Copies of All Correspondence*, p. 48.

2 *ibid.*

3 *Hobart Town Gazette*, 1 April 1825.

4 *ibid.*

5 *ibid.*, 22 April 1825.

6 The *Tasmanian*, 18 April 1825.

7 *Hobart Town Gazette*, 29 April 1825.

8 TAHO CSO 762 and Plomley, *Jorgen Jorgenson*, p. 88.

9 *Colonial Times*, 29 September 1826.

10 Plomley, *Jorgen Jorgenson*, pp. 94–95.

11 Plomley, *Friendly Mission*, 2nd edn, p. 118.

12 *Hobart Town Gazette*, 12 November 1825.

13   *ibid.*, 4 February 1826.
14   TAHO CSO1/316/7578, p. 762.
15   Jones deposition to Anstey, quoted in Plomley, *Jorgen Jorgenson*, p. 95.
16   Plomley, *Jorgen Jorgenson*, pp. 87–88.
17   *ibid.*
18   *Colonial Times*, 6 January 1826.
19   Roderic O'Connor, in *Van Diemen's Land: Copies of All Correspondence*, p. 55.
20   *Colonial Times*, 13 January 1826.
21   http://bonesinthebelfry.com/cubit/james.html#

Chapter 9 ~ *'Parrawa, parrawa!* Go away!'

1   TAHO CSO 792.
2   *Hobart Town Gazette*, 4 February 1826.
3   *ibid.*
4   This death was otherwise unrecorded.
5   Nyman, *East Coasters*, pp. 55–56.
6   *Hobart Town Gazette*, 15 April 1826.
7   *ibid.*, 20 May 1826; Plomley, *Friendly Mission* p. 314. In *Steps to the Scaffold* I wrongly identified Colley as the man slain the previous month during the raid on Buxton's.
8   *Colonial Times*, 12 May 1826.
9   *Hobart Town Gazette*, 6 May 1826.
10   TAHO CSO 832.
11   TAHO CSO 832, 846.
12   TAHO CSO 832.
13   *Colonial Times*, 16 June 1826.
14   *Hobart Town Gazette*, 29 September 1826.
15   *ibid.*, 22 September 1826.
16   Cox, *Steps to the Scaffold*, p. 78.
17   *Hobart Town Gazette*, 30 September 1826.
18   *Van Diemen's Land: Copies of All Correspondence*, p. 51.
19   Robinson to Lascelles, 17 November 1828, TAHO CSO1/331, pp. 168–177.
20   *Colonial Times*, 21 December 1826.
21   *Colonial Advocate*, 1 July 1828, quoted in Calder, *Brady, McCabe et alia*, p. 161.
22   *Hobart Town Gazette*, 21 October 1826.
23   *ibid.*, 14 October 1826.
24   *ibid.*
25   Plomley, *Aboriginal/Settler Clash,* p. 61.
26   *ibid.*
27   *Colonial Times*, 10 November 1826.
28   *Hobart Town Gazette*, 11 November 1826.
29   *Colonial Times*, 10 November 1826.
30   *Hobart Town Gazette*, 18 November 1826.
31   *ibid.*
32   *Colonial Times*, 10 November 1826.
33   *ibid.* The men's fate is unknown.
34   Carter to Burnett, 5 March 1828, TAHO CSO 1/316/7578, p. 115.
35   *Hobart Town Gazette*, 4 November 1826.
36   Rush to Simpson, 22 June 1828, TAHO CSO1/316, p. 141.
37   *Colonial Times*, 17 November 1826.

38   *ibid.* The 'three murders' were of Guinea, Reynolds, and George Taylor, who was slain after Guinea and Reynolds but whose death was described before theirs in the *Gazette*'s report.

39   *Hobart Town Gazette*, 18 November 1826.

40   *ibid.*

41   *ibid.*, 2 December 1826.

42   *Colonial Times*, 24 November 1826, *Hobart Town Gazette*, 25 November 1826.

43   *Hobart Town Gazette*, 2 December 1826.

44   TAHO CSO 1/316/7578, p. 12.

45   *Hobart Town Gazette*, 2 December 1826.

46   TAHO CSO 12. 792.

47   *Hobart Town Gazette*, 2 December 1826.

48   *Colonial Times*, 1 December 1826, TAHO CSO 762.

49   *ibid.*, 19 January 1827

Chapter 10 ~ 'You white bugger, give me some bread'

1   *ibid.*, 24 November 1826.

2   *ibid.*, 15 December 1826.

3   *Hobart Town Gazette*, 9 December 1826.

4   *Colonial Times*, 15 December 1826.

5   *Hobart Town Gazette*, 16 December 1826.

6   On 27 September 1828 the *Hobart Town Courier*, in a belated report of Palawa attacks, complained that 'We are sorry that these distressing events should occur, and that no one concerned or acquainted with them should think it worth his while to communicate the circumstances to us, while we are almost invariably left to gather our information, from verbal [*sic*: oral] reports, often exaggerated, and sometimes entirely unfounded'.

7   Gilbert Robertson, minutes of evidence before the Committee for the Affairs of the Aborigines, 3 March 1830, *British Parliamentary Papers, Colonies, Australia,* 4, p. 221.

8   Pybus, 'Robinson and Robertson' in *Whitewash*, p. 274.

9   Bonwick, *Last of the Tasmanians*, p. 202.

10   *ibid.*, p. 272.

11   Cox, *Baptised in Blood*, pp. 196–197, 281.

12   The *Colonist* (Sydney), 31 October 1838.

13   Roy Bridges, *That Yesterday was Home*, Sydney, Australasian Publishing Company, 1948, p. 69. Seventeen years earlier, in an article titled 'In the Black War: Perils of Tasmanian Pioneers', Bridges had first mentioned 'Lang' chasing Black Tom up the valley (*Australasian,* 11 July 1931).

14   Roy Bridges, letter to W. H. Hudspeth, 19 October 1937, TAHO NS690/68.

15   TAHO CSO1/331/7578, pp. 194–195.

16   Breen, *Contested Places*, pp. 30–31.

17   Roslynn D. Haynes, *Tasmanian Visions: Landscapes in Writing, Art and Photography,* Sandy Bay, Polymath Press, 2006, p. 79.

18   Pybus, 'Robinson and Robertson' in *Whitewash*, p. 272.

19   Laing, *Memoir.*

20   TAHO CSO1/8 pp. 60–61.

21   Reynolds, *Fate of a Free People*, p. 97.

22   *Van Diemen's Land: Copies of All Correspondence*, p. 20.

23   *Colonial Times*, 19 January 1827.

Chapter 11 ~ 'Beset by these black furies'

1   *ibid.*, 13 January 1827.
2   *ibid.*, 5 January 1827.
3   *ibid.*, 26 January 1827.
4   *ibid.*, 26 January 1827 and 2 February 1827.
5   *Hobart Town Gazette*, 23 June 1827.
6   *ibid.*, 10 February 1827.
7   *Colonial Times*, 9 February 1827.
8   *ibid.*, 20 April 1827.
9   *ibid.* Whether Johnson survived his wounds is not recorded.
10 *Hobart Town Gazette*, 5 May 1827; *Colonial Tines*, 4 May 1827.
11 *Colonial Times*, 4 May 1827.
12 *ibid.*
13 *Hobart Town Gazette*, 5 May 1827.
14 *Colonial Times*, 11 May 1827.
15 *ibid.*, 25 May 1827.
16 *ibid.*, 4 May 1827.
17 *ibid.*, 3 August 1827.
18 *ibid.*, 1 June 1827.
19 *Hobart Town Gazette*, 23 June 1827, *Colonial Times*, 6 July 1827 and 13 July 1827. He later served in the Field Police.
20 *Hobart Town Gazette*, 23 June 1827.
21 TAHO CSO1/316/7578, p. 24.
22 TAHO CSO 41 (1/7/27).
23 *Colonial Times*, 6 July 1827.
24 *ibid.*
25 *ibid.*
26 *ibid.* While such bellicose editorials undoubtedly reflected the sentiments of many colonists, if the report of so many Palawa slain in cold blood were accurate, all the perpetrators were *prima facie* guilty of murder. But it is extraordinary and shameful that no colonist was ever punished by the British for murdering a Palawa.
27 *Colonial Times*, 27 July 1827.
28 *ibid.*, 3 August 1827.
29 TAHO CSO 799 (10.1.1831).
30 *Colonial Times*, 21 September 1827.
31 *ibid.*
32 The *Tasmanian*, 18 October 1827.
33 *Sydney Gazette*, 9 November 1827, quoting the *Tasmanian* of 18 October 1827. Also *Hobart Town Courier*, 20 October 1827 and 3 November 1827.
34 The *Tasmanian*, 18 October 1827.
35 *ibid.*, 1 November 1827.
36 *ibid.*, 13 July 1827.
37 *ibid.*
38 *Hobart Town Courier*, 24 November 1827.
39 McKinlay, *Forgotten Tasmanians*, pp. 41–42. Bryn Estyn is now the site of a sewage treatment works.
40 *Hobart Town Courier*, 17 November 1827.
41 The *Tasmanian*, 16 November 1827.

Chapter 12 ~ 'He has aided in many murders'

1   Arthur to Goderich, 10 January 1828, quoted in *Van Diemen's Land: Copies of All Correspondence*, p. 3.
2   *Hobart Town Courier*, 1 December 1827.
3   Executive Council Minutes, 14 December 1827. TAHO EC4/1/1 pp. 236–237.
4   Reynolds, *Fate of a Free People*, p. 104.
5   Extracted from Plomley, *Aboriginal/Settler Clash*, pp. 65–70.
6   Arthur to Colonial Secretary Huskisson, quoted in *Van Diemen's Land: Copies of All Correspondence*, pp. 4–5.
7   *ibid.*
8   Executive Council Minutes, 10 April 1828. TAHO EC4/1/1 p. 303.
9   Plomley, *Jorgen Jorgenson*, p. 19.
10 Quoted in Melville, *History of Van Diemen's Land*, pp. 75–76.
11 *Hobart Town Courier*, 5 January 1828.
12 *Hobart Town Gazette,* 5 January 1828.
13 Arthur arrived in the *Malabar* in 1821 with a seven-year sentence and in 1827 was condemned to death in Launceston for 'unlawfully shooting at one James Gurd' (*Colonial Times*, 26 January 1827). The sentence was commuted to life imprisonment.
14 Clements, *Black War*, p. 110.
15 Plomley, *Weep in Silence*, p. 325.
16 *Hobart Town Courier*, 19 July 1828. According to the *Tasmanian (Hobart)* of 18 July, Kikatapula was discharged on the 15th of that month, but court records state that it was the 17th. The Criminal Minute Book for the 17 July 1828 session of the Supreme Court provides no additional information. (Ref: TAHO SC32/1/1, unnumbered page, online image 324.)
17 Robertson to Arthur, 6 July 1828, TAHO MM115/1/9 no. 50, n.p.
18 Hobler, *Journal*, 29 July 1828. Colonists' fears of being attacked by Palawa with stolen firearms never materialised.

Chapter 13 ~ 'Murder shakes her bloody spear'

1   Longman, 'Songs of the Tasmanian Aborigines as Recorded by Mrs. Fanny Cochrane Smith', p. 80. Translation presumably Cochrane Smith's.
2   *Hobart Town Courier*, 13 September 1828.
3   The Macquarie River correspondent is identifiable as a Campbell Town farmer named Taylor vide a letter, reproduced in part below, 'from Mr. Taylor of Campbell Town' that was quoted in the *Examiner* nearly a century later (13 June 1925). The wording of the first half of Taylor's undated letter is nearly identical to the report from the *Courier*'s unnamed Macquarie River correspondent, showing both were written at the same time by the same man. Taylor was one of the sons of farmer George Taylor, possibly Robert, the eldest, who had inherited Valleyfield, the family farm, after his father's death in April that year, although other Taylor sons farmed adjoining lands. The relevant part of the letter reads 'The natives have been on my farm again. As soon as the floods go down I expect a further attack. A report states that Black Tom is again in the district, and the Police Magistrate is swearing in respectable settlers as special constables and the whole neighbourhood is standing together to resist the tribe.'
4   *Hobart Town Courier*, 27 September 1828.
5   *Colonial Advocate and Tasmanian Monthly Review and Register*, 1 October 1828, p. 393.
6   TAHO CSO1/1/170, p. 74.
7   *ibid.*, p. 75. The *Tasmanian*, 15 August 1828.

8   TAHO CSO1/1/170, p. 76.

9   See for instance Plomley, *Friendly Mission*, 31 May 1829. Plomley also noted that 'These legendary beliefs in relation to "England" are probably no more than an indication that the place was distant and somewhere to the north' (*ibid.*, 1st edn, p. 465 n. 205).

10   Drummond to Anstey, 13 October 1828, TAHO CSO1/316, p. 173.

Chapter 14 ~ 'Now I like catch all dat black un'

1   *HRA* 3/9: 644–645.

2   *Hobart Town Courier*, 1 November 1828.

3   Henry Reynolds quoting Plomley's estimate in Reynolds, 'The Written Record', in B. Attwood and A.G. Foster (eds), *Frontier Conflict, The Australian Experience*, Canberra, National Museum of Australia, 2003, p. 82.

4   Anstey to Arthur, 4 December 1827, quoted in Plomley, *Jorgen Jorgenson*, p. 19.

5   *Van Diemen's Land: Copies of All Correspondence*, p. 7.

6   Quoted in Alastair H. Campbell, *John Batman and the Aborigines*, Malmsbury, Kibble Books, 1987, p. 54.

7   Reynolds, *Fate of a Free People*, p. 71.

8   Brown to AC, TAHO CSO1/323/7578, p. 146.

9   *Hobart Town Courier*, 15 December 1827.

10   On 3 November according to the *Tasmanian* of 21 November 1828.

11   *Hobart Town Courier*, 8 November 1828.

12   The boat, hired out on the Derwent by the government at 10 shillings a week, earned the four Palawa slightly more than £18 between September 1831 and May 1832. On the night of 19 May 1832 it was lost after drifting from its mooring. Plomley, *Friendly Mission*, 1st edn, p. 801, n. 4.

13   Quoted in Melville, *History of Van Diemen's Land*, pp. 75–76.

14   *Tasmanian*, 21 November 1828. Plomley's *Aboriginal/Settler Clash* records only one killing on the east coast 'opposite Maria Island' in October/November: that of John Bailey on 25 October.

15   Unless otherwise cited, information about Robertson's capture of Umarrah is mostly from *M.S.S. Journal*, quoted in Melville, *History of Van Diemen's Land*, pp. 79–81n.

16   Robertson told the Aborigines Committee in 1830 that he had followed Umarrah's mob from Oyster Bay to Maloneys Sugar Loaf, meaning from the Oyster Bay *region* – that is, somewhere unnamed on the east coast – subsequently encountering the Lieutenant Governor. See *Van Diemen's Land: Copies of All Correspondence*, p. 48.

17   *Hobart Town Gazette*, 29 October 1824.

18   Plomley, *Friendly Mission*, 23 October 1831.

19   Plomley, *Tasmanian Aboriginal Place Names*, p. 36.

20   Robertson's party had taken on a convict named Robert Lee who was picked up opposite Maria Island, which he had apparently escaped from, around the time the party camped with the Lieutenant Governor's entourage. Although Robertson praised his part in the capture of Umarrah's mob, Lee seems to have been an unsavoury character. He was a lifer, an old lag whose conduct sheet was annotated 'A worse character cannot well be conceived'. Although Lieutenant Governor Arthur, who was aware of Lee's reputation, agreed to his joining Robertson's party rather than being returned to Maria Island, it was on the strict understanding he would not be granted a ticket of leave, as the other convicts in the party had been promised, regardless of his contribution to the party. (Robertson to James Gordon 20 February 1830, TAHO CSO1/332/7578, p. 197.)

21 Melville, *History of Van Diemen's Land,* p. 86.
22 Hugh Murray was the brother of David Murray, whose farm, Twickenham, was adjacent to where Palawa battled pursuing colonists in April 1827, sparking false reports of Kikatapula's death.
23 *Hobart Town Courier,* 4 April 1829.
24 See Plomley, *Weep in Silence,* p. 806, entry for Luckerrermicticwockenner.
25 Plomley, *Friendly Mission,* 21 October 1831.
26 The *Tasmanian,* 21 November 1828.
27 *Hobart Town Courier,* 22 November 1828.
28 The *Tasmanian,* 21 November 1828.
29 TAHO CSO1/331/7578, p. 159.
30 Executive Council Minutes 19 November 1828, TAHO EC4/1/1 p. 383.
31 TAHO CSO 41/1/1, pp. 185–186.
32 *M.S.S. Journal,* quoted in Melville, *History of Van Diemen's Land,* p. 81n.
33 Robertson, Journal of the Proceedings, TAHO CSO 1/332/7578, p. 115.
34 *ibid.,* p. 117.
35 Bonwick, *Lost Tasmanian Race,* p. 114; TAHO CSO1/320/7578, pp. 341–342.
36 Robertson, Journal of the Proceedings, TAHO CSO1/332/7578, p. 123.
37 Cowertenninner was reunited with Grant's detachment a few days after absconding.
38 Plomley, *Friendly Mission,* 8 January 1831.
39 Robertson, Journal of the Proceedings, TAHO CSO1/332/7578, p. 137.
40 *ibid.*
41 The unnamed victim appears to have been an employee of J.W.T. Bell. He was ambushed at Cummings Folly (Little Swanport region) on 24 February and died in hospital on the 27th. (*Hobart Town Courier,* 28 February 1829; *Launceston Advertiser,* 2 March 1829.)
42 Robertson, Journal of the Proceedings, TAHO CSO1/332/7578, p. 141.
43 *ibid.,* p. 142.
44 *ibid.,* p. 143.
45 Grant's detachment had captured the lone old Palawa man thought to have been responsible for lighting the fires that Robertson noted in his journal on 31 January 1829.
46 Robertson, Memorandum for a Journal, TAHO CSO1/331/7578, p. 80.
47 *ibid.,* p. 84.
48 TAHO CSO41/1/1, p. 356.
49 *ibid.*
50 *Hobart Town Courier,* 27 June 1829.
51 TAHO CSO1/320/7578, section F, p. 367. The letter of complaint is mentioned in a marginal note Anstey wrote on a William Grant report that Cowertenninner refused to follow a Palawa track, but archival searches for Robson's letter were unsuccessful.
52 TAHO CSO1/320/7578, p. 368.
53 *ibid.,* pp. 373–374.
54 Plomley, *Friendly Mission,* 1st edn, p. 109, n. 69.
55 *Hobart Town Courier,* 5 September 1829.
56 *ibid.,* 7 March 1829.
57 Quoted in Alastair H. Campbell, *John Batman and the Aborigines,* Malmsbury, Kibble Books, 1987, p. 54; West, *History of Tasmania,* p. 279.
58 *Hobart Town Gazette,* 18 August 1827. Crawn eventually became licensee of the Crown Inn at Pontville.

59   TAHO CSO1/332/7578, pp. 190–192.
60   *ibid.*
61   TAHO CSO1/1/330/7578, pp. 49–50.
62   TAHO CSO41/1/1, p. 339.
63   Robertson, Memorandum for a Journal, 14 November 1829, p. 89.
64   *Hobart Town Courier*, 13 March 1830.
65   TAHO CSO1/320/7578, pp. 322–323.
66   Quoted in Bonwick, *Last of the Tasmanians*, pp. 186–187.
67   TAHO CSO1/320/7578, p. 367.
68   *ibid.*
69   Extracted from Plomley, *Aboriginal/Settler Clash*, pp. 77–83.
70   TAHO CSO41/1, p. 355.
71   TAHO CSO1/332/7578, pp. 210–212.

Chapter 15 ~ 'I entertain great hopes of the assistance of Tom'

1   See for instance Cassandra Pybus, 'Robinson and Robertson' in *Whitewash*, pp. 262–263.
2   *Hobart Town Courier*, 7 March 1829.
3   Ryan, *Aboriginal Tasmanians*, p. 124.
4   *ibid.*, p. 129.
5   *Hobart Town Courier*, 20 June 1829.
6   *ibid.*
7   Robinson, Speech to the Australian Aborigines Protection Society, 1838.
8   Plomley, *Friendly Mission*, 1st edn, p. 89.
9   *ibid.*
10 Robertson to Burnett, TAHO CSO1/332/7578, pp. 210–212.
11 Plomley, *Friendly Mission*, 26 December 1829.
12 *ibid.*, 10 January 1830.
13 *ibid.*, 11 January 1830.
14 *ibid.*, 17 January 1830.
15 *ibid.*, 3 February 1830.

Chapter 16 ~ 'Mountain tiers as far as the eye could reach'

1   Reynolds, *Fate of a Free People*, p. 136.
2   Paul Collins, *Hell's Gates: The Terrible Journey of Alexander Pearce, Van Diemen's Land Cannibal*, South Yarra, Hardie, 2002, p. 79.
3   Cox, *A Compulsion to Kill*, p. 37.
4   Plomley, *Friendly Mission*, 3 February 1830.
5   *ibid.*, 4 February 1830.
6   *ibid.*, 6 February 1830.
7   *ibid.*
8   *ibid.*, 11 February 1830.
9   *ibid.*, 19 February 1830.
10 *ibid.*, 5 March 1830.
11 *ibid.*, 7 March 1830.
12 *ibid.*, 12 March 1830.
13 Denison King, quoted in Plomley, *Friendly Mission*, 1st edn, pp. 227–228.
14 Plomley, *Friendly Mission*, 25 March 1830.
15 *ibid.*, 26 March 1830.

16 *ibid.*
17 *Hobart Town Gazette*, 21 July 1827 and *Colonial Times*, 27 July 1827. However, according to a contemporary Palawa 'Any such status placed on Aborigines anywhere in Australia was a false one that was intended to win over the tribe by recognising their leaders with [such titles as] queen, king, chief, etc, and really nothing of significance in reality to Aboriginal society ... Also, it was used as a means of early ideas of assimilation, as George Augustus Robinson did at Wybalenna. He gave Aborigines there names such as Queen Alexandra, King Albert, that sort of thing to give Aborigines a sense of being accepted in white society. It's quite possible of course that Kikatapula's wife would be given such a title to win the trust of Kikatapula' (Jim Everett, pers. comm.).
18 Journal of Charles Sterling, Clerk, for 15 July 1829, quoted in Plomley, *Friendly Mission*, 2nd edn, p. 128.
19 Plomley, *Friendly Mission*, 1st edn, p. 981.
20 *Hobart Town Courier*, 17 April 1830.
21 *Sydney Gazette*, 18 May 1830, quoting the *Tasmanian* of 30 April 1830.
22 *Tasmanian*, 7 May 1830.
23 Plomley, *Friendly Mission*, 18 April 1830.
24 *Hobart Town Courier*, 8 May 1830.
25 Plomley, *Friendly Mission*, 9 May 1830.
26 *ibid.*, 23 May 1830.
27 *ibid.*
28 *ibid.*, 12 June 1830.
29 *ibid.*, 7 August 1830.
30 Extracted from Plomley, *Aboriginal/Settler Clash*, pp. 85–91. The figures are imprecise because some attack reports lack specific dates. Possibly subsequent deaths from wounds were not recorded.
31 Plomley, *Friendly Mission*, 23 June 1830.

Chapter 17 ~ 'They are desperate people and will spear us'

1 *ibid.*, 5 September 1830.
2 Plomley, *Friendly Mission*, 1st edn, p. 243.
3 *ibid.*
4 See for instance Plomley, *Friendly Mission*, 5 September 1830; 1st edn, p. 237 n. 60; and pp. 435–436 n. 6.
5 *ibid.*, 2 October 1830.
6 *ibid.*, 1st edn, p. 435, n. 6.
7 *ibid.*, 20 October 1830.
8 *ibid.*, 1 November 1830 and *ibid.*, 1st edn, p. 438, n. 41.
9 *ibid.*, 1st edn, p. 438, n. 43.
10 *ibid.*, pp. 438–439, n. 44.
11 *Hobart Town Courier*, 22 January 1831.
12 Cox, *Baptised in Blood*, p. 273.
13 The site subsequently became the Port Arthur penal settlement.
14 *Hobart Town Courier*, 27 November 1830.
15 Plomley, *Friendly Mission*, 26 November 1830.
16 *ibid.*, 20 December 1830.

Chapter 18 ~ 'Tucker said he would shoot Black Tom'

1 *ibid.*, 1st edn, p. 450, n. 119.
2 *Colonial Times*, 22 June 1827.

3 Henry Laing's journal, quoted in Plomley, *Friendly Mission*, 1st edn, p. 451, n. 123.
4 *ibid.*, p. 452, n. 130.
5 Plomley, *Friendly Mission*, 30 April 1831. On 29 April Robinson had noted 'Jack convalescent'.
6 *ibid.*, 1st edn, p. 462, n. 174.
7 *ibid.*, 8 July 1831.
8 *ibid.*, 17 July 1831.
9 *Launceston Advertiser*, 1 August 1831.
10 *Friendly Mission*, 13 August 1831.
11 *ibid.*, 8 November 1831.
12 *ibid.*, 6 August 1831.
13 *ibid.*, 12 August 1831.
14 *ibid.*, 25 August 1821.
15 *ibid.*, 17 October 1831.
16 *Launceston Advertiser*, 5 September 1831.
17 Surridge to Aborigines Committee, February 1832, TAHO CSO1/321/7578, pp. 393–400.
18 Plomley, *Friendly Mission*, 13 September 1831.
19 *ibid.*, 1st edn, p. 687 n. 19, also *ibid.*, 3 October 1831.
20 *ibid.* This account was apparently not paid for some time. Plomley noted that 'Letters written at this time to the Colonial Secretary included one on 24 March [1832] asking for the money due to the natives for the hire of their boat to be sent at once (an account for goods purchased for Black Tom and WOORRADY from Isaac Sherwin at Launceston)' amounting to £7.10.8.
21 The *Independent* (Launceston), 8 October 1831.

Chapter 19 ~ 'This man Tom is a bad character'

1 Plomley, *Friendly Mission*, 10 November 1831.
2 *ibid.*, 28 October 1831.
3 *ibid.*, 15 November 1831.
4 *ibid.*, 19 November 1831.
5 The *Courier*, 10 December 1831.
6 Burnett to Robinson, 23 November 1831, quoted in Plomley, *Friendly Mission*, 1st edn, p. 583 n. 89.
7 *ibid.*
8 *Friendly Mission*, 1st edn, p. 570.
9 Nicholas Shakespeare, *In Tasmania*, Sydney, Random House, 2004, pp. 160–161.
10 Plomley, *Jorgen Jorgenson*, p. 113.
11 Robinson, official report dated 25 January 1832, quoted in *Friendly Mission*, 1st edn, pp. 570–571. Also Robinson, Speech to the Australian Aborigines Protection Society.
12 The child was Tukalunginta's son Paparamina. He died soon after the Palawa were taken to Flinders Island.
13 Robinson, Speech to the Australian Aborigines Protection Society.
14 *Friendly Mission*, 3 November 1831.
15 In 1835 Bothwell residents presented Robinson with a silver cup to commemorate his removing all the Palawa from the district. The Queen Victoria Museum and Art Gallery, Launceston, now houses it.

Chapter 20 ~ 'I greatly deplored the loss of this aborigine'

1 *Friendly Mission*, 1st edn, p. 572.

2   Plomley, *Jorgen Jorgenson*, p. 114 (which wrongly dates the attack to September); Plomley, *Aboriginal/Settler Clash*, p. 98; *Hobart Town Courier*, 20 August 1831. Details of the attack are in *Friendly Mission*, 8 November and 14 December 1831.
3   *Friendly Mission*, 1st edn, p. 585, n. 96.
4   The Castle Hotel was the town's respectable inn. The only other hotel in the town was the Plough and Harrow, a 'low sort of tavern' (Mary Ramsay, Bothwell Historical Society, pers. comm.). See also http://www.bothwellhistoricalsociety.org.au/Bothwell%20Chronology.html
5   Robinson, Speech to the Australian Aborigines Protection Society.
6   George Russell, *The Narrative of George Russell of Golf Hill with Russellania and Selected Papers*, London, Oxford University Press, 1935, p. 61.
7   Plomley, *Jorgen Jorgenson*, p. 114.
8   Plomley, *Friendly Mission*, 1st edn, p. 572.
9   *Hobart Town Courier*, 7 January 1832.
10 *Colonial Times*, 11 January 1832.
11 *Hobart Town Courier*, 14 January 1832.
12 The *Independent* (Launceston), 14 January 1832.
13 Plomley, *Friendly Mission*, 1st edn, p. 589. Also *ibid.*, p. 685 n. 17, and *FM* 1 March 1832.
14 *ibid.*, p. 681 n. 2.
15 Plomley, *Friendly Mission*, 1st edn, p. 689, n. 40.
16 *ibid.*, 22 May 1832.

Epilogue

1   Brodie, *The Vandemonian War*, p. 377.
2   *Bent's News and Tasmanian Three-penny Register*, 2 April 1836.
3   The *Mercury*, 28 November 1872.
4   David Thompson, pers. comm.
5   Elizabeth Jones, *Richmond – Tasmania: A Crossing Place,* Richmond, Richmond Preservation and Development Trust, 1973.
6   William Thorne in Plomley, *The Westlake Papers: Records of Interviews in Tasmania by Ernest Westlake, 1908–1910*, Launceston, Queen Victoria Museum & Art Gallery, n.d., p. 76.
7   Horace B. Pithouse, *The Luck of 1825: Tasmanian Historical Romance*, Melbourne, Alexander McCubbin, 1922. Chapter 5, 'Musquito's Retreat', was published in the *Circular Head Chronicle* on 13 December 1922.
8   *Advocate*, 27 September 1928 and 29 August 1931.
9   *ibid.*, 14 October 1933.
10 Cox, *Steps to the Scaffold*, p. 118.
11 *Tasmanian News*, 20 August 1884, and *Mercury*, 23 August 1884.
12 Bonwick, *Last of the Tasmanians*, p. 95.
13 Plomley, *Weep in Silence*, p. 909.
14 Quoted in Taylor, *Into the Heart of Tasmania*, p. 88.
15 Quoted in Powell, *Musquito*, p. 166. Translator unknown. A somewhat different translation, presumably by Cochrane Smith herself, is in Longman, 'Songs of the Tasmanian Aborigines', p. 84.

Appendix 1

1   Plomley, *Friendly Mission*, 17 May 1832.
2   *ibid.*, 22 May 1832.
3   *Advocate*, 27 September 1928.

4 *ibid.*, 29 August 1931.
5 *ibid.*, 14 October 1933.
6 *ibid.*
7 Brian Rollins, pers. comm.

Appendix 2

1 http://www.law.mq.edu.au/sctas/html/r_v_musquito__1824.html
2 *Hobart Town Gazette*, 27 August 1825. Since the authorities possibly forced Radford to commit perjury, it might be thought unfair to censure him for doing so. He was, after all, still a prisoner at the time of the trial and thus subject to the government's orders and pressure. He might also have been compelled to omit any mention of Kikatapula's part in the affray because of the Sarah Birch connection and the administration's desire to shield her from scandal. Self-exculpation, however, was undoubtedly a major factor.
3 Cox, *Baptised in Blood*, p. 327 n. 15.
4 Calder, *Native Tribes of Tasmania*, p. 54.

Appendix 3

1 See Cox, *Compulsion to Kill*, p. 90 *et seq.*
2 See Cox, *Baptised in Blood*, pp. 158–159.
3 TAHO CSO 1/108/2631, p. 62.
4 *ibid.*, p. 60. Laing had been Chief District Constable for only three years at that time, although a constable for seven.
5 That was the month of the Matthew Brady raid on Sorell. I have suggested elsewhere (*Baptised in Blood*, pp. 164–165) that Laing was suffering from post-traumatic stress as a result of what happened to him during the raid; TAHO CSO 1/108/2631, p. 60.
6 *ibid.*, p. 66.
7 G.T. Lloyd, *Thirty Three Years in Tasmania and Victoria*, London, Houlston and Wright, 1862, p. 269.
8 *Tasmanian (Hobart)*, 9 February 1828.
9 See *Bent's News and Tasmanian Three-penny Register* of 19 March 1836 and the *True Colonist* of 13 May 1836 and 24 June 1836.
10 Quoted in Laing's *Memoir.*
11 *ibid.*
12 Because of physical proximity to and synchrony with other nominated attacks, Laing must be referring here to Thomas Pratt, killed on 16 October 1830. Another of Stacey's shepherds, John Priest, had been slain by Palawa on 21 September 1828.

Index

Index

Printed in Australia
AUHW011451290422
362941AU00003B/3

9 781743 058671